I0105035

The Labyrinth of Multitude and Other Reality Checks on Being Latino/X

Julio Marzán

Critical Perspectives on Social Science

VERNON PRESS

Copyright © 2024 Julio Marzán.

All rights reserved. No part of this publication may be reproduced, stored in a retrieval system, or transmitted in any form or by any means, electronic, mechanical, photocopying, recording, or otherwise, without the prior permission of Vernon Art and Science Inc.
www.vernonpress.com

In the Americas:
Vernon Press
1000 N West Street, Suite 1200,
Wilmington, Delaware 19801
United States

In the rest of the world:
Vernon Press
C/Sancti Espiritu 17,
Malaga, 29006
Spain

Critical Perspectives on Social Science

Library of Congress Control Number: 2023936349

ISBN: 978-1-64889-834-1

Also available: 978-1-64889-677-4 [Hardback]; 978-1-64889-803-7 [PDF, E-Book]

Product and company names mentioned in this work are the trademarks of their respective owners. While every care has been taken in preparing this work, neither the authors nor Vernon Art and Science Inc. may be held responsible for any loss or damage caused or alleged to be caused directly or indirectly by the information contained in it.

Every effort has been made to trace all copyright holders, but if any have been inadvertently overlooked the publisher will be pleased to include any necessary credits in any subsequent reprint or edition.

Cover design by Vernon Press using image designed by Zarubin-leonid / Freepik.

For Clarissa, Janese, and Olivia

Much the same thing happens with... people at a certain critical moment of their development. They ask themselves what are we and how can we fulfill our obligations to ourselves as we are?

–Octavio Paz, "The Pachuco and Other Extremes"

TABLE OF CONTENTS

ACKNOWLEDGMENTS

A shorter, earlier version of "William Carlos Williams, Lin-Manuel Miranda and the Enigma of Identity," was published as "Lin-Manuel, Meet William Carlos" in *New English Review*, 2016.

"Harvard Patrols the Border," was first published as guest article in *Black Renaissance Noir*, New York University, ed. Quincy Troupe, Summer 2010.

"Does Your Child Speak Another Language at Home?" was published under the title "Found in Translation: Reflections of a Bilingual American," in *Bilingual Games: Some Literary Investigations*, ed. Doris Sommer, Palgrave/MacMillan, 2003.

"Pablo Neruda's Dilemma," first appeared in *The Massachusetts Review*, 40th Anniversary Issue, Spring 2000. It was reprinted in *Pablo Neruda and the U.S. Culture Industry*, ed. Teresa Longo, 2002.

INTRODUCTION:
WHEN BE IS THE FINALE OF SEEM

This was a skit on *Saturday Night Live* in May 1982. That week Argentina had invaded the off-shore islands it calls Las Malvinas to reclaim them from the UK that knows them as The Falkland Islands. Solomon, played by Eddie Murphy, reads from a newspaper and asks his friend Pudge at the piano, played by Joe Piscopo, what he thought about those Puerto Ricans down in the Falklands. Pudge clarifies: "They ain't no Puerto Ricans, man, they Argentine." Solomon scowls skeptically, "I seen them in *Newsweek*: they Argen-Ricans." Comic irony in Solomon's being a black man for whom all Latinos looked alike.

Solomon was also parroting Joe White Guy in seeing no difference between one group of Spanish speakers in New York probably up to no good and another the length of a hemisphere away invading islands the home to some decent English-speaking folk. On the plus side, Pudge's clarification that the invaders were specifically Argentine demonstrated that by the eighties Latin America had advanced beyond the traditional Spanish lumping: in the seventies, after its political and literary emergence, Latin America came into sharper focus in the sight of a generation of educated Americans now more cognizant of discrete Americas nations as distinct political and socioeconomic theaters, no longer monolithic Spanish.

Still, Solomon, a man more of the people, couldn't be blamed for repeating the established popular homogenization of Spanish speakers. One day in the seventies the Spanish playwright José Ruibal, frequently invited to universities in both halves of the country, quipped "Oh I'm used to it. In the West I'm Mexican and in the East I'm Puerto Rican." One night in the seventies, a non-Hispanic couple and I were looking for a Spanish restaurant in the Wall Street district where our New York Rican woman friend, a flamenco dancer, was to perform. We asked a carrot-topped, presumably Irish, passerby if he knew of a Spanish restaurant in the immediate area. He shook his head and, with no nuance of irony, answered "No, I don't know of any Puerto Rican restaurants around here."

As late as the mid-1980's in English the two "Spanish" points of reference for most Americans were still Mexican Americans in the West and Puerto Ricans in the East understood as encompassing the identity "U.S. Hispanics"[1] that in the sixties spoke for Spanish-speaking minorities in the Civil Rights Movement. Long before then, of course, Mexican Americans and both mainland and island Puerto Ricans were distanced *latinos,* fraternal descendants of the same Spanish-speaking heritage, sharing the same music, art, and literature of a then-monolithic Hispanic culture. Still, except for the more sophisticated or well-traveled members of those communities, other than an assumed parallel Hispanic minority experience and cliches about a shared Spanish heritage, neither knew much about the other.

In the seventies both communities rediscovered shared hemispheric roots in emergent Latin America that became the grand theater of Third World liberation, symbolized politically by the Cuban Revolution and intellectually by its joining the ranks of world-class culture with a body of literature whose explosion the French termed a literary Boom. We U.S. Hispanics basked in this new Latin America, which suddenly gave our challenge to Anglo-Saxon presumptions of cultural supremacy an international dimension and a patina of prestige. After all, as the voices of Latin America in Anglo America, U.S. Hispanics fought for the civil rights of all *hispanos.*

Unforeseen in the U.S. Hispanic civil rights gains was that making the United States a more just and equitable place for all *hispanos* also meant making this country an even more attractive refuge from Latin American poverty and political oppression as well as a vehicle for the upward mobility of its better off. For even though most Latin Americans were compelled to escape their own countries by a legitimate spectrum of grievances on which international attention mainly focused, the promise of post-civil rights minority equality and entitlements provided additional incentive for the northbound migration that began in the early eighties, the majority Mexican.

By the 90's that immigration significantly changed the nation, with the composite of native Hispanics and immigrant Latin Americans projected to become the new century's largest minority. This massive Latin American influx also revitalized the original seventies roots-consciousness, prompting my revolutionary U.S. Hispanic generation to identify with Latin America and making trendy our identifying as *latinos,* the Spanish shorthand for Latin American. In short time, its Anglicization, Latino, caught on in the national media to encompass both native and the recently-immigrated "Latinos."

---

[1] Cubans, having started to arrive earlier in that decade, were still neither perceived nor had yet announced themselves as Americans, and in subsequent years with the arrival of the *marielitos,* they didn't identify with racial plight of any kind, especially voiced by the Civil Rights Movement, which conservative America resisted as a communist subversion.

I was all for this new epithet, understanding that it performed as did Spanish *latino,* one sweet fruit being the new Latin American writing's coattails extending to U.S. Hispanic writers because the two had dovetailed to become what publishers identified as a "Latino" market. After all, a publishing niche is better than none. But it was also in response to publishing's influence on school reading assignments, that I began to have questions about the semantics of English Latino. In schools, post-civil rights curricular correctives promoted assigning multicultural readings, and Latin American translations were read alongside or as surrogate U.S. Hispanic writings. Over time in the media and in conversations one heard this fusion of discrete demographics and not always aligned cultural experiences –hemispheric Latin America, immigrant *latino,* and U.S. Hispanic– referred to as simply Latino.

As a writer I had been writing from the perspective of what I understood to be a discretely Puerto Rican culture whose specificity as Spanish *latino* had not changed. Meanwhile, out in America, I was now a Latino, the epithet having evolved from trending to being the most politically correct. Everywhere homonymic "Latino," pronounced as the embedded Spanish *latino,* ricocheted in media and pop cultural venues not always signifying consistently and more reliably defined as a political epithet. Latino had become a voting bloc that could tilt presidential elections or secure funding for programs or campaign for laws or policies.

Native Latinos and immigrant *latinos* all seemed fine with being conflated until, as the latter settled in, that pan-Latin American romance wore off, and I more sharply appreciated that Latino was becoming the public harmonic cover over how communities actually think of each other and themselves, not always in unity. Latinos and *latinos* were on the same screen when on Univisión and rubbing shoulders on the dance floor to *musica latina,* but that shared pop culture camouflaged not always being on the same cultural page. Still, an appearance of unity afforded a political empowerment that superseded not always making linguistic or intellectual or cultural sense. Many who culturally preferred Hispanic saw the political advantage of publicly acceding to Latino even though it did not mean the same as the *latino* they used when interacting among other *latinos* in Spanish.

Presumed to translate *latino,* and even pronounced to highlight its Latinate sound, Latino is actually a transliteration that once coined immediately began diverging semantically from its Spanish source word. *Latino* is a heritage epithet that is only figuratively a cultural epithet but resonances of *latino* allowed Latino to suggest that it was a cultural epithet. This veneer of authenticity warranted its flourishing unexamined, assumed to be a politically-correct self-generated American identity that gave cultural backing to a united Democratic Latino vote and a consolidated Latino approval of policy. But presidential elections began to tell a different story as Republicans could also win a sizeable Latino vote, disrupting the presumption of a monolithic Latino.

While *latino* invoked Spanish culture and language rooted in a threading Romanic heritage, culturally amorphous Latino had a distinctly American political and racial function, with a conflicted array of applications in American English that at times contradicted what *latino* signified in Spanish. In this divergence, Latino proceeded to sow cultural confusion, generating solidarity as satisfying a millennial generation's aspiration for a defined American identity also rooted in *latinidad,* an aspiration so anxious that in optimism it deluded itself into having found that identity, making, to borrow from Wallace Stevens, Be the finale of Seem.

In politics, Anglophone Latino is presumed to represent all Latinos/ *latinos* when, except passively in socioeconomic and political self-interest, not all subgroups identify with Latino consistently or at all. Latino is the public mask of a labyrinth of multitude that consists of rhetorically homogenized subgroups, camouflaging what in reality is a competition between one better-heeled community against another less fortunate, between whiter and darker demographics, each subgroup its own discrete theater of internecine cultural, social, and political drama blurred by boilerplate American interpretations. On the other hand, Latino came into existence because its time had come, responding to the aspiration for a more unified, participatory, self-identifying, less foreign-sounding American identity.

Latino was also fast-tracked in English because it satisfied a post-sixties mainstream need for a handle on Hispanics as Americans. Latino was turned by American media into the popular forum from which all variants of Hispanic citizens addressed American society although in this endeavor Latino and American attempt to put behind them a history of working at cross purposes. American culture's traditional proclivity to racialize "Hispanic," especially in the southwest, extended that proclivity to marginalize Latino. Emerging post-sixties, multicultural America presumably corrected that traditional racialized demotion of cultural value, and born on a cresting wave of post-sixties multicultural optimism, Latino promised much as an American identity in what appeared to be a changing America.

That prospect encouraged younger immigrant *latinos* to replace their origin cultures with Latino, which residually reserved being also *latino,* signifying a preservation of *latino*'s Romanic and Hispanic roots. But Latino itself couldn't actually provide a heritage because it had burned itself into mainstream America as a racial minority consciousness. Instead, in this evolving confusion, Latino threatened to racialize *latino,* prompting rejection from some member subgroups although any internecine distinction had no effect on Latino as a public entity. It meant nothing to Americans who advocated the building of

Trump's wall out of simple racism against a brown associated with all Latinos/ *latinos*.

And that is where Latino stands today, at times invoking a *latino* culture, which strictly speaking doesn't exist (*latino* being the heritage of many cultures), while engaged in combating the racism among less-educated popular America, riled up by policymakers who use race as a fuse, ostensibly against Latino as America's browning but really because underlying Latino is a historical rival Hispanic culture whose "cultural assault" threatens to redefine traditional America.

In the post-sixties, racialized Latino as consciousness started out emulating the early African American model, oscillating between identifying as a culture and a race. But younger Latinos did not follow the African American arc in coming to see that, while race was a political unifier, it was not the foundation of a cultural identity. Tribes are racial; cultures are transracial. African American identity expanded beyond politics and activism and even race to encompass ideation, critical discourse, and especially its particular contribution to history as also American history, history being the component that Latino pretends to be able to shed in political overcorrectness.

Needless to say, history remains important to many Latino scholars, but they are overshadowed by the numbers of Latinos who define themselves by a sociopolitical presentism. For those Latinos, identifying with Hispanic means identifying with white conquerors, and so the more populist, racialized Latino discourse is based on a liberation from its white history, implying a purer other history.

That Latino mindset often situationally borrows *latino* as cultural consciousness or even promotes Latino as a culture discounting that a culture is fundamentally a history. The canceling of a Hispanic history is the canceling of a Hispanic culture, leaving a sui generis Latino to reinvent itself against the Hispanic claims of its *latino* roots while proceeding, thanks to an American education, unaware of the Hispanic heritage in American cultural history that Latinos inherit as Americans.

My witnessing Latino become the currency despite its dysfunction as a chaotic semantic plane inspired my writing the essays that became this book. In the first part, I revisit the semantics of Latino as epithet and its consequences as consciousness, inquiring into much taken for granted in the twin reliance on both oral "you know what I mean" reasoning, and the preeminence of political solidarity. The body of this book consists of essays that, although in the first-person, are not about their author but that chronicle first-hand my experience with earlier segues to Latino in the Puerto Rican experience, in all cases revisions of established Latino perspectives on cultural milestones and familiar iconic personages.

My thesis on Latino as a rhetorical unifier of actually discrete subcultures is not original. Latino Studies scholars have researched, chiefly from a social science perspective, the discrepancy between a public Latino unity and an underlying disunity. The bulk of that study examines the influence of political and economic forces at work in the making of a market or the inventing of a people from the multitude of subgroups. The originality of this book is its contemplating the Latino condition through the methodology of the humanities.

Latino Studies presumes as core the social sciences, having established the convention of assigning to the humanities the ancillary role of providing graphic or entertaining representations of social science insight. This book questions that convention not as an academic vendetta but as the inescapable result of carrying out what humanities disciplines do: apply critical thinking using a more exacting distrust of language. In examining the semantics of Latino, this book incurs into cultural consequences of Latino on which social science research provides data as evidence but does not put conclusions on trial for consequential nuances or intellectual soundness. Nor is there the political will to perform such testing because, as I will demonstrate, Latino Studies struggles with giving primacy to cultural criticism over solidarity with popular community perceptions.

Culturally undefined while performing as if culturally defined, Latino allows a bundle of semantic possibilities, an amorphousness that invites creativity. The most notable example is the circumventing of true introspection by something that poses as an intellectual discussion, correcting an invented grammatical gender bias in English. This tinkering in stages produced today's Latinx, which the more woke extended to express a generational questioning of binary identities.

That activism is piggy-backed onto the use of gender-correcting Latinx, claiming an identity neutrality represented by a supposedly Latinx people. Do Latinos who adopt Latinx to express simply gender awareness know that they are also advocating a dismantling of identity? And should they discover that application of Latino, do they betray their solidarity to gender consciousness and not use Latinx? Into the churning stream of creative possibilities enters yet another obfuscating variant of Latino.

Nevertheless, motivated by solidarity and a desire to advance social justice, institutions and organizations quickly adopted Latinx, whose actual usage, according to polls that I will cite, do not exceed 3%. In other words, if Latino became institutionalized almost immediately, Latinx remains an advocacy, staying alive as a gender corrective higher moral ground while functioning as a Trojan Horse on binary identities.

As I write, the nation's oldest Latino civil rights organization, the League of United Latin American Citizens, has instructed its staff to drop Latinx from the group's official communications. What are they actually rejecting? Latinx's gender consciousness, its distorting Spanish in claiming that it has no gender neutrality only binaries, its not being a Latinate word and so stripped of vestige evocations of *latino*? There remains much more to be discussed in greater detail not immediately visible on the surface of that Latino v. Latinx debate, understanding that Latinx is just the latest displacement of the deeper conversation that fails to take place on the identity conundrum of Hispanic-heritaged citizens as Americans.

For that reason, against that background, I focus on the original Latino as the hub of the identity conundrum, discussing where Latinx might need a closer look to complete my argument. Latino's foundational contradictory nuances, questionable readings of history, and inconsistent evocations underlay Latinx's ostensibly novel insight, so both identically obfuscate the cultural context from which I presumably write as a Latino.

Through filters of activism, generations, class, race, and education levels, Latino emits multiple, conflicted senses. Such is its semantic flexibility that applications of Latino that I discuss may not seem immediately recognizable to every Latino, for which even different geographies give different emphases. For example, for those who simply understand Latino to be a more updated identifier than the older umbrella Hispanic and do not follow more academic discussions may respond to my reading of Latino as advocating the canceling of its Hispanic history as exaggerated. On the other hand, because the solidarity semantic feature of Latino tolerates that both viewpoints are validly Latino, that contradiction may be overlooked.

My focus is not on viewpoints or political stances but on Latino as an English word determined by English ethnocentricity that can subvert what bilinguals believe they are making English say. Anglophone Latino, so much a victim of that subversion, saying so many contradictory things, often injects meanings and evocations that are not what the speaker intended if thinking that by saying Latino they are uttering *latino*.

Not out of academic snobbery nor out of a nostalgia for a Hispanic past nor in search of another epithet for which I want to be credited as having invented am I motivated to write cultural criticism on Latino. My effort with this book is to make sense to myself of what today purports to be my Latino American identity, a discussion that I posit needs more critical nuance than the present discourse that as a writer I hear, an undisciplined creativity that defines and refines in search of an identity perfection that winds up serving politically at the expense of making cultural and intellectual sense. If those who romanticize Hispanic history blind themselves to its role in historical racial oppression, Latino's political effectiveness is sustained at the cost of romanticizing an ignorance of historical facts, that ignorance feeding a racial oversimplification of what is Hispanic and the delusion that an antipathy toward Hispanic as being simply white changes them culturally.

Nor do I presume to define Latino, what no one person can, why there exists literature and art and public intellectual discussion. In this book, I apply my authority as writer and linguist to examine the semantics of the epithets Latino and the newer Latinx as X-rays of our conflicted communal thought process, language usage providing empirical evidence of what we think we are thinking for ourselves and more often are just repeating unexamined.

Like any X-ray, this book is intended to provide a picture of underlying flaws or structural weaknesses, defects that, in this case, require more collective introspection. My search is for the intellectual functionality that any consciousness must have to make cultural and intellectual, not just political and racial, sense, and this book invites today's Latino/*latino* demographic to begin a needed collective introspection, and not just in academe, of what it means or should or could mean to be Latino and American.

I proceed aware of endangering my Latino credentials by disrespecting its solidarity feature with elitist critical thought, in other words, of taking it seriously as an intellectual subject. A siege mentality protects as *nuestro* even conflicting understandings of Latino, so any criticism, including constructive self-criticism, smacks of self-loathing or of a whitening. Intending to keep house as Jack Spicer asks of himself in the epigraph to Part I, I glean encouragement from the experience that I describe in the final essay of this book on my encounter with Pablo Neruda in New York.

Please read it by way of the preceding essays intended to clean up Latino's intellectual clutter that in solidarity we overlook, forgive, convince ourselves that the matter really isn't that important. In fact, that clutter threatens mature Latino/*latino* self-reflection and Latinos' becoming more empowered than passive, ward-culture citizens--whether or not this nation becomes a multicultural country.

PART ONE:
KEEPING HOUSE

Is there some rhetoric
To make me think that I have kept a house
While playing dolls?

–Jack Spicer,
    from "Imaginary Elegies"[1]

---

[1] "Imaginary Elegies," in *The New American Poetry: 1945-1960*, ed. David Allen (Berkeley and Los Angeles University of California Press, 1999), 147.

1.

THE LABYRINTH OF MULTITUDE:
THE LATINO/X MASK

> Strange word, lacking a specific meaning,
> or more precisely stated, is loaded, like all
> popular inventions, with a plethora of meanings!
>
> –from *The Labyrinth of Solitude*,
> Octavio Paz

FROM "SPANISH" TO "HISPANIC" TO "LATINO" TO "LATINX": AN OVERVIEW

In the opening essay of *The Labyrinth of Solitude* (1950), "The Pachuco and Other Extremes," Octavio Paz explains that his contemplation of Mexican culture began with his interest in better understanding Mexican American culture in Los Angeles. Paz detected that in the L.A. air the Mexican qualities of Mexican Americans floated persistent while resistant to blending. Mexican Americans outwardly displayed their difference while betraying an inner insecurity about what they were: "Even though their attitude reveals an obstinate and almost fanatical will to be, that will affirms nothing more concrete than the decision ambiguous, as we shall see, not to be like those people that surround them."[1]

Paz was in the U.S. on a Guggenheim Fellowship from 1943 to1945, wartime years when a fashion among Mexican-American young men was to dress in the flashy zoot suit of the *pachuco*, whose eye-catching array of wide-brimmed hat, baggy pants, long suit jacket, and looping watch-chain expressed a double-edged defiance against both anonymity among Anglo bigotry and an older Mexican self-marginality. Paz interpreted that, expressive of the floating Mexican American culture in not having a clear cause, the *pachuco's* rebellion also fell short: "[he] doesn't want to return to his Mexican origins, nor to all

---

[1] Octavio Paz, *The Labyrinth of Solitude*, Translated by Lysander Kemp (New York: Grove Press, 1991), 14.

appearances does he desire to join the life of the Anglo American. Everything in him is the impulse that denies itself, a knot of contradictions."[2]

Paz noted that the *pachuco* and other Mexican Americans, although different, were still Mexican, making the *pachuco* and Mexican Americans also illustrations of what Paz ascribed to all Mexicans, their wearing a public mask to hide solitude. In the case of the *pachuco*, his mask of rebellion welcomes confrontation with American society that otherwise turns its back on him, who feels excluded. In other words, in reconciling a life divided as Mexican and American, the *pachuco* resorted to a paradoxical psyche: "Persecution redeems him and breaks his solitude: his salvation depends on his becoming a part of the very society he appears to deny."[3]

In 1979 Luis Valdez's play *Zoot Suit* came from the West Coast to Broadway. Set in Los Angeles, it was based on the 1942 Sleepy Lagoon Murder scandal, the railroading of a *pachuco* gang after a rival gang member was found killed actually by a member of a third gang, an injustice overturned on appeal in 1944. In Valdez's play, El Pachuco, a zoot-suited Greek-chorus figure, narrates events as the inner voice of Henry Reyna, a member of The 38th Street Gang. The play reenacts the history of the scandal, so the murder takes place and a bigoted jury ignores the evidence that should have exonerated Henry and his posse.

Henry languishes in prison as subplots have his lawyer fighting for justice and Henry falling in love with the Anglo woman journalist who advocates on his behalf. One might argue that Valdez was answering Paz's claim that Mexican Americans didn't know what they were or wanted to be, that from Valdez's El Pachuco we should infer a cultural consciousness that a Mexican American intuitively understands beyond the grasp of a Mexican. That was my assumption when I first saw *Zoot Suit*, impressed that Valdez could be what seemed so confident about understanding what it means to be Mexican American while I, along with my Puerto Rican second generation, was trying to figure out what Puerto Rican meant in English.

But in time I came to see that, the Pachuco's cool demeanor notwithstanding, both Valdez and the play were ambivalent about for what the Pachuco actually stood. In the rising action, the Pachuco parades the self-assurance of his identity although we never get a sense of what that is beyond his being a cool *pachuco*. More cultural dimensions are suggested than are represented on stage beyond Henry's surname, the motive for the conflict, and the bigotry toward him and the other gang members. In the descending second half, once Henry is jailed and must engage with the legal process and ponder the

---

[2] Paz, *The Labyrinth of Solitude*, 14.

[3] Paz, *The Labyrinth of Solitude*, 16.

consequences, El Pachuco shrinks in importance. Before Henry and his gang got caught up in the Anglo justice system, El Pachuco had broadcast a hip confidence, colorfully expressed in bilingual L.A. *vato* slang, with the swagger of having the ear of Henry, who as gang member listened to his inner Pachuco.

But as citizen, Henry has to fight within the system to be released and confront his integration into society whether as a smitten lover of his Anglo journalist advocate or as his Chicana girlfriend's husband. At that point, El Pachuco loses interest, ostensibly out of frustration with Anglo injustice, but really also because he could play no meaningful role as inner voice: Henry as engaged citizen simply outgrows him. The Pachuco gestures frustration and simply exits without a soliloquy.

Ultimately Henry as *pachuco* performs as Paz underscored, the expression of contrast to the Anglo world but also its embodiment in his English and his civic and social consciousness, Mexican yet a member of the Anglo world, a "knot of contradictions." The play ends admitting to the playwright's uncertainty about its protagonist's fate, asking the audience to contemplate possible endings: either Henry's returning to gang life as if that were his cultural identity, or his joining the armed services and dying as a war hero, or his marrying his girlfriend, in both cases becoming the proper Mexican-American citizen.

Zoot Suit came to Broadway after a decade of Mexican-American and Puerto Rican alliance in the civil rights struggle, the collective minority identified as "U.S. Hispanics." My watching on stage Henry's plight in California evoked sympathy that was both universal and associated with our then still-monolithic Spanish consciousness that made us "Hispanics." That fraternally-shared heritage had always made us culturally if discretely Latin American (Mexican/Puerto Rican), but in the seventies, a decade of Latin America's political and cultural emergence, U.S. Hispanics were prompted to stand with their Latin American roots, sowing the trend to speak of being also *latinos*.

In the eighties, incrementing Latin American immigration, primarily Mexican in the west and Dominican in the east, prompted a broader exuberance to stand as *latinos*, especially as the composite was on schedule to form the new largest minority, which by the millennium would be acknowledged and mainstreamed as Latino. At that time, looking back at Valdez's seventies play, I realized that our transition from Hispanics to Latinos produced the semantic consequence of also making Luis Valdez and me virtually *paisans*.

"Hispanics" as an umbrella covered distinct cultures with a common heritage, Latino homogenized. That Valdez and I were now Latino writers made *Zoot Suit* retroactively seem even more emphatically about my personal experience, and given Latino's racialization, our connection as writers was also tacitly genetic. I asked myself how, under the epithets *hispano* and *latino* and even Latin or

Spanish or Hispanic, Valdez and I were not assumed to write from the same culture while English Latino more strongly suggested that our cultural backgrounds were identical.

I have no Aztec heritage, and Valdez did not grow up conscious of Taíno and African-Caribbean roots. Our communities' shared *latino* consciousness came not from a direct identification with each other but through the convergence of a shared Hispanic cultural and linguistic heritage received from our origin cultures, each having cultivated a differently-flavored Hispanic consciousness informed by respective non-European heritages in the Americas mélange. Each community has its unique history and participation in U.S. American history, and except for what respective shibboleths about each as Hispanics that American culture perpetuates, unless as subject of formal study, members of our respective cultures really have little knowledge of the other.

Meanwhile, both communities embody a central confusion spun by traditional America. Both are racialized and marginalized as of-color minorities while both are actually multiracial communities. Both are also ethnic communities and mythologized as immigrant when neither is an "immigrant community," a term that invokes the traditional immigration mythos. U.S. Hispanics are a native U.S. American consciousness shaped by American history, Mexican Americans absorbed with the southwest acquisition, and Puerto Ricans made citizens after the island became of booty of the Spanish American War.

As Americans, both groups are addressed as reiterations of the American experience while neither constitutes an actual race, both being in fact multiracial, including members of European descent. One can say that Latino as allowed to be understood popularly is a concession to American expectations of its being a minority and defined by American racial history even though, in fact, each group's understanding of itself, as well as each's particular relationship to American culture, is a consequence of a respective, discrete cultural history.

Let's see how well "Latino" serves as consciousness after detailing how Mexican Americans and Puerto Ricans are different from each other and how they are related--and how it is not their homogenized racial interface but their cultural particularity that informs their relationship with American culture. The two cultural histories will also reveal the deeper origins of the divergence of Latino from *latino* and account for the contradictory nuances of Latino. I will start with what I know best, Puerto Ricans as Americans, which happens to be the paradigm about which other Latinos (although I can say also a good number of Puerto Ricans) know more shibboleth than substance.

Puerto Ricans as Americans are a hologram of social science clichés about the post-WWII diaspora mythologized in *West Side Story*, the community that later became the east coast Hispanic actors in the Civil Rights Movement from which the second-generation emerged self-racialized, turning their mainland story into one of race in America.[4] Glossed over in that simplified narrative was that diaspora's also being the story of race in Puerto Rico and the second chapter of an earlier segue migration[5] that had started before World War II.

Smaller, predominantly white and skilled, the prewar migration formed part of the New York *hispano* community that included Spaniards and trickles from Latin America. Those earlier migrants experienced traditional ethnic bigotry but later benefitted from America's turnaround toward Latin America in The Good Neighbor Policy. New York popular speech of that time homogenized them with other Spanish-speakers as "Spanish,"[6] translating from their own homogenizing identity as *hispanos*, how Latin Americans had traditionally identified themselves, especially vis a vis Anglo-Saxons, up to the seventies.

From their first presence on the mainland, Puerto Ricans identified as *hispanos* not out of a retrograde nostalgia, as it might seem from today's Latino perspective, but—to reiterate—because all Latin Americans still identified as *hispanos* and because throughout its entire history, Puerto Rico had not just been a figurative child of the *Madre Patria* but a literal colonial extension of Spain. In1898, as booty of The Spanish American War, the island became an American territory/colony, and in the first half of the twentieth century, Puerto Rico's cultured class aggressively reinstated the Spanish cultural model to preserve the island's *hispanidad* against the U.S. effort to impose what was interpreted as a barbarian Teutonic and Protestant culture.

That was the consciousness exported by both prewar and postwar migrations to the mainland, explaining why Spanish language and a loyalty to generic Hispanic culture were the foundations of New York Puerto Rican history, dominating the identity of even the poorer and more racially mixed post-WWII diaspora, whose first generation lived in New York's *hispano* world.

---

[4] The counter mythos that influenced Steven Spielberg's 2022 remake of the film version.

[5] I write of migration and not of immigration because citizenship had been extended to Puerto Ricans as an amendment to the Jones Shipping Act of 1917.

[6] Into the late eighties, publishers still used "Spanish" as the traditional encompassing epithet, releasing anthologies that would introduce the new Latin American writing as part of Spanish writing and therefore alongside Iberian writers. Two examples are John A. Crow's edition of *An Anthology of Spanish Poetry: From the Beginnings to the Present Day, Including Both Spain and Spanish America* (1980) and Angel Flores' textbook reader *Spanish Stories* (originally published in 1960 and re-released in 1987), which also includes Latin American writing.

As I grew up, I realized that the diaspora's second generation was split: the more culturally conscious identified with New York's *hispano* world while, commensurate with socioeconomic and racial marginalization, *hispanidad* lost importance, a tension that would eventually surface because the postwar migration was built on the default white community founded by the prewar diaspora. A survey of U.S. flamenco dancers of the second half of the twentieth century would reveal the surprising number of Puerto Ricans who studied it in the fifties. As a little kid, I had to accompany my mother to my sister's flamenco classes. My earliest childhood was instilled with a monolithic yet eclectic *hispano* consciousness that encompassed both Spain and Latin America, the cultural world of my aunt and mother, not sophisticated women.

The music I heard growing up in my aunt's apartment as a child came from wax records whose content spanned the *hispano* world, Spanish *cante jondo*, Gardel's tangos, trios that sang *boleros*, *plenas* from Puerto Rico as well as *mambo* from both Puerto Rico and Cuba, *merengues* from the Dominican Republic, and of course, Mexico's songwriting genius in love ballads and *rancheras*, to which I never saw anybody actually dance until I traveled to the southwest. One can only deduce that class and racial differences among Puerto Ricans determined the sequence of pre-eminence given that musical range but that composite was the music of the popular *hispano* world.

Its movies chiefly came from Spain and Mexico. My mother especially swooned over the handsome and singing Mexican *galanes* in films distributed by Mexico's powerful, often Hollywood-partnered film industry. I was five or six when my beautiful young mother took me along to see her heartthrob, the screen mariachi Jorge Negrete, who had come directly from Mexico to perform in the Bronx Theater on 138th Street before a sold-out crowd of *hispano* fans, all Puerto Rican. He emerged on stage on horseback and, after the performance, in jealousy I tried to pull my mother away when he wrapped an arm around her shoulder to pose for a photograph.

My childhood was actually steeped in the fading end of that consciousness in New York and, although I spent my summers in Puerto Rico while growing up, I came of age in the Civil Rights Era. From my summers in Puerto Rico and the example of my family's qualified relationship to *americanos*, I had always understood *puertorriqueño* independently of its American citizenship. In the late sixties, while the mainland community was really still thinking of itself as *puertorriqueña*, my Puerto Rican second generation took on a national American identity as "U.S. Hispanics" in alliance with Mexican Americans in The Civil Rights movement. Mexican Americans' American credentials were over a century older, but the Puerto Rican diaspora provided a national broadcasting of Hispanic, no longer just regional southwestern "Mexican" but *hispano* as also coming out of Chicago and New York and Boston.

The Civil Rights Movement, although underscoring civil rights and racial equality, was subtextually also about cultural equality, which in advocating, sowed an enhanced appreciation of *roots*. But while roots may suggest a steeping in ethnic consciousness, it was concomitantly a contemplation of participation in American culture. Against this multi-layered background, and U.S Hispanics' being influenced by a racial pride consciousness picked up in the civil rights struggle (for distinct reasons rooted in each group's history on which I will expand later), younger Mexican Americans and Puerto Ricans came to define their American identity racially.

"Puerto Rican" came to be understood by the diaspora's second generation as a racial identity in an American conversation that I could never have with my extended island family. From the perspective of a *puertorriqueño*, I was still a member of the Hispanic and Latin American cultural fraternity. But on the mainland by the late seventies, the distribution "white, black, or Puerto Rican" invoked a racial fraternity with Mexican Americans whose more revolutionary Chicano consciousness was proudly self-identifying with indigenous roots as brown. Our talked-up political alliance and our coinciding in identifying racially in English tricked my Puerto Rican mind into thinking it knew Mexican Americans until one day I realized that, as "Puerto Rican" I knew nothing about Mexican Americans, having only always known them as Mexican from seeing them through my eyes as *puertorriqueño*.

This is what "Puerto Rican" knew about "Mexican" in those days into the sixties. American culture stereotyped Mexicans as risible or dangerous ("bad hombres"). In a Disney animation that I watched with my daughter, a fat frog was essentially a sleazy mustached Mexican, meaning from a Mexico that was backward, always "down in old Mexico," *mañana* sleepy, whose emblem was a humble peasant beside a burro. This image was diametrically the opposite of Mexicans seen through my eyes as *puertorriqueño* since my early childhood as part of the New York *hispano* world that I had earlier described.

Racial and cultural perspectives intertwined so the second mainland generation grew up politically in solidarity with racialized "Puerto Rican" if culturally understanding itself as *puertorriqueño* although what that meant often did not surpass a folkloric nostalgia. In the seventies, after Latin America emerged breaking up monolithic "Spanish," discrete national Latin American cultures came into clearer focus, including *puertorriqueño*, to which I will return, and as well my *puertorriqueño* view of "Mexican" through its literature.

In graduate school I switched from an English concentration in American literature to a doctorate in Latin American Literature, in which I more fully appreciated that Mexico was a motherlode of Latin American intellectual, literary, and performance genius, a fact that Americans learned through its literature in the seventies and decades later though Oscar-winning films and with the success of Univisión, a television network whose audience dwarfs any English language network.

The Spanish-language television that my mother in her later years watched would primarily be Mexican, notably the soap operas to which my mother could become addicted when she lived on the island and later in Florida and could continue watching uninterrupted when she flew back to Puerto Rico and could have just as well caught up in Los Angeles, Santa Fe, Tucson, Fayetteville, and scores of other Mexican-strong metropolitan broadcast areas to which she has never traveled. Yet, my mother, who toured Mediterranean Europe several times, but had never been to the southwest, needed no hands to count the Mexican Americans she was conscious of ever having met because for her they were Mexican.

The looming image of a discrete Mexican American first came into my view channeled through the publication of "U.S Hispanic" writers. Notable was the contribution of Nicolás Kanellos, who founded *Revista Chicana-Riqueña* and Arte Público Press, from whose list of Chicano works generations of Puerto Rican college students discovered Mexican American culturally and not just as remote Hispanic political allies. But that revelation was chiefly taking place in academe. In society, both mainland and island Puerto Ricans have always been and continue to be more directly in touch with and know Mexicans.[7]

As I worked on this book, the U.S. Post Office released a stamp honoring Laura Mendoza, star of *Tejano* (Texas Mexican) music, about whom as a listener of N.Y. Spanish-language radio, I confess I knew nothing. I first heard Tejano music one fortuitous weekend in San Antonio when a two-day annual festival included day-long concerts on several stages of the best *conjunto* bands, whose obviously popular stars were unknown to me.

This glossing over Mexican Americans continued back in New York. The new Mexican immigration to Manhattan, which had started occupying the formerly all-Puerto Rican El Barrio, soon had its own a radio station devoted to that Mexico-centered demographic, playing selections of regional Mexican music. Meanwhile, New York's generic Spanish-language radio stations have always played, among a galaxy of *musica latina* from throughout Latin America and Spain, the releases of the more urbane Mexican artists. No New York radio

---

[7] In the nineties New York's El Barrio in East Harlem, the original geographic symbol of the Puerto Rican migration, began to receive Mexican immigrants, and despite what cultural kindredness is implied, this encounter produced territorial friction. Those Mexicans straight from Mexico themselves have little history in the U.S., unfamiliar with Mexican Americans and particularly Southwestern American culture, and although living among them, Puerto Ricans are no closer to knowing Mexican American life.

station played Mexican American or *Tejano* music in my time and less so today as stations struggle with generationally diverse musical tastes influencing hemispheric *música latina*. And there's another reason.

In the lopsided cultural communication between the two Latino communities, Puerto Ricans, both mainland and island, disproportionately produce the popular music that all Latin America consumes, including Mexican Americans.[8] Several generations of Mexican Americans already knew "Oye Como Va" by Puerto Rico's Tito Puente playing the *timbales* decades before Carlos Santana recorded it playing the electric guitar. This flow of music from east to west, long the pattern, continues in the present generation with the southwestern fandom of Marc Anthony and Jennifer Lopez and more recently the Dominican-Puerto Rican Romeo Santos and island singers such as Gilberto Santa Rosa and Chayanne and Luis Fonsi and Ricky Martin.

In the opposite direction, west to east, while both mainland and island Puerto Ricans are constantly in tune with the music popular throughout Latin America that includes Mexican artists, Puerto Rican appreciation of Mexican American talent only comes as it does for the rest of the country, in the diversification of mainstream American media entertainments. Consequently, for Puerto Ricans as for any other easterner, decades would separate the sensation of Richie Valens' 1958 rock and roll version of the Mexican folk song "La Bamba," to which Anglo America couldn't help dancing however, and Freddy Fender's 1974 country ballad hit "Before the Next Teardrop Falls," and the coming to national prominence of guitarist Carlos Santana and the singer Linda Ronstadt. Puerto Ricans learned about the Texas-born singer Selena Quintanilla when the news broke of her murder, after the media coverage of her story and then the film, ironically starring the New York Rican Jennifer Lopez.

This Puerto Rican appreciation of Mexican American only seen through a mainstream national lens extended beyond music to other entertainments. On Spanish-language television, not just on Univisión and Telemundo but as well on the myriad other smaller Mexican cable stations, Mexican American is hardly if ever nationally visible. It was in the post-sixties' cultural diversification

---

[8] Cuban music, such as the Buena Vista Social Club, has greater cachet in the U.S., but Cuban artists are rarely heard in New York and, except for sophicates, relatively less heard in Latin America, where Puerto Rican performers are more widely known. During a month-long visit to Madrid, I listened to much radio, where *latino* or Latin American music is very much in vogue. On a station of strictly *latino* music, an average of four to five Puerto Rican artists were played amid every eight selections of singers from various countries, occasionally one from Cuba. To the Spanish, shared culture trumps nationalities, so the selection would include Andalusian renditions of Mexican classics and identifying the New York Rican star "La India" provincially as *la neoyorquina*.

of American film and television that, along with the rest of the country, both mainland and island Puerto Ricans discovered Cheech and Chong and director Robert Rodriguez's *Spy Kids* series. In the next decades, mainstream television would introduce the comedians George Lopez and Jimmy Kimmel, whose Uncle Guillermo constantly reminds us of his nephew's origins.

The difference between the communities, of course, extends beyond entertainments as each is conjoined with American culture from the perspective of discrete and contrasting histories. Mexican Americans, of course, descend from Mexico, inheriting as roots an epic history over a vast landmass, and as well an ancient anger over Cortés' pummeling native Mexicans with the brunt of Spanish brutality. Cortés, who can be said to have personally created the modern Mexican, took on as concubine an Aztec woman, in Spanish named Doña Marina and more popularly memorialized as La Malinche, who as translator betrayed her people by helping Cortés conquer, why Mexicans refer to themselves as *los hijos de la chigada*, or children of the rape.

In contrast, Puerto Rican roots are planted on an island colony of three hundred square miles descended from a more meager history of Spanish abandonment. Its "conqueror" was Ponce de León, more oblique than Cortés, who first provided military assistance to island Taínos under the threat of the fierce, presumably cannibalistic Caribs advancing north from Venezuela. Taínos were rescued only to have to fight their rescuers. With the Taínos' eventual demise, through disease and intermarriage, that cultural past did not fertilize a strong nationalist consciousness compared to indigenous Mexicans.

The different yet subtle parallel histories of violent founding are dramatized in each's respective literature. Mexico's story, inherited by Mexican Americans, is today retold in many genres of world literature, the drama of Moctezuma who, guided by an astrological conviction that the white invaders were ordained, acted conciliatory toward them. As one version of that legend tells it, he was stoned to death by his people and replaced by his nephew Cuauhtémoc, who resisted Cortés until his final breath. Cortés triumphed and Mexico today officially speaks Spanish. Even though Americans associate Mexico with "Montezuma," Cuauhtémoc is the Mexican's true hero.

René Marqués short story "Three Men by the River"[9] is based on Puerto Rico's less known legend about two brother chiefs with identical names, Agüeybaná. The older one, then the *cacique*, was conciliatory to the Spanish, convinced that they were gods, immortal, possibly owing to the protection of armor. On his death, his skeptical younger brother Agüeybaná "El Bravo" arranged an experiment to prove Spanish mortality: Diego Salcedo, a young Spaniard who asked to be

---

[9] *En una Ciudad llamada San Juan* (Río Piedras: Editorial Cultural, 1970), 19.

carried across a river, was invited to rest, dine, and continue his journey the following day. The next day he was carried into the river and drowned. Agüeybaná had three men witness that the corpse remained dead for three days—based on white men's preaching about Jesus' having risen on the third day— proof of mortality that set the stage for war.[10]

In the nineteenth century, when Latin American Spanish colonies seethed with visions of nationhood, sprawling Mexico became a vast theater of regional, class, and racial inner conflict, between Mexican Spaniards competing for power against colonially empowered Spaniards, between the Church with its own interests and Mexico's political forces, between descendants of indigenous and non-indigenous sectors of Mexico. Ultimately independence came to an ungovernable Mexico although that milestone cannot be traced to one heroic military victory as much to the breakdown of authority in Spain where the monarchy struggled to reign against the threat of constitutional rule.

From this complex drama whose violence and instability would extend into the twentieth century arises one important metaphor: the symbolism sown in 1566 by Martín Cortés, son of the union of Cortés and La Malinche, making making Martín the Mexican *mestizo*, the Mexican Adam. Throughout a history of external intervention in Mexico –Spanish, French, American– his *mestizaje* embodies the mythos of Mexican national identity, the origin from whom descended the also now world iconography of actors who fought to define Mexico yet again in the 1917 Mexican Revolution.

In the decades after that revolution, American imperialism would intervene and redefine Mexico yet again by taking possession of about half of its landmass, absorbing its native Mexicans, who had to reconcile now also being American. But even though the American southwest was no longer northern Mexico, it was Mexican history that Mexican Americans looked back at as their roots although today a more radical Latino looks further back solely to indigenous roots before the creation of modern Mexico.

In contrast, in Puerto Rico, the nineteenth-century sense of nationhood that erupted throughout Latin America was not as strong, militarily or psychically, against Spain's increased oppression. Because Puerto Rico was geopolitically strategic as the navigable gateway to America's waters[11] and being Spain's last hope of possibly regaining its lost empire, the island was virtually shackled to compel fealty, also serving as the exile haven of last resort to those Spaniards

---

[10] More historically precise, it was the cacique Guaironex, of another Taíno tribe, who suggested to Agüeybaná to carry out the experiment, according to https://quizlet.com/69939695/tres-hombres-junto-al-rio-analisis-literario-flash-cards/.

[11] Therefore, valuable to Spain for the same reason that it has always been to the United States.

expelled from former colonies, their presence augmenting island loyalty to Spain.

After the island's becoming a U.S. colony in 1898, against U.S. efforts to Anglicize island culture, even though a century before Puerto Ricans had contemplated independence from the Spanish, the island's cultured class rekindled the conviction that Spanish culture was the foundation of Puerto Rican culture. Not just politically and culturally motivated was the preservation of a Hispanic consciousness, there was also the confrontation of Hispanic Catholicism and Anglo Protestantism: while the U.S. governance of Puerto Rico connected it to Washington and its judiciary to the First Circuit Court, the island's soul, so to speak, remained in the Spanish-speaking world as its Catholic church remained connected to Spain, which provided its priests.

In that tradition, the island remained culturally and religiously, a Spanish *patria chica*, and during the Spanish Civil War (1941-1943), as cultural resistance to Anglo-Americanization, Puerto Rico welcomed exiled Spanish writers, artists, and intellectuals, who reinforced Hispanic culture. Among them figured the world-acclaimed cellist Pablo Casals, whose mother was Puerto Rican, and poet Juan Ramón Jiménez who while a resident of Puerto Rico, his wife's birthplace, received the Nobel Prize.

These discrete histories of Mexican Americans and Puerto Ricans resulted in contrasting perspectives on their shared Hispanic heritage and their American consciousness. Mexican-Americans have a longer history debating among themselves their connection to that Mexican history as Americans, producing generations that have identified strongly with its more recent American history, or with only its Hispanic heritage or its Mexican history or with only its indigenous history.

In that latter tradition, influenced by the civil rights struggle and the awareness of race as fundamental to the American experience, the more radical adopted the epithet Chicano (from the Aztec Xcano), identifying as indigenously brown, rejecting Hispanic as white oppression. Behind the southwestern Hispanic canceling operated the romanticization of a racial purity before the conquest, a purity that Mexican Americans and Puerto Ricans could not contemplate on the same footing.

Puerto Ricans don't inherit a prodigious indigenous legacy on which to create even the simulacrum of an alternate pre-Columbian founding. Instead, in those anti-imperialist seventies, when Latin America emerged as its own civilization breaking up the traditional Spanish monolith, activist Puerto Ricans were adopting a *latinoamericano* consciousness as implicitly revolutionary but did not promote the canceling of Hispanic.

Even as a heightened, more Latin American consciousness stressed *latino* over *hispano*, among the most radical Puerto Ricans there did not exist a shared brown racial consciousness, instead extending island ideological progressivism, which included solidarity with Nativist Latin America and a rediscovery of Taíno and Afro-Caribbean roots, to mainland self-racialization as "Puerto Rican," which passively aligned Puerto Ricans with Chicanos in drifting toward a racialized Latino.

Because Mexican-American is demographically hegemonic, Latino as Chicano brown was mainstreamed although inconsistently, alternately both canceling Hispanic and invoking it, spreading a politically-correct cloud over the trunk of the legacy tree from which Mexican Americans and Puerto Ricans are distinct branches.

Hispanic culture, misunderstood as a devotion to Castilian Spain, presumably redacts a history of racial oppression that, in the nature of historical ironies, is still fundamental to the creation of Latin America, which is largely Spanish-speaking. Anglophone Latinos, many who possess an oral but not literate Spanish, and for whom Spanish-speaking is often more functional than fluent, could facilely cancel Hispanic but Latin America, including Puerto Rico, which see the world through Spanish's linguistic history certainly could not. The Latin American emergence was a flowering of its having taken possession of Hispanic and Spanish in the same way that Americans and Canadians and Jamaicans have redefined Anglo culture in a functional appreciation that requires no cancellation of that history.

Puerto Ricans also sharply contrast with Mexican Americans in the influence of their respective non-European heritages and how that influence affects each's coming to terms with race. Mexican Americans inherit a history in which from the very beginning race consciously figured in the struggle to define the Mexican people. As noted in my brief Mexican history, from the start Mexicans were conscious of the role of race in their cultural destiny, symbolized by Martín Cortés, a legacy of racial consciousness that powerfully informs also Mexican Americans.[12]

A classic celebration of Mexicans' coming to terms with their multiracialism is José Vasconcelos *La Raza Cósmica* (*The Cosmic Race*, 1925),[13] which announced a Latin American mission to be a future "fifth race" in the Americas, composed of all the world's races. It is believed that Vasconcelos' idealization,

---

[12] This brief discussion addresses race as a factor of national identity, which does not mean that racism, also as an expression of class superiority, doesn't exist, either toward darker indigenous or Afro Mexicans.

[13] José Vasconcelos, *La Raza Cósmica* (Madrid: Editorial Verbum, 2021).

some say romanticization, of *raza* inspired sixties Chicanos/Mexican Americans to refer to their community as *la raza* and in the post-sixties influenced a rediscovering of roots in the former northern half of Mexico, now the American southwest, although younger Chicanos cultivated a consciousness centered on their indigenous pre-Columbian history.

In contrast, Puerto Ricans, owing to the hegemony of a white *criollo* consciousness, have always wrestled with their racial history, which except to mythologize the Taíno, hardly figured in Puerto Rico's nationalist vision. After the decimation of the native Taíno and the importation of Africans, Puerto Rico gained an Afro-Caribbean culture that primarily came to define a working class that although mythologized as integrated evolved socially marginalized from the whiter upper classes that preserved the mythos of the island as a land foremost of descendants of Spain, *criollos.* This vision facilitated perpetuating the popular mythos of Puerto Rico as the land of the country-poor yet implicitly white *jíbaro.*

After the U.S.'s 1898 taking possession of the island, Afro-Puerto Ricans were generally seen as favoring U.S. statehood, presumably envisioning more possibility of equality. Meanwhile, the great icon and martyr of independence, Pedro Albizu Campos, was Afro-Puerto Rican, and as product of his generation, fought for independence to preserve the island's Hispanic culture and defend its Catholic heritage against Protestant America. But except for the highly visible paradox of Albizu Campos, independence has primarily been a *criollo* aspiration.

Otherwise, race as subject in Puerto Rico had been kept chiefly a subtext until it reared its head early in the twentieth century in reaction to the Hispanophilia promoted by the island's cultured class to resist U.S. efforts to the island's being Anglo-Americanized. The aforementioned infusion of Spanish artists and intellectuals during the Spanish Civil War, while reinforcing Puerto Rico's Hispanist consciousness, demoted Puerto Rican uniqueness. This *hispanismo* therefore prompted a nativist reaction expressive of the twentieth-century Latin American discovery of the overlooked interiors of America's nations, their darker demographic components as part of every country's total patrimony.

Puerto Rico's Afro-Caribbean heritage came to the forefront in the 20's crossover popularity of the *plena* as dance and song, until then considered solely for *negros.* In that same decade, the actually white poet Luis Palés Matos published his Afro-Antillean poetry, through which he celebrated his vision of the Caribbean teeming with African spirits from whose inheritance even whites were not immune. For Palés Matos, Puerto Rico's being informed by Afro-Caribbean spirits was what distinguished Puerto Rican from Spanish culture.

Palés Matos' obsession with his African inheritance began from the perspective of the racist, mocking *criollo*, influenced as well by Vachel Lindsay's poems on the white man's "Dark Continent." White islanders dismissed his allegedly distorting true island culture, and in the sixties Palés' poems were misread as racist. Palés reputation had better luck outside the island: his indelible imagery and rhythms are credited with sowing a *poesía negra* movement throughout Latin America. Today, his Afro-Antillean vision continues to inspire later generations, notably the Afro-Puerto Rican novelists Luis Rafael Sánchez and Mayra Santos Febre, both writers whose renewed African-rooted cultural consciousness challenges the traditionally narrower interpretation of Puerto Rican culture as monolithically *criollo.*

The racial divide symbolized by Palés Matos' rebellion was a subtext of both prewar and postwar migrations to the mainland as in both cases it was the traditional *criollo* consciousness that was exported.[14] A photo exhibit of the Museum of the City of New York in conjunction with Hunter College's Center for Puerto Rican Studies showed the prewar migration arriving on steamships as first-class passengers.[15] That lingering white and skilled first impression had a great deal to do with the island government's convincing New York City to accommodate a large postwar migration of islanders to replace upwardly mobile Jewish workers in the garment industry.

That white image, as noted earlier, endured into the postwar migration, influencing the writing of *West Side Story* and prompting the correction of that more racially mixed diaspora's second generation, which came of age in the Civil Rights Era and experienced the racial rejection not experienced by the earlier migration. That generation began to speak of their American Otherness in racial terms, "white, black or Puerto Rican."

This proclivity also came from other sources. In the Civil Rights Era, there was the youthful agenda to gain national visibility, race being the strongest currency in national discourse. Additionally, self-racialization had become an expression of anti-imperialist pride, in this case also pride in the face of island rejection. These became the public expression of the diaspora's more racially-conscious second generation's frustration with the white image of Puerto Ricans planted in New York by the prewar migration.

---

[14] It is worth noting that while the diaspora's second generation acquired an appreciation of the same racial impurity that Sánchez and Santos Febre celebrate in their writings, a transracial rivalry and island holistic rejection of the diaspora supersedes acknowledging the also racial motive for cancelling the mainland as also germane to those authors' challenge to traditional Puerto Rican identity.

[15] I cite here from having attended this exhibit at the Museum of the City of New York.

But if Puerto Rican cultural history has been strongly defined by racism, that racism was never attributed to Puerto Rico's being *hispano*, the heritage that bulwarked against Anglo-Protestant United States. On the mainland, the prewar migration had experienced xenophobic ethnic hostility but not in any way to trigger that it was racial, while the youth of the more racially-mixed postwar diaspora, coming of age in the Civil Rights struggle, had experienced explicit racial bigotry and began to voice a racial consciousness. But their rebellion against *criollo* racism was not identified as originating from their being *hispanos*.

Mainland Puerto Rican racial consciousness was also not, as implied in English, about being brown;[16] it was about being black. The operative Caribbean colors are black and white. The racially-sensitive mainland Rican consciousness began to question the island's traditional *criollo* mythos of the *jíbaro*, and for a time influenced by the Cuban Revolution's multiracial pride consciousness, coincided with the island's younger revolutionary generation that was envisioning a Puerto Rican nationalism now based on truer culture, a confluence of island culture as the merging of Hispanic and Afro-Antillean roots. That idyll faded with the seventies' revolutionary consciousness after which mainland and island diverged again, this time with island *criollismo* more deeply entrenched and mainland popular talk of "white, black, or Puerto Rican" creating a proprietary racial metaphor, which never, strictly speaking, had a color although suggesting a blending of white and black or, tacitly, brown.

Of course, multiracial and racially-conflicted Puerto Ricans do not constitute a separate race in the way that younger Anglophone Ricans were finding more revolutionary to speak of themselves as their American identity. In fact, mainland Puerto Rican's racial consciousness was more figurative and rhetorical than real, never replacing the consciousness of historically internecine black and white racial island differences sharing *hispano* roots, never producing an explicitly racial political action like the Chicano's Brown Power movement, and not inspiring the intuitive adoption of brown as a racial-identity alternate to "Puerto Rican."

The racialization of Hispanic was not always interpreted as racial hostility by the first generation of the postwar Puerto Rican diaspora, but it was the racial experience of the more Americanized and explicit second generation that publicly identified with references to "black and brown" and "of color" communities, nomenclature not used in internecine personal conversations. No Puerto Rican, in discussing racial marginalization as American, would actually utter to another, "Because I am brown" for "because I am Puerto Rican." An

---

[16] I am discounting here the social, not political distinction, of being *trigueño*.

Afro-Puerto Rican who feels Puerto Rican might identify as *negro* as Puerto Rican and even say in English "I am black" while not while not necessarily conveying an assimilation as African American.

Nevertheless, at least in venting the frustrated racial consciousness of the mainland Rican if not exactly matching the colors, racialized Latino publicly bonded Chicano and mainland Puerto Rican communities, this time not culturally as Hispanic had done, but racially, mainly in politically sharing being of color and publicly falling into the available color distribution already adopted by Chicanos, which Puerto Ricans themselves never used in English except to translate *trigueño,* the color brown.

This passivity was further encouraged by the racialization of Latino's really also being a collaboration with white America's having already racialized Hispanic and seventies white progressive's having romanticized racial pride as revolutionary, defying and defanging white obsession with race. Liberals' and progressives' receptivity to the idea of a "protected class" augmented the credence to being racialized Latinos over cultural *latinos,* providing a louder and trendier forum in the then-quintessentially American racial conversation, and so Latino became committed to the racial consciousness that *latino* never evoked.

I have revisited the discrete histories and cultural and racial dynamics of Mexican Americans and Puerto Ricans with the purpose of restoring the more complicated discrete cultural causes that converged in the adoption of Latino. The more popular political understanding of that adoption oversimplifies in an American redaction, a racial reductionism that effectively homogenizes the two discrete cultural histories as the traditional shedding of the past that is presumed irrelevant to contemporary Latino American lives, which should echo the racial model of African Americans. But it was owing to their discrete histories, of course in the context of their shared American experience, that both coincided at unifying under a racialized Latino while their respective, different motives offer one reason why Latino semantically fluctuates in usage.

The adoption of racialized Latino must also be seen as accommodating the white American management of Hispanics, giving credibility to the political promotion of Latinos as cast in an American racial drama when, in fact, race is used to camouflage what most concerns Americans about Hispanics, their being a cultural threat. Americans intuitively know that the racialization of Hispanic[17] is really just political rhetoric, Hispanic being a transracial

---

[17] I refer here to Hispanics' being nationally racialized by white America as brown and the Chicano embrace of brown as defiant pride. But the subsequent wholesale Latino rejection of Hispanic racializes the epithet as a white-washing, as well as, ironically –as I

cultural identifier. Hispanic has never been seriously treated as constituting a literal race, never prompting a racial pseudoscience, a fear of miscegenation, and that ambiguity also carries over to "Latino." For even though its popular racialization provides the nation's media with a journalistic racial shorthand (black and brown communities) and the gristle for Latinos who cancel Hispanic, the greater number of Latinos invoke Latino tacitly also meaning Hispanic as motive for ethnic or cultural pride, and still many older others don't even agree with the adoption of Latino, for them an implied acceptance of the racialization of Hispanic.

The Mexican-American Richard Rodriguez dismissed the racializing of Hispanics. In his April 14, 2003 Bradley Lecture before The American Enterprise Institute, "The Invention of Hispanics and the Reinvention of America," Rodriguez proposed that racialized Hispanic was created by Nixon: "I grew up in a black and white America, which had no place to put brown. ...But in 1972, in a document called 'Statistical Directive 15,' Richard Nixon invented Hispanics. President Nixon in that same year also invented Asians and Pacific Islanders."[18]

Nixon "invented" Hispanic, according to Rodriguez, as a unit to define a racial voting bloc and so counteract emergent, unified African Americans, a guaranteed Democratic vote. But, Rodriguez underscored, Nixon was making a false comparison, between cultural and racial categories: "You cannot compare Hispanics to African Americans. Hispanic, indeed, is not a racial category; it is a cultural category." Rodriguez was speaking to conservative white America but also to his Chicano generation that advocated Third World solidarity and their membership as racially brown.

Of course, Hispanic had always existed as a summary cultural category, a translation of *hispano*. The novelty was its being racialized, what Rodriguez found useful to hyperbolize in the claim Nixon "invented" Hispanics. Actually, younger Hispanics, most prominently Chicanos, were also self-racializing in leftist defiance to having been racialized, the racialization in which Nixon didn't have to believe as literal to co-opt politically. Owing to Mexican American national hegemony, that popular anthropology prevailed for Nixon to pick up.

The national brown racial homogenization of Hispanic was fully operative by the eighties when Mexican Americans and mainland Puerto Ricans were identifying with the Latin American immigration as *latinos*, fast-tracked in the media as Latino. Latino offered a less-foreign-sounding alternative to Hispanic while

---

will discuss in more detail later– promotes the Castilian Fascist vision of a white Spain against its actually multicultural and multiracial composition.

[18] *The Invention of Hispanics and the Reinvention of America,* May 1, 2013, AEI, https://www.aei.org/articles/the-invention-of-hispanics-and-the-reinvention-of-america-2/

was not transracial, a tribal culture. From that that also *latino*, synonym of *hispano*, was not transracial, a tribal culture. From that point on, driven largely by southwestern grievances in the national discourse, Latino started taking on a semantic life of its own. This new narrative declared Hispanic as only white against which Latinos should assume the same proud defiance shown against white America in the sixties, embracing the brown to which white America had already racialized Hispanic.

Latino, in other words, was also a product of simplistic boilerplate that epitomized what younger Hispanics knew about traditional American culture, that it was racist and a mirror of conquering Spain in a narrative of racial injustice. Latino was an investment in post-civil rights hubris, not thinking that American change would be more complex, that America still consisted of forces working to obstruct progress toward "a more perfect union."

Mainstream America's racialization of Hispanic/Latino as brown was actually a manipulation of popular white proclivities, using political-base patriotic ignorance as the front line in the cultural war being waged to undo the assault on traditional cultural that had been the Civil Rights Movement. Intellectually, of course, traditionalist America saw another assaulting wave in the more recent massive immigration from Latin America, the real Hispanic threat not racial but cultural. In other words, while popular America squabbled fixated on racial equality, Washington thinkers knew that the civil rights triumph's greatest threat was its positing a multicultural America.

Multiculturalism by the eighties had gained traction from the emergence of minorities after post-civil rights recognition, its threat further epitomized by the massive immigration of Latin Americans, more Hispanics who historically have never satisfactorily assimilated and, in preserving their multicultural particularity, threatened traditional American identity. Not just in retaining Spanish but because *hispanos* as *latinos* arrive from multiracial societies and bring different attitudes toward race. If African Americans were iconic of the civil rights struggle, Latinos/*latinos* were the more apt icons of multiculturalism.

The conservative fear-mongering portrays Hispanics as an adulteration of a pure Anglo-Protestant America, a posture that veils the truth that America never was pure and that multiculturalism is not a novel post-sixties threat but a constant challenge since the English settlement. One vein of that multiculturalism dating to a century before that settlement is the Hispanic history that has been a major tributary of American cultural history. The English relied on Spanish cartography to perform its exploring. The oldest American city, Saint Augustine, was founded by the Spanish in 1565. Spanish literature was the foundation of American literature: the first effort at a novel, *Father Bombo's Pilgrimage* (1770) by Hugh Henry Brackenridge and Philip Freneau and the first modern American novel, *Huckleberry Finn* (1885) descend from Cervantes. Hispanic is also native because of the history of American expansion. Today's national geographic configuration is a map of the Hispanic heritage that the country absorbed.

These historical facts educated Americans know but true American patriotism is proved not by ignorance of those facts but by knowing them and discounting their importance. The "land of immigrants" mythos layered over American multicultural fact produces the impulse to cry out that Hispanics either assimilate or go back to their country, a wish that disintegrates in the historical reality that in the southwest, Mexican Americans had always been in their country and the U.S. occupied Puerto Rico.

And the absence of their contribution in the American education of "U.S. Hispanics" is instead filled with obsessing with American racial history, Latino popularly understood as a racialized unit juxtaposed to the equally fictitious monolithic, racially hostile Anglo culture. Of neither of their two cultural heritages were U.S. Hispanics taught nuanced reality and their education left them responding according to the rules of the game, not questioning it. In relation to each other, of their *latino* heritage they didn't know enough about Latin Americans to realize that, although politically defined by their racialized relation to American culture, what we call Latino mirrors the relationship of the discrete countries of their Latin American origins.

Politically discrete Latin American countries are a plane of ideological variety yet, sharing both Iberian and non-European cultural and intellectual heritages, they are threaded by that defining merger, the bonding idiosyncrasy cited by Carlos Fuentes regarding its writings: twenty nations with a single literature, which we can expand to a single artistic expression. We therefore read a Latin American literature and contemplate a Latin American art spoken of as the expression of a single cultural consciousness. Gabriel García Márquez's *One Hundred Years of Solitude* (1967) is at once a fictional history of Colombia and a Latin American Book of Genesis. Envisioning a pan-America, in 1891 Martí published *Nuestra América*, and in the seventies Hispanics were inspired by that vision to adopt *latino* as an extension of their Latin American roots in the U.S.

But, while ideal, that *latindad* fraternity in Latin America is alternately figurative, dissolved at a soccer match and occasional wars, with demarcations of profound ideological differences especially dredged up during the Cold War. Seventies U.S. Hispanic idealism, however, blinded from that more nuanced fact. My seventies generation extrapolated the Latin America of the literary "Boom" and the paradigmatic theater of Third World liberation from social injustice symbolized by the Cuban Revolution, not factoring in that Latin American were also the iconic generals, the Cuban *exilio*, the oligarchies.

That more nuanced Latin America arrived with immigration and the settling of discrete immigrant communities whose *latinidad* bond began to exert its influence on the collective Hispanic-American identity. But, as in Latin America, that collective bonding was limited to cultural expressions –even though Latino writing and art were as yet emergent– more prominently through pop culture and entertainments. Ironically, if *latinidad* bonding in Latin America is diluted in political difference, Latino Americans give the appearance of being politically bonded by their public mask of unity. But this is not the reality. Under that mask, the subgroups don't politically gel into a community anymore than Latin American nations form a single nation—as has now become apparent especially since the election of Trump.

Because Latino is the public face, however, native Latinos and those who adopt Latino politically represent all Hispanics. The immigration that had sowed a sense of *latinidad* as a cultural solidarity did not behoove getting versed in Latin American cultural particularities; sheer numbers empowered generalized Latino as the largest American minority. Moreover, the "U.S. Hispanic" consciousness that in the seventies had rediscovered Latin American "roots," nourishing a *latino* pride, inadvertently also resulted in a comparison of the new American egalitarianism with racial and class inequities in home cultures. This conflicted "U.S. Hispanic" view of Latin American roots was harbored into the eighties and nineties, overshadowed for a while by the cultural empowerment of Latinos' being projected to form the new largest minority, but ultimately informing the Anglophone Latino consciousness.

That consciousness veered from its originally culture-defining source *latino* to become the sociopolitical portal of criticism of *latino* as being synonymous with *hispano*. If in the past Hispanic unity came from monolithic Spanish as the bonding heritage and more recently Latin America had defined its own civilization that inspired Hispanics' identifying as *latinos*, in the millennium Anglophone Latino dropped its Latin American model, the roots era bygone, and established an Anglophone-understood Latinidad, the American bonding of U.S. Hispanic as a racialized political consciousness. To underscore, being anti-Hispanic is Latino's most radical stance. Still meaningful to greater numbers of Latinos is *latino* as a heritage epithet synonymous with *hispano*, while that traditional meaning overlapped with those Latinos who, not wanting to glorify a racist past, now championed Latin America's native and African heritages as their new roots.

But all that buzz was contained to the hive, having no impact on the public performance of Latinos as Americans. White Americans still understood Latinos to be a racialized voting bloc, a source of crime, a victim of socioeconomic injustice, and the cast of border dramas. The pitting of Latino against Hispanic was a refinement of no importance to the American general public, which continued to use Latino and Hispanic interchangeably. The great irony and indicator of Latino disconnect as an American identity was that while America had racialized Hispanic as brown, youthful Latino was racializing Hispanic as white.

There are other ironies and inconsistencies. Outside of its political and racial role, except what cultural vestiges Latino suggests as carried over from *latino*, Latino conveys no clear cultural sense, its semantic amorphousness inviting political and commercial exploitation and much creativity in defining it according to the context in which it is being used. Latino's range of possible meanings accommodates even contradictory usages: assumed to signify many self-evident things (such as the assumption that it is also *latino*), Latino's presumed *latino* cultural sense, Hispanic, can be invoked as it is tacitly denied. At the most extreme point of semantic diversion, Latino can denote an assimilation while *latino* denotes a preserved cultural distinction. And that simplified contrast glosses over that even when Latino and *latino* denote the same, they connote differently.

One sign of the semantic deficiency of "Latino" is a constant need to refine it, making nomenclature refinements to correct for or express gender equality in "Latino," discussions that are really displacements of confronting Latino's broader inadequacy squarely but that provide Latino a simulacrum of cultural content. This gender correction was grandfathered from Spanish grammatical gender consciousness: Spanish with its masculine terminal -o as predominant prompted the need to correct, or express gender equality.

Based on that argument "Latino" evolved to become Latino/a then Latin@ then Latinx, a history that explains much and that summarizing here overlooks much, requiring my returning to it later in appropriate detail. But Latinx does beg being more immediately addressed before proceeding because of the underlying questions that its advocacy raises that are really a questioning of Latino, a bespeaking more obviously than previous tweaks of an urgency to improve on Latino and not just to correct gender consciousness.

This admission comes out in Ed Morales *Latinx: The New Force in American Politics and Culture* (2018). Morales describes his book as a study of "Latinxs' occupation of the middle ground in America's racial binary."[19] He explains his having chosen Latinx as epithet: "I'm attempting, like the mostly young folks that are embracing this label, to engage with several threads of thinking about

---

[19] Ed Morales, *Latinx: The New Force in American Politics and Culture* (New York: Verso 2018), 45

identity and naming, recognizing and evaluating the potential of such a label's elasticity and ability to evade categorization."[20]

His book, on the one hand, is a thoroughly researched history of Hispanic racial consciousness that traces the origins of today's Latinx. On the other hand, while its focus on the Latinx consciousness as cutting edge does demonstrate that such a generational avante garde cries out for its own space and that Latinx does threaten to undermine or redefine the older notions of race and identity, Morales' book isn't about Latinx's having achieved that change; rather, it is a hyping of its novelty, on whose broader impact ultimately Morales is prophesizing.

Seeing as positive Latinx's "elasticity and ability to evade categorization," Morales refers to a "Latinx people" whom he avers are "the primary destabilizers of American and by extension Western identity."[21] Latinx, if one understands Morales correctly, is not what Latinos are or have been but what those "younger folks" want them to become, which is conscious of a history of binary impositions on race and identity. "Latinx people" are actually Latinos convinced they should be calling themselves Latinx because Latinx presumably obliterates identity binaries—although the epithet is also used by gender-conscious Latinos who may have no idea of being Western identity destabilizers.

Morales himself proceeds to be tentative about Latinx. He had opened with an acknowledgment that Latinx is an epithet hard to warm up to: "…the term has a technocratic emptiness that makes it hard to warm up to. It feels like a mathematician's null set, and many are unsure of how to pronounce it."[22] So why does Morales express such solidarity to a hollow-feeling and semantically amorphous word? Because solidarity is, as the expression goes and I posit here, what Latino and by extension Latinx are primarily all about, especially since one gleans from Morales' discussion that Latinx is predominantly an oral consciousness. While Morales cites from past Spanish texts very effectively and uses a metaphor adopted from poet Audrey Lourde, and does cite Latino writing as cross-pollinated and bilingual, his evidence of Latinx hybrid identities is predominantly from oral and pop culture, the default of Latino.

Latinx's semantic elasticity allows it to signify anything a Latinx can claim or what Morales can interpret, among them a recycling of things that are described as new. One major example is that Latinx, in rejecting Hispanic or Latin binaries, is really just a mode of assimilating in presumably a more advanced woke

---

[20] Morales, *Latinx: The New Force in American Politics and Culture*, 3.

[21] Morales, *Latinx: The New Force in American Politics and Culture*, 3.

[22] Morales, *Latinx: The New Force in American Politics and Culture*, 4.

America: "The real power of the term and its true meaning, however, erupts from its final syllable. After years of Latin lovers, Latin looks, Latin music, and Latin America, the word describes something that is not as much Latin ...as it is an alternative America, the unexpected X factor in America's race debate."[23] In that alternative America, Latinx envisions being neither black nor white but presumably self-identified and nonbinary of-color.

In other words, if Latino shed a Hispanic heritage as politically incorrect, Latinx sheds Latin altogether and becomes a wholly American identity, a rejection of what is intolerable about home cultures to be corrected in a woke America, in which presumably Latinx does not have to invoke a fixed identity either. In that case, this interpretation of Latinx is really derivative, a trendier way of expressing "ex-Latin" because Latino had already made that shift after having diverged from *latino*, racialized Latino implying membership in a redeeming multicultural America—except that Latino didn't proselytize a third racial way of undefined elasticity although open to it by being semantically amorphous.

That recycling of a Latino elasticity nuance is one example of Morales' emphasizing the novelty of Latinx that really isn't, at times overreaching in describing things as new. For example, he credits Latinx for creating "hybrid identities," the "today" term for multiracial, hyphenated identities, familiar terrain upgraded in words that presumably resonate with those "mostly young folks." This pattern goes a bit far:

> Yet the widespread creation of hybrid and hyphenated identities such as Nuyorican, Chicano, Dominican-York, Tejano, Miami Cuban has created space for excluded identities to assert themselves.
>
> For Latinx in the United States this relatively new process of creating hybrid identities dates back to the end of the Mexican-American War and the absorption of the Southwest territories in 1848.[24]

"Excluded identities," as he had earlier explained, included "gender identifications,"[25] whose role in defining *The New Force in American Politics and Culture* remains unclear. Excluded identities that did factor into the making of a communal consciousness have been asserting themselves since the American Revolution, starting with women and African Americans although Morales describes the process of creating hybrid identities for Latinxs as "relatively new," and yet dating "back to the end of the Mexican-American

[23] Morales, *Latinx: The New Force in American Politics and Culture*, 4.

[24] Morales, *Latinx: The New Force in American Politics and Culture*, 6.

[25] Morales, *Latinx: The New Force in American Politics and Culture*, 4-5.

War and the absorption of the Southwest territories in 1848." Something that dates back to 1848 is a historical, not a new process.

What is new here is not those excluded identities but simply calling them in a new way, which at times in this book gets chaotic, notably in the use of "Latinx": "But as I've alluded to in Chapter 1, the race narrative of Latin America, which is transmitted through the social mores of Latinx that emigrate to the United States...." In a book that explains Latinx as a new force in American culture, Latinx also corrects the epithet "Latin American." Morales apparently found himself at the crossroads of either having to fall back on Latin American as *latino* or muddy up his argument a bit and choose solidarity, sticking by Latinx, producing "Latinx that emigrate."

To summarize, notwithstanding Morales' thesis of novelty about Latinx, it is a younger folks' tagging of Latino with newness that is really, including its gender statement, a recycling of Latino never thought through in the first place but now their generations' very own binary-conscious identity "that allows them to cross boundaries more easily and construct identities or self-images that include a wide variety of racial, national, and even gender identifications."[26]

In other words, Latinx resolves Latino's semantic amorphousness by embracing it. But "crossing boundaries" was not an idea that produced Latinx, which was academically spun from the originally gender-correcting X, based on a binary concept of gender: "nonbinary" Latinx was a biproduct of the application of the creative semantic feature of semantically amorphous, undefined Latino.

Otherwise, aside from providing space-age-sounding novelty, except for those who feel they have no identity nor need one, in more widespread actual usage semantically Latinx remains the gender-correcting reiteration of Anglophone Latino. Semantically, both Latino and Latinx are our latter-day versions of something not clearly defined, making Paz's summary of the *pachuco* applicable both to Latino and Latinx: "Strange word, lacking a specific meaning, or more precisely stated, is loaded, like all popular inventions, with a plethora of meanings!" A plethora that Morales celebrates as "elasticity."

In other words, for all its ostensible novelty Latinx comes with Latino's original contradictions as baggage. Latino can cancel the history that made it Hispanic, a purging passed on to Latinx, yet in his book, Morales needs to recount a Hispanic history to arrive at Latinx. Latino/x wants to correct Latin American racial consciousness, inherited as Hispanic default white and redeemed by a woke American multiracialism that now should also be nonbinary, allowing for Latinx as, theoretically, no fixed identity, in other words,

---

[26] Morales, *Latinx: The New Force in American Politics and Culture*, 4-5.

do what Latino had earlier was intended to do, escape *latino* binaries (its machismo, racism, classism) by finding a space of political purity.

Perhaps because Latinos/*latinos* intuit Latinx's celebrating the very cultural confusion that Latino evokes, which "the Latino community" shies from intellectually confronting head-on, Latinx has not gotten very far in winning converts from Latino, even to express gender consciousness. Notwithstanding what percentages are crossing identity boundaries in Latinx, much like the flashy fashion displayed on runways but that only a select actually wear, Latinx remains a statement more than natural usage. And this is our present state of affairs as the first Latino/x generations advance toward maturity with "elastic" or semantically amorphous notions of their American identity, stuck in the presentism of a brief Latino history.

So far, I have traced that trajectory sketchily, sufficient as a political or social science summation, but not useful as cultural introspection to confront challenges ahead because it glosses over causes and consequences that require the scope of a more intellectually detailed history. To embark on that journey, however, requires my proceeding to do the un-Latino thing of being critical, more meticulously descriptive, suspending solidarity and the epistemology of literalness, arguing that one is not solely defined by political and racial consciousness, by immediate social "issues," but as well by cultural and linguistic inheritances, by ideas and their history that influence our thoughts. For however conscious we may believe we are of who we are, culture implants thoughts and feelings, a programming from one's past that one cannot circumvent or control without a knowledge of that history. But history is that problematic background that Latino either explicitly or tacitly works to cancel, in this case, two cultural histories, both Latin American and Anglo American, to which converging contexts I must return Latino in order to recover the history of how we got here.

YOU SAY YOU WANT A REVOLUTION: HOW WE GOT HERE

"When I use a word," Humpty Dumpty said in rather a scornful tone, "it means just what I choose it to mean – neither more nor less."
"The question is," said Alice, "whether you can make words mean so many different things." –Lewis Carroll, *Through the Looking Glass*

The Civil Rights Movement politically worked to secure the social integration of minority citizens in the courts while culturally challenging traditional white assumptions of supremacy, awakening African Americans to shed their second-class consciousness and self-define their American identity. In forcing white America to apply in legal practice democratic principles that it had historically betrayed, African Americans became the model for all Americans and The Third World to emulate. Culturally, that triumph was expressed in a resurgent pride in African roots, a resurgence also emulated by U.S. Hispanics in rediscovering their roots.

To re-summarize, the most radical Mexican Americans traced their origins to purely indigenous roots predating Hispanic Mexico, the mythic land of Atzlán, self-identifying as Chicanos. In the east, mainland and island Puerto Rican youth revitalized an ever subtextual nationalist desire for an independent Puerto Rico while challenging island racial attitudes, stirring up a historical racial controversy. Meanwhile, the composite "U.S. Hispanic" demographic reaffirmed roots in emerging, revolutionary Latin America.

This background usually serves to trace a generalized cultural motive for a Latino political trajectory, glossing over a more substantive cultural vacuum that to fill requires more nuance, much that is assumed, overlooked, invented, or simply repeated as assumed truth. To illustrate, when we say Latino, we summon archived images. We don't immediately think, say, about New Mexicans, who do not traditionally identify as Mexican Americans. Having preserved a consciousness more directly connected to both indigenous and Spanish roots, they identify as *hispanos*. Santa Fe has been one of the world's showcases of flamenco dance.

In the sixties and seventies, the activist Reies López Tijerina (1926-2015) organized indigenous and *hispano* groups to restore New Mexican land grants to the descendants of their Spanish colonial and Mexican owners, grants guaranteed by the Treaty of Guadalupe Hidalgo (1848) that ended the U.S. war with Mexico. His story of action and activism survives as both legend and controversy, even among Mexican Americans, and does not coincide with facile racializations of Hispanic as white. Chicanos supported his rebellion, political solidarity that overlooked his disagreement with their view of history. López Tijerena, who was born in Texas and over the span of his life alternated living in the U.S. and Mexico, preferred the epithet *indohispano*.

Also, little-contemplated on the gestation of Latino, is the background influence of The Cold War on all liberating minorities. From the start, F.B.I. founder and director J. Edgar Hoover had monitored the Negro demand for civil rights as a Communist-induced threat. Hoover and the Right viewed Martin Luther King, Jr. as a Communist infiltrator while Hispanics were identifying with Latin America that, after the Cuban Revolution, had become for mainstream America practically synonymous with the threat of Communism. The fear of that contagion was reinforced by the 1970 democratic election of the Chilean socialist president Salvador Allende.

That fear or appearance of threat was not completely unfounded as young U.S. Hispanics increasingly contextualized their minority struggle in The Third World, in which Latin America was now globally most visible. Moreover, the validation of Hispanic roots consciousness by liberal America had empowered young Hispanics who expressed their cultural views in liberal/progressive diction. For my generation, therefore, Latin America's political resistance to U.S. imperial domination made their Latin American "roots" the world's emblem of the Third World, the mental site where we then-Hispanics envisioned our U.S communities on the geopolitical globe, Chicanos and Puerto Ricans rooted in one giant leftist metaphor, Latin America.

That broad metaphor also applied in celebrating Latin America's cultural emergence apart from monolithic Spanish as expressed in its world-class writings. In that decade before the start of Latin American immigration, as noted earlier, U.S. Hispanics had started to adopt *latino,* which was translated as Latino, homogenizing everything *latino.* Salsa, the musical genre created by mainland Puerto Ricans in New York, in English became the emblematic music of a total Latin America. American book reviewers associated all Latin American novels with the revolutionary aesthetics of Magical Realism, really a Caribbean basin surreal imagination quite distinct from the psychological and metaphysical-fantasy exercises of the Southern Cone. Every newly booming Latin American writer was presumed part of a revolutionary wave, whether political or literary or both. Needless to say, that ostensibly monolithic Latin America was in reality more politically and culturally complicated and subtle, but who kept count of how many of its iconic figures were actually leftist?

Certainly not all were, as Latin America actually comprised a less hyped spectrum of political ideologies. Nobel Prizes went to the Communist Pablo Neruda and the Fidel Castro-admiring Gabriel García Márquez. But Latin America's literary emergence also included the future Nobel laureate Mario Vargas Llosa and Jorge Luis Borges, who spoke for a middle-to-oligarchical right, a posture that surely cost Borges the Nobel Prize. The poet Nicanor Parra, who at first aligned his works with the left, later famously forsook it for a personal anarchism, neither left nor right. In addition, even more far right were Christian-right Cuban exiles, the Nicaraguan anti-Sandinistas, and committed Westernists like the generals Pinochet and Varela. But for my seventies generation that far-right was the vestige of a historical mistake. For us Hispanics, there was only a single-entity Latin America, with Cuba the hemispheric model of social commitment and literary *compromiso*, harbingers of everybody's revolution just around the corner.[27]

Consequently, Cuban writers were read for politically-correct guidance, most influential for this discussion Roberto Fernández Retamar, conventionally called by his maternal surname Retamar. In 1971 Retamar published his book-length essay *Calibán*, a revolutionary response to the Uruguayan José Enrique Rodó's late-Romantic classic essay *Ariel* (1900), which critiqued Latin America's envy of Anglo-American material achievement. For Rodó, Shakespeare's Ariel was the proper metaphor of the positive and non-materialist values that should serve as Latin America's more sublime intellectual model against the crass paradigm Caliban, beast driven by negativity and the basest human urges, a slave to the material world. Retamar counterargued that Shakespeare's Caliban was the proper symbol of Spanish imperial dehumanization of Latin America.

Retamar also channeled his nineteenth-century mentor, the Cuban poet José Martí (1853-1895), today ironically canonized as both the inspiration of the Cuban Revolution and the spiritual patron of the anti-Communist Miami *exilio*. Martí is a testament to the fact that Latin American intellectual emergence had really begun in the nineteenth-century.

In his almost two decades of exiled residency in New York City plotting Cuban independence from Spain, Martí published his most important poems and volumes of journalism, cultural criticism, and reviews of literature and art, a couple of essays in English. In some anthologies of Latino writing the New Yorker Martí is acknowledged as an antecedent. Among his works is the book-length essay that contemplates a pan-Latin America, *Nuestra America* (*Our America*), a call to guard against the United States' imperial appetite. Originally published in 1892, its English translation was first published in 1977, making it part of the Latin American translation Boom at the right moment to inspire U.S. Hispanics with its central idea of Our America, in which we were rediscovering our roots. In channeling Martí, Retamar was writing not just as Cuban but as Latin American, *Calibán*'s subtitle is *Apuntes sobre la cultura de nuestra américa*.

A patently American influence was the post-civil rights practice of liberating through nomenclature (Negro to Black, girl to woman, Indian to Native American), and Retamar advanced that in identifying Latin America as *Hispanoamérica*, the prefix *hispano* celebrated Spain, the hemisphere's original enslaver, honoring Spanish imperialism and not those who struggled

---

[27] We were not alone but encouraged as well by our American times: mainstream America, after its support of the Civil Rights cause, had joined the era of Radical Chic. The actress Jane Fonda traveled to Hanoi. We were all on board the same world-saving schooner of our time.

to be liberated. *Hispanoamérica* also distorted hemispheric history by isolating Spanish-speaking countries from their French and Portuguese sister former colonies, which also descend from Romanic roots and survived colonialism. That struggle, according to Retamar, is the defining experience of Latin America and should be acknowledged by a change in nomenclature, so *Hispanoamérica* to identify Our America should be retired never again to be used as synonym of its more authentic traditional alternates *Latinoamérica* or *América Latina*.[28] Thus was born the political correctness of *latino* over *hispano*.

This call from Cuba, the world's revolutionary Oracle, behooved that international political correctness immediately stop honoring that imperialist Spanish past. In the U.S., graduate students of Spanish and Romance Language departments, where Latin American literature was replacing Iberian hegemony, immediately ceased and desisted, making the correction and correcting others. Those who continued to use *hispano* and *hispanoamericano* suddenly sounded like those retrograde souls that continued to use *colored* or *Negro*. By the late seventies and early eighties, the correction spread outside academe where it resonated with politically active Hispanics[29] still gestating a newly acquired post-civil rights racial consciousness as the Latin American immigration was beginning and planting the idea of their also being *latinos*.

Retamar's call, of course, was a lettered distinction. In popular Spanish usage *latino* and *hispano* had historically been and continued to be synonymous. But for college-educated U.S. Hispanics, Retamar's call was consistent with seventies revolutionary consciousness and began to make even more sense into the eighties with incrementing Latin American immigration. By the late nineties, with U.S. demographics auguring a new largest minority, *latino* was definitely the trend, and by the millennium, Spanish-language TV had standardized *latino* that phonetically encompassed its huge native Hispanic and immigrant *latino* market, and even competing English-language media adopted the epithet, using the Anglicized Latino.

By then, almost three decades after the publication of *Calibán*, *latino* in popular Latin American usage and even among immigrant *latinos*, who had picked up the trendy usage because Latinos had made it standard but not to affirm any political point, still tacitly understood *latino* to be synonymous with *hispano*. Former U.S. Hispanics, now Latinos, however, conserved the epithet's

---

[28] The history of *latinoamérica* has a couple of tellings, notably repeated is that the coiner is reputedly a French diplomat, who changed the traditional *hispanoamérica*, and thus *hispano* to *latino*, to encompass French interests in the hemisphere.

[29] At that time Mexican Americans and mainland Puerto Ricans, with exiled Cubans as yet still not identifying as American.

seventies politicization with ideological passion, Americanizing it one step further into a racial epithet while a second generation of the Cuban *exilio* would reject Latino as part of the leftist world that supported the Cuban Revolution.

Into the millennium, an older generation still considered Latino a younger generation's misguided consciousness. In *A Hispanic View: American Politics and the Politics of Immigration* (2002), California journalist Raoul Contreras Lowery expressed his generation's reaction, arguing that most Mexican Americans didn't identify with either the then-politically-radioactive Latino or the radical Chicano: "Most middle-class people with Spanish surnames reject the word Latino. Many immigrants from Spanish-speaking countries also reject the term."[30] The replacement of Hispanic with Latino was a self-inflicted cultural diminishment.[31]

Contreras Lowry blamed the *Los Angeles Times* for mainstreaming the new epithet by authorizing the most outspoken young Mexican Americans who had made Latino a code word for progressivism.[32] The *Times*' picking it up as cutting edge started a domino effect that spread eastward until across the country Hispanic gave way to Latino.

Contreras Lowry's *Hispanic View* was taken through a traditional Hispanic cultural lens. It also exhibited the racial fault line that *latino* transracialism blurs and yet socially sustains not in genetics-consciousness but in classed, including cultured, distinctions ("middle-class Spanish-speaking people") that were prompting younger Latinos to racialize Hispanic.

Contreras Lowry did not explicitly articulate but really objected to the racialized reduction that was Latino, a subject one has to extrapolate from his cultural response to how Latino influenced the gestating American identity of the cohort-consciousness that began with the sixties alliance of Mexican Americans and Puerto Ricans. The racial emphasis is indeed an influence of white American racial objectives to discredit culture, but race is also a subtext of internecine borders in both communities with their root cultures, the Mexican American with Mexican and mainland Puerto Rican with islander Puerto Rican.

In Mexican culture, racism has always been the subject "del que nadie quiere hablar," wrote Marcos González Díaz in underscoring that the dormant race debate surfaced in response to the killing of George Floyd. Marcos started out

---

[30] Raoul Contreras Lowery, *A Hispanic View: American Politics and the Politics of Immigration* (New York: Writers Club Press, 2002), 3.

[31] Contreras Lowery, *A Hispanic View: American Politics and the Politics of Immigration,* 9.

[32] Contreras Lowery, *A Hispanic View: American Politics and the Politics of Immigration,* 2.

by noting that Latin Americans harbor the shibboleth that they are less racist than Anglo Americans despite the fact that in Mexico itself "más de la mitad de la población **reconoce que se le insulta por el color de su piel,** según el Consejo Nacional para Prevenir la Discriminación [more than half the population acknowledges being **insulted because of their skin color**, according to the National Council to Prevent Discrimination]."[33]

On October 25, 2021, the United Nations' *Noticias ONU* reported on María Celeste Sánchez Sugía, the first senator in Mexican history who openly identifies as Afro-descendant, and her struggle to "lograr el reconocimiento no sólo de la existencia de los pueblos afromexicanos, sino de sus aportaciones al país y de la necesidad de hacer efectivos sus derechos. Dejar atrás la herencia de invisibilidad y olvido a la que han sido sometidas las personas afrodescendientes desde hace 500 años [achieve the acknowledgment not just of the existence of Afro-Mexican communities but as well of their contributions to the country and the need to uphold their civil rights, leave behind the inheritance of invisibility and oblivion to which people of African descent have been subjected for 500 years]."[34]

On the subject of racism in Mexico, books and articles abound that need not be cited here to make the point that in interpreting Retamar's call to retire the idea of an *hispanoamérica,* Chicanos were responding to an endemic Mexican racial tension when they identified with pre-Hispanic racial origins, a historical context lost in the simpler American discourse of a brown minority group expressing racial pride before white America. And that historical context gives credence to the Chicano argument that preserving Hispanic as cultural refinement is fraught with racial implications, that defending Mexican Americans as primarily Hispanic can also be setting up racial gradations.

In other words, Contreras Lowry's history of Latino traced the demise of the Hispanic consciousness omitting any racial evocations that Hispanic might have, so his generalizing that the *L.A. Times'* adopting Latino started a domino effect that eventually spread Latino eastward amounted to his saying that Latino simply became the latest fad that eastern Puerto Ricans picked up. But as with Mexican Americans, and specifically Chicanos, the adoption of Latino by Puerto Ricans came as a convergence of their own racial issues, and as noted

[33] Marco González Díaz, "Racismo en México: cómo la muerte de George Floyd desató en el país un debate 'del que nadie quiere hablar,'" *BBC News Mundo,* last modified June 5, 2020, https://www.bbc.com/mundo/noticias-america-latina-52931479

[34] "Celeste Sánchez y la lucha por el reconocimiento legal de las poblaciones afrodescendientes en México," *Noticias ONU,* last modified October 25, 2021, https://news.un.org/es/story/2021/10/1496012

earlier, in their case, was not concomitant with a demonization or racialization of Hispanic but, as with Mexican Americans, also resulted from a discrete Puerto Rican racial history.

As noted earlier, after Puerto Rico's becoming a U.S. colony in 1898, cultured islanders resisted the agenda to Anglo Americanize Puerto Rico by reviving its Hispanic heritage to keep the island Spanish-speaking. In that Puerto Rico, black culture was considered a folkloric component but not a defining essence of Puerto Rican. That island racial debate was exported to New York subtextually in both the prewar and the postwar diasporas. The earlier, mainly white prewar community had experienced traditional ethnic bigotry but was essentially treated as white; that *criollo* population was in turn racist. A paradigm of that dynamic is the Afro-Puerto Rican historian Arturo Alfonso Schomburg (1874-1938), who before the 1898 American annexation of Puerto Rico had worked in New York with the island's independence movement. Schomburg's response to Puerto Rican racism is often finessed, as is evident in this *Encyclopedia of Puerto Rico* biography:

> The Spanish-American War (also known as Spanish-Cuban-American War) of 1898 added an unexpected twist to the political destinies of Cuba and Puerto Rico. After the U.S. invasion of the islands, many separatists returned to their island homelands while others remained in their countries of exile. For Schomburg, the postwar years marked a growing estrangement from New York's Puerto Rican community and an increased connection with his black roots and the African American community. Married to an African American woman, he Anglicized his name and moved to the black section of Harlem. There he developed long-standing friendships with many prominent black intellectuals and artists from the United States and the Caribbean and joined the Pan-African movement that also influenced the work of many leading figures of the Harlem Renaissance.[35]

The "unexpected twist" included a dimming of independence prospects for Puerto Rico and, as would unfold, a general Afro-Puerto Rican interest in statehood. The phrasing "growing estrangement" finesses the resentment that Schomburg felt toward his compatriot's racial attitudes, which prompted his "growing estrangement from New York's [understood as white *criollo*] Puerto Rican community" and his increasingly identifying as a global African and African American, his moving to West Harlem, and his relocating his extensive library of Africana that the New York Public Library would acquire as the

---

[35] "Arturo Alfonso Schomburg," *Encyclopedia of Puerto Rico*, last modified May 18, 2021, https://en.enciclopediapr.org/content/arturo-alfonso-schomburg/

foundation of what would become the Schomburg Center for Research in Black Culture.

Schomburg predated the pre-WWII *criollo* diaspora that started after a 1917 amendment to the Jones Shipping Act extended citizenship to Puerto Ricans. That first, chiefly white diaspora would serve as ironic prologue to the post-WWII diaspora, which would arrive racially mixed to a New York that had already known Puerto Ricans as predominantly white. Ironically as well, the second generation of this more massive diaspora came of age with The Civil Rights Movement and challenged the first generation that rationalized conflicted Puerto Rican racial attitudes.

Emblematic of the Puerto Rican racial dilemma was the island's treatment of The Young Lords Party, founded in 1968, a Chicago street gang that evolved into a political activist organization, which then expanded nationally, its most visible chapter in New York. Its leadership was chiefly Afro-Puerto Rican. The Lords advocated island independence and implemented service programs that earned the entire community's respect. Paradigms of *latino* transracialism, the Lords modeled themselves after and allied with The Black Panthers and other race-based organizations as a Third World revolutionary movement, but never explicitly as a racial movement. When the Lords opened an office in San Juan to join the independence movement, however, they were rebuffed—the rejection couched nonracially in the mainland organization's assumed irrelevance to island affairs but the rejection was equally as racially motivated. Internal divisions and F.B.I. persecution led to its being disbanded in 1989.

Ironically, a decade later, in the late seventies and early eighties, young progressive islanders who came to the mainland joined the nativist chorus of revolutionary Latin America by advocating a more inclusive Puerto Rican racial consciousness, acknowledging as well the postwar diaspora. In the spirit of those times, as an industrialized Puerto Rico was identifying with emergent Latin America and its left was emulating Cuba's recognition of its multiracialism, the island's nationalist movement tried to gain the support of working-class mainland cousins. Their bi-weekly newspaper *Claridad* was distributed in colleges with large Puerto Rican student enrollment, including New York University where I was doing graduate studies.

But even though politically left in being anti-colonial and wanting to emulate Cuba on the question of race, *independentistas* could only bring themselves to recruit the mainland as an asset while remaining culturally traditionalist, *criollo,* unable to incorporate meaningfully either the island's also being Afro-

Caribbean[36] or the more racially-conscious mainland Puerto Ricans. In response to a general sense of alienation from their cultural origins, including the symbolism of the treatment of the Young Lords on the island, younger mainland Puerto Ricans had started embracing racialized "Puerto Rican" as their American identity.

This mainland consciousness had been expressing itself among New York Ricans in a population shift in Manhattan. As the first generation, island-centric *boricuas* died off or returned to the island, second-and third-generation Ricans had been drifting to Manhattan's Lower East Side, the Barrio vacancy filled by arriving Mexican immigrants. Meanwhile, the Lower East Side took on the character of a discrete community, dubbed Loisaida. El Barrio and Loisaida properly symbolized the cultural distinctions between island-centricity – institutionalized in Hunter College's Center of Puerto Rican Studies– and the newly distinct mainland consciousness of Loisaida, whose unofficial cultural institution[37] was becoming the Nuyorican Poets Café, which promoted the "Nuyorican" mainland mythos, essentially racialized Puerto Rican.

Through the even international fame of the Nuyorican Poets Café, especially by way of its most famous poet and playwright Miguel Piñero, Nuyorican became a brand, a marketing myth that distorted the less colorful but sober reality that, by then, what one called the "mainland Puerto Rican community" had extended beyond New York, encompassing several northeastern states, as well as Chicago, the city of Orlando, out to Hawaii. Nevertheless, in loose pop speech, the mainland Rican American identity was routinely identified as tacitly racialized Nuyorican, segue to Latino.

Contreras Lowry was right in observing that Latino over Hispanic got its strongest impetus from the southwest, where Retamar's seventies call struck a particular chord with Mexican American historical anger at Hispanic. Contreras Lowry did address the Chicano movement's racially homogenizing the entire Mexican American community as Brown when his generation still identified as Hispanic. But he did not account for Latinos becoming the national epithet beyond the Mexican American contribution. That nationalization resulted owing to the same generation of mainland Puerto Ricans' having racialized the

---

[36] As previously noted, the island's black leadership had always been associated with the statehood movement presumably against the classist culture that compartmentalized black islanders although ironically the icon of the independence movement, Pedro Albizu Campus, was Afro-Puerto Rican.

[37] The Cafe still exists but as a performance poetry and theater space largely disconnected from the immediate community around which it was originally created. For a more detailed history and discussion, please see "The Making of Miguel Piñero and 'The Nuyorican Experience'."

entire mainland demographic as racially "Puerto Rican," only adopting the racialized Nuyorican in response to their own internecine drama, Nuyorican deferring nationally to unifying Latino.

But, to reiterate, even though Nuyorican as a tacitly racial consciousness adopted to defy racial marginalization, mainland Puerto Ricans never actually racialized Hispanic as did Chicanos. This paradox was passed on to the adoption of Nuyorican, which was never explicitly spoken of as a racial consciousness—encompassing both racialized white and nonwhite Nuyoricans— in part because Nuyorican was a pop culture epithet without more complicating intellectual dimensions.

But even in its lightness, Nuyorican illustrated how Puerto Ricans have a hard time separating themselves racially, whether owing to an inherent transracial consciousness or to a racial self-censorship at work in the Rican psyche— something for the individual to interpret. In contrast, if on the one hand, race is the subject about which Mexicans "don't want to speak," as Ed Morales' history of Hispanic racial consciousness demonstrates, race has been in the front of the Hispanic mind for five hundred years, and not solely because of racist attitudes that Spain sowed with the Conquest but as well because Spain was a target of Western racism.

For in their converging self-racialization as Latino Americans and their implied or explicit racialization of Hispanic as white, Chicanos and Puerto Ricans evince a shared ignorance of the Western racialization of Spain. This racialization began with England's rivalry against Spain's expansion into the Americas. After the publication of Bartolomé de las Casas' *Brevísima relación de la destrucción de las Indias* (*A Short Account of the Destruction of the Indies*, 1552), a condemnation of the conquistadors' ruthlessness, the English coopted that portrayal to promote their future settlement as destined to be more civilized. Allied with the Dutch, who were combating Spanish rule, the *leyenda negra* or Black Legend of Spain racialized as savage was cranked out of printing presses and disseminated throughout Europe.

That racialization of Spain, which began as a response to its brutal conquest of the Americas, evolved over time to express European condescension to Spain's admixture of cultures and races, a departure from European purity critiqued by Dominque Dufour de Pradt in his 1816 *Mémoires historiques sur la révolution d'Espagne*, which portrayed Spain as really where Africa begins:

> It is an error of geography to have assigned Spain to Europe; it belongs to Africa: blood, manners, language, the way of life and making war, in Spain everything is African. The two nations have been mixed up for too long, the Carthaginians who came from Africa to Spain, the Vandals who left Spain for Africa, the Moors who stayed in Spain for 700 years for such

a long cohabitation not to have confused the race and customs of the two countries. If the Spaniard were Mohammedan, he would be completely African; it is religion that has kept it in Europe.[38]

The running phrase today, whose original source is debated, is that "Europe ends at the Pyrenees" or "Africa begins at the Pyrenees."

Spain's Iberian impurity, William Carlos Williams argued in *In the American Grain*,[39] sowed in the Americas a multiracial consciousness, the quintessentially American "mingling spirit." The racially purist English colonizers lacked that spirit and could not sow it, being incapable of touching the natives. In contrast, the Spanish came to "lay hands" and baptize them, the Church acknowledging their humanity with souls to harvest. Williams finessed Spanish cruelty, including the Church's cruelty, but was not wrong in underscoring the major difference that the Spanish came "to marry" America, what the English saw as bestiality.

In their supposedly savage difference, then, the Spanish sowed, according to Williams, the inclusive American spirit, the inherently American impurity that Anglo America has historically resisted acknowledging of its own uniqueness to preserve its narrative of Euro-descended purity. This "mingling spirit" sprang from Spain's convergence of Roman, Jewish, Northern African Arab, producing the multicultural/ multiracial consciousness that it planted in the Americas, including the United States, making Spain the more American inheritance than the British. This was the subject of Williams' talk at the University of Puerto Rico in 1941, "An Informal Discussion on Poetic Form":

> For in many ways 16th and 17th century Spain and Spaniards are nearer to us in the U.S. today than, perhaps, England ever was. It is a point worth at least taking under consideration. We in the United States are climactically as by latitude and weather much nearer Spain than England, as also in the volatility of our spirits, in racial mixture—much more like Gothic and Moorish Spain.[40]

Today's racially-conscious purists may dismiss Williams' defense of his Spanish roots as half-baked liberalism compared to the more rigorous racial sensibilities of our time. But he was not wrong in seeing the Spanish cup half full because of the Church's humanizing of the Other and because the Spaniards

---

[38] Translation cited from "The Kingdom of Andalusia," *Deviantart*, https://www.deviant art.com/mobiyuz/art/The-Kingdom-of-Andalusia-870078657

[39] William Carlos Williams, *In the American Grain* (New York: New Directions, 1925).

[40] William Carlos Williams, "An Informal Discussion of Poetic Form." *Revista de la Asociación de Mujeres Graduadas de la Universidad de Puerto Rico* (July, 1941), 45.

married interracially, sowing the hemisphere's multiracial consciousness. Williams wrote not indicating if he was aware that Latin Americans celebrate on October 12 not Columbus Day but *El Día de la Raza*. On that day Latin Americans mark the birth, despite a horrible rape, of a common humanistic spirit, an acknowledgment of one good that survived being *hispano*, the sowing of Christian egalitarianism even if Christianity itself started out as an instrument of conquest.

My effort here is not to romanticize the Spanish but to add nuance to a simplistic presentism that confuses a multicultural and multiracial Hispanic legacy with Francisco Franco's dream of a monolithic white Spain under the monarchy of Castile. Human history is all impure; the nation that longest condoned slavery is still the world's beacon of democracy. The worst Spaniards slaughtered and enslaved native Americans while nobler others, notably among the Church, worked to protect them as Hollywood depicted in *Black Robe* (of course, after other less noble of the Church subdued those indigenous by spiritual conquest in a gray past brackish with good and evil). And it was the Church that, to defend the native from being extinguished by slave labor, misjudged in allowing the exportation of the slave trade practiced among African tribes, an adoption whose true sinfulness later enlightenment would prompt the Church to first condemn. Indeed, the forced imposition of Catholicism, the cruelties that Bartolomé de Las Casas recorded, the introduction of slavery all constitute a horrific legacy if properly propagandized.

On the other hand, one should be wary of simplistic political correctness. In his 1947 classic work on slave history, *Slave and Citizen: The Negro in America*, Frank Tannenbaum demonstrated how slavery contrasted profoundly in Anglo-Protestant United States and in the hemisphere's Catholic countries.[41] Protestantism never affirmed the humanity of Africans and even elaborated Biblical justification for their destiny of enslavement. In contrast, Catholicism perceived slavery nonracially, as a civil status that did not discount the humanity of slaves, whose equality was their souls, which belonged to God. Spanish Catholicism, therefore, acknowledged the human rights of slaves, which had been acknowledged long before the African slave trade, in the reconquest of Iberia from the Moors.

Enslaved captive Moors had inalienable human rights to property, to marry and have children. By royal and Church decree, families were sacred and could not be fragmented by selling off members. That decree was passed on to slavery in the Americas. Consequently, masters were strategically imposed the honor of becoming baptizing godparents, who at some point, as a gift, gave their

---

[41] Frank Tannenbaum, *Slave and Citizen: The Negro in America* (New York: Vintage Books, 1947).

godchildren freedom. With the right to property, slaves also generated income and could purchase their freedom. Haiti came to exist as fruit of French Catholic slavery.

Of course, there were devout Catholic masters and then there were hypocritical Catholics whom slaves had to endure and against whom they had to appeal to the Church for succor. Better than the Protestant version, but this was still slavery, which in the Americas Catholic countries also first had the epiphany of condemning. This sharp contrast in Catholic and Protestant racial attitudes explains why French Louisiana was where American slaves hoped to escape, Nat Turner's envisioned destination. In contrast, as Protestants refused to come to terms with African humanity, they acknowledged no inherent African human rights, instead generating a metaphysical and even theological justification for white supremacy.

Tannenbaum did not incur into American Catholic slavery, which introduces the additional dimension investigated by *New York Times*' contributing writer Rachel L. Swarns in *The 272: Families Who Were Enslaved and Sold to Build the American Catholic Church.*[42] Swarns recovered a personal family history of ancestors who had been enslaved and sold, among many others, by slaveholding parishes and clerics, the profit from their sale footing the bill for the founding of Georgetown University and the first Catholic seminary. "The sale of few unnecessary Negroes," helped to cover expenses for the seminary, "John Carroll, the nation's first Catholic bishop, wrote in 1805."[43]

The American Catholic Church was a cultural product of Irish immigrants who adopted the white supremacy of American Protestantism. Swarns summed up the general attitude among clerics by citing "what they called 'the peculiar dispositions and habits' of Black people." Germane to our conversation is that, factoring in Tennenbaum's comparison of slavery under Spanish and French Catholicism versus Anglo Protestantism, even more fundamental to the profound difference between the two is the Southern European or *latino* humanism that opposed slavery, for which Texans and Cubans fought for the freedom to practice.

Additionally significant to appreciating some Latinos' confusion with Hispanic is Swarns' commitment to her Catholic faith in spite of its racial history, as underscored in her title "My Church Was Part of the Slave Trade. This Has Not Shaken My Faith." The reason she gives is that "the church was bigger

---

[42] Rachel L. Swarns, *The 272: Families Who Were Enslaved and Sold to Build the American Catholic Church* (New York: Random House, 2023).

[43] "My Church Was Part of the Slave Trade. This Has Not Shaken My Faith," *The New York Times,* June 17, 2023.

than the sinful white men within it." We can translate that reasoning: faith or belief are the essence of defining oneself a Catholic and not the individual, imperfect Catholics one comes across. Latinos who inherit Hispanic humanism essentially inherited Hispanic Catholic values or *latino* Catholic values as Swarns inherited her faith. But some Latinos confuse their Hispanic heritage with the conquerors and the Catholics who failed to see then what Latinos can see now about the sin of imperialism. Swarns traces her faith lineage as an enduring idea; some Latinos hold a grudge against a lineage of individuals.

In other words, the racial divide that today's Latinos draw between Hispanic and Latino is a really simplistic writing of Latin American and Spanish cultural history. In that history, race indeed figured in the Conquest but, notwithstanding that there are supremacists who interpret that event as the triumph of white Western Civilization, the cultural component that had made *hispano* and *latino* synonymous in popular usage was the underlying humanism expressed in the Spanish-language and Hispanic Catholic values. The aforementioned Mexican philosopher José Vasconcelos celebrated multiracial Latin America's defining humanism in La *Raza Cósmica* (*The Cosmic Race*) and that humanism is understood as the bonding celebrated on October 12 as Latin America's *Día de la Raza*.

If for Anglophones *latinos* are threaded by their Spanish language and if Latinos understand themselves as chiefly defined by how they are racialized in English, for Latin Americans, *latino* actually means the transracial kinship of a humanistic consciousness that is their Hispanic Catholic inheritance, their being also *hispanos*. Latinos mistakenly ascribe their multicultural/multiracial consciousness to progressive American post-civil rights enlightenment when in fact they gravitate to American progressivism as a consequence of the very Hispanic heritage that some seek to purge. This very high-minded purging of a presumed inherited Hispanic racism is done in a political bubble unappreciative that their stance naively emulates the anti-Hispanic and now anti-Latino bias in American tradition and layers a patina of white supremacy to progressivism as redeeming Latino of its presumably pathetic Hispanic roots. Recall Octavio Paz on the *pachuco*: a "knot of contradictions."

Culturally speaking, then, what is "Latino," what sense does it make? For the present, the epithet's function is chiefly political, the subject of social science-tracing and a motive to generate pop-cultural solidarity. For more than pop culture, Latino milks whatever cultural sense from its being confused with *latino* because by itself Latino has no cultural content. Combined, the homonyms Latino/*latino* blur distinctions between native Latinos and immigrant *latinos*, between Latinos in the U.S. and *latinos* in Latin America (recall Morales' referring to "Latinx that emigrate") while not all Hispanics identify as Latinos. The Latino political agenda to present a single face racialized as brown before white America masks the underlying semantic and cultural disparity of Latino and *latino* because the homonyms Latino/ *latino* are presumed to be a single epithet or mutual translations that evoke and signify the same things, which they don't, not actually being mutual translations.

LATINO AND *LATINO*

Latinos/ *latinos* are wont to insert Spanish words and phrases into their English, and owing to this practice, Latino is usually presumed to be the Spanish *latino*, pronounced emphasizing its Latinate vowels. The syllable "tin" does not sound like the mineral but like the adolescent, teen. Speakers might think they are embedding Spanish *latino* or believe that Latino simply means the same in English, which explains Latinos' often being modified as "U.S. Latino," marking a distinction from non-U.S. Latino, or *latino*. To repeat, Latino is assumed to be a translation when, in fact, it is a *transliteration* diverged from the semantics of its source word.

A truer translation of Spanish *latino* is the older Latin, as in Latin music, generally understood as the musical expression of Latin America although *música latina* actually encompasses Spanish and even Italian artists who sing in Spanish. *Música latina* is not translatable to Latino Music. Latino has no identifiable music. Latinos listen to anything from La India to Adele to Snoop Doggy Dog. To create the musical *Hamilton*, Lin Manuel Miranda didn't compose Latin Music or a Latino Music, adapting popular American forms to his musical redaction of the country's founding. Miranda's being Latino does not make his music Latino, and while the phrase Latino music can phonetically exist, as yet it conveys a speaker's ignorance of the genre Latin music.

At the 2006, still-called Latin Grammy Awards ceremony, held in Spanish, the lead singer of the winning band in *reggaetón*, a Spanish-language hip-hop, held up the award and shouted out *¡Latino!* No Spanish-listening ear heard the masculine form *Latino* modifying the feminine *música* nor did that ejaculation celebrate, in the plural, all present as *latinos*, so it was highly probable that the *reggaetón* artist shouted out a linguistic interference to celebrate the cultural unity evoked by Anglophone Latino. But independent of his conscious intention, the ejaculation celebrated his *latino* as those present would have understood it: their Romanic heritage shared by discrete cultures gifted with a warmer humanistic view of the world, how Latin Americans ideally see themselves.

In Rome our Neapolitan taxi driver inquired about my origins from my Italian-fluent Argentine lady. She answered, of course, that "lui" was American from Puerto Rico. He nodded contemplatively, "Parlano spagnolo lì, giusto?" ("They speak Spanish there, right.") She nodded and he thought more seconds before shrugging his shoulders to conclude that "Tutti siamo latini." He meant, of course, we three who came from different Latin cultures were therefore all *latinos* and more freely expressed the humanistic warmth that, as he told us, as a Neapolitan he enjoys in southern Italy, why he never ventured north of Rome to the snow-capped attitudes of more Teutonic northern regions, for him not Italy.

That cabbie's consciousness was, of course, *latino*, the shared heritage of discrete cultures, and not "Latino," the racialized American minority identity although often used to mean *latino*. Instead of a shared heritage of discrete cultures, in its contrast with Anglo-Saxon, Latino assumes the posture of an actual culture, ironically channeling the unifying mythos of Martí's Our America. Consequently, recent *latino* immigrants, for whom back home *latinidad* was a poetic or figurative oneness, accept as their American condition being perceived as culturally one and embrace *latinidad* literally, picking up the notion of possibly forming one people. Celia Cruz could therefore sing: *Latinos en Estados Unidos/Vamos a unirnos,/vamos a unirnos/Claro que sí!* [*"Latinos* in the United States/Let's unite, let's unite/Definitely!"] This unity is a project, "vamos a unirnos," not a feit accompli.

There is irony in rediscovering this idea of unity in the U.S., a lost dream that began with Simón Bolívar, resurrected by José Martí, and recycled by the Argentine revolutionary Ernesto "Che" Guevara, both in his memoir *The Motorcycle Diaries* and his acting on that ideal in committing his life to the liberation of Cuba. As a young novelist the also Argentine Reina Roffé, on her way to the Iowa Writers Workshop, stopped to give a talk at N.Y.U., of when she felt that she first really discovered Latin America only after having traveled north from Argentina. Her country's oligarchical myths had separated institutionally white Argentina from multiracial Latin America. This exceptionalism was what she was taught since childhood and having discovered Latin America first-hand, felt betrayed, lied to, because what she met in her travels was a hemisphere of peoples with whom she felt fraternal.[44] That transracial and transcultural Latino American fraternity that Roffé discovered is conveyed by *latino*, popularly synonymous with *hispano*, acknowledging Spain as conduit to the Romanic humanism that our Neapolitan taxi driver celebrated as a Southern Italian.

In other words, Retamar's thesis that *hispanoamérica* honored Spain as oppressor was his Marxist challenge to Latin Americans who, despite their history of oppression under imperialism, preserve an appreciation of their *Hispanidad* lineage, Retamar's critique written in literate Spanish, of course.

---

[44] I am citing from personal experience, having attended her talk as a graduate student.

Marxism was more absolutist about history than most Latin Americans in understanding that being hemispheric Americans, as opposed to European, meant by definition being impure, brackish. All Americas nations originate with Western defaults as a consequence of history, inheriting, like Retamar, a Western language and philosophies and civil structures that integrate Latin American societies to the Western world.

That default doesn't necessarily reflect the racial reality of *latino* societies because every American nation is also informed in varying degrees by indigenous or African cultures that have also been, with isolated exceptions, Westernized. Haiti is racially African yet culturally French. Mélange, or what Williams called "the mingling spirit," is the defining American fact throughout the entire hemisphere: nationalities and institutions, including in the United States, were created/imposed by white Westerners and the predominant languages reflect that default and the final product. Despite conservative movements to keep Western Culture proprietary to whites, the expansion to America and later Imperialism made Western Culture transracial.

Consequently, just as Latino is a mask for public intercourse with American society, in many Latin American societies, indigenous or African peoples preserve their culture among themselves but use the postal system, use credit cards, rely on the internet and speak the national language. A Latino idealism may aspire for an Americas indigenous purity, a reversal of the Conquest, but what makes those nations modern is their expanding in their own particular way the original limitations of Western consciousness. The Mexican and Cuban revolutions were efforts to make that correction, not a wiping out of Western consciousness. The Civil Rights Movement was the African-American response, applying Western philosophical, political and moral principles to challenge white Westernist hegemony.

Owing to U.S. hegemonic influence, the Civil Rights Movement reawakened Latin America's multiracial consciousness, a confluence with Vasconcelos' appreciation of a cosmic mixture of races and the Movement as reinvented Western multiculturalism. This concatenation is hemispheric America's history, sown by the "mingling spirit" of its founding Hispanic heritage. To cite Celia Cruz again: *Venimos de la América del Indio/ Del Negro y del Español.* [We come from the America of the Indian, of the Black and of the Spaniard.] *Latino* idealizes a humanism that embraces that impurity while overcoming the component of founding white supremacy (essentially Retamar's definition)— which expressed itself differently in the U.S. but no less consistently in the histories of discrete Latin American nationalities, racially circumstances if expressed differently than in the U.S.

But that complexity is not conveyed by "Latino" as epithet of a simplified actual culture. *Latino* signifies a membership based on one's being *latino* of a distinct subculture. *Latinos* may be motivated to unite as Americans, but still, a person is *latino* who embodies a specific, discrete, multiracial Latin American culture, say Dominican or Ecuadorean. Only Anglophone Latinos see themselves as culturally Latinos dissociated from a specific *latino* culture as well as from foundational *hispano*.

The Newyorican Marc Anthony paired with the Cuban band Gente de Zona to record "La Gozadera," a celebration of *latino: si tú eres latino, saca tu bandera* [if you're *latino*, show your flag]. Typical of Caribbean *música latina*, their song blends beats and lyrics that are a joyous marriage of African and Hispanic heritages of Caribbean *latino*. The song's subtext, of course, is the pan-Latin American ideal of Martí's *Nuestra América*, the notion of a racially unifying Hispanic, the multicultural/multiracial heritage that makes *latino* and *hispano* synonymous, that Latin American admixture giving *latino* a *gozadera* (essentially a joie de vivre–which English needs to express in another Latinate language) expressed in the exuberance of the lyrics. Marc Anthony can wave the Puerto Rican flag, just as Oscar de la Hoya carries a Mexican flag into the ring. There is no Latino flag.

Nevertheless, Anglophone Latino idealizes a multicultural United States predominantly defined by its nonwhite heritage and a romance of Latin America before the Conquest, in other words before the sowing of *latino*. As much a product of white America's historical racialization of Hispanic and of an American education's popularist perspectives on Latin America, Latino embraces with pride a racial brown defined less by race or even culture than by socioeconomic condition and political solidarity. Blond and blue-eyed Latinos are culturally constructed as also brown.

This racial homogenization puts off, whether out of racial consciousness or just identity confusion, many immigrant *latinos* who must live with the fact that Latino is nevertheless their public American identity. The United States' census may preserve Hispanic as both white and nonwhite, but before America's popular Cyclopean eye, Latino and *latino* are obliged to form a single line, which Americans randomly call either Hispanic or Latino, both racialized by default.

The racialized political reality of hegemonic Latino cannot be circumvented no matter how Teutonically white a *latino* may be because when Latinos and *latinos* perform as citizens their internecine racial distinctions are irrelevant. This circumstance of imposed racialization offers a *latino* motive to identify with the political right to reinforce racial difference. One other ironic influence of the Latino/*latino* conflation is that today one might hear white *latinos*, who don't consider themselves racially brown, not realize that they have referred to Anglo Americans as *blancos*.

Latino's dissolution of discrete *latino* subcultural identity is one reason for why white *exilio* Cuban Americans do not identify as Latinos. The other is Latino's commencing as a seventies advocacy of youth that celebrated the multiracialism of the Cuban Revolution. Diverging further, second-generation Cuban Americans started identifying as white *latinos* on a par with white America. Similarly, white islander Puerto Ricans started coming to the mainland assuming white parity as *latinos,* preserving their traditionally understood white *puertorriqueñidad* against becoming racialized among mainland Puerto Ricans, quintessentially Latinos. Immigrants from South America's more predominantly European countries, Argentina and Uruguay, which harbor being exceptions to Latin American stereotypes, arrive also assuming the same racial marginality from Latino. Are these groups all preserving traditionally default white Hispanic cultural history? Indubitably.

That default is the cultural fact of Latin America with its own built-in revisions in the same way that the U.S. started with a Constitution of established principles that its all-white, all-male signers contradicted by also allowing slavery. Again, that default was also why there were Mexican and Cuban revolutions and the Civil Rights Movement. In the U.S., the true America for us Latinos and other minorities was never traditional America but the promised "more perfect union." Otherwise, Latinos drink from a predominantly white cultural history every day and speak the language of originally monarchic England. Latinx advocates the breakdown of binaries, allowing for other possible identities, as if that concept were an intellectual novelty: that breakdown has always been expressed in Americas impurities that rigid categorization cannot sustain, the broad spectrum that comprises both Anglo and Latin America.

Nevertheless, Latinos repeat the mantra that America is a racist country but launch no campaign to correct being called American as some do in canceling Hispanic as white racism and cancel being identified as Hispanic out of racial consciousness. It is considered deep-thinking political consciousness to summarize Hispanic as white and advocate cleaning the slate in total ignorance of impure but inherited cultural dimensions that produced modern Latin America, what Marc Anthony and Gente de Zona joyfully celebrate. Latin Americans express that impurity in their music and their literature. Those Latinos who interpret Hispanic solely by its white Spanish origins and not by its transracial evolution, redact history in a way that excuses canceling it.

Not just in response to that history as a memory of racial oppression is it cancelled but as well because of Latino's commitment to presentism to rationalize its being spoken of as an actual culture. Proclaiming a culture suggests Latino's having a history, a body of thought and a grammar of myths. All those are suggested in Latino's having what is called a "Latino literature," a problematic phrase because, strictly speaking, a literature is not the bibliography of writings but a bibliography of those writings canonized by a reading culture. Does that reading consciousness as yet exist? Are literate Puerto Ricans and Mexican Americans intellectually compelled to read not just their own but each other's essential Latino authors? There are signs that a Latino/*latino* reading culture is looming but as yet thrives as a chick lit and young adult market.

Novelist Ernesto Quiñones, author of *Bodega Dreams*, identifies as a Latino in an interview for the e-zine *The Latin Post* (leaving aside the use of "Latin" in the website's name): "I am a Latino, so my work deals with Latino issues. But it is no different than James Joyce romanticizing the Irish culture, or Faulkner romanticizing Southern culture. I do the same for Latino culture."[45] Of course, unless in the etymological sense of writing novels neither Joyce nor Faulkner "romanticize" their culture as they wrote critically to inquire what it means to be Irish or Southern. Their novels are also written with a historical consciousness, their prose making graphic cultural themes reiterated over generations. Quiñones' comparing Latino to Irish and Southern culture suggests that Latino too has such a historical consciousness, one not exhibited in his novel, about a dream of creating a thriving community of El Barrio.

Latino was coined to *begin* a history. Spanish *latino* is a bonding by heritage and therefore a summation of a history. Latin American writings branch out of Spanish literary traditions, a continuity of themes. In contrast, as I will discuss later in greater detail, Latino writing does not address themes, focused instead on social and political "issues." "Issues" is the word evocative of the sociopolitical substance of Latino, which doesn't handle literary ideas or themes or history, but is conventionally expected to document social and political and always contemporary circumstances, the presentism evoked by "issues." Quiñones: "I am a Latino, so my work deals with Latino issues."

Quiñones' next response illustrates that, in contrast to *latino*, which implicitly addresses an adult consciousness, "Latino" implicitly addresses youth: "That's the real question for me. What kind of Latino American am I. ...what are you going to do tomorrow morning to show everyone that you are proud? What actions are you taking? Do you have a vision? A plan? Are you in school? Working? Bettering your life for your kids?" Although the reference to having kids tosses in an adult circumstance, the catalog of questions that Quiñones poses really addresses a person growing up. School is not college and not

---

[45] Nicole Akoukou Thompson, "Novelist Ernesto Quiñonez Discusses the Young Lords Party and Inspiration," *Latin Post*, last modified October 29, 214, http://www.latinpost.com/articles/23608/20141029/novelist-ernesto-qui%C3%B1onez-discusses-young-lords-party-inspiration.htm

presumed to be the source of knowledge or civic or intellectual preparation but as the means to getting a job and so "bettering your life for your kids."

Again, presuming that Latino is a defined culture, the "real question" for Quiñones is to do something to live up to that definition although he also understands Latino to be a social stigma that requires showing "everyone that you are proud." One also extrapolates from that interview Latino's implying that, literacy, learning Spanish, and history, especially one's own personal cultural history (Quiñones is Ecuadorean-Puerto Rican) defer in importance to one's social place in the American scheme, not an actual overview of one's personal or cultural life but the confrontation with "issues" from which one can come up "proud."

In Junot Díaz's novel, *The Brief Wondrous Life of Oscar Wao* (2007), in which Latino is never discussed, the two principal male characters embody the semantic contrast of Latino and *latino*. Oscar, fat and unattractive, needs to have sex lest he die a virgin and not a true Dominican. Out of a spontaneous interest to learn more about himself, he flies to the Dominican Republic where he falls in love with a prostitute who happens to be the main squeeze of a henchman of the ruling dictator, the legendary Rafael Trujillo. He touches the girl's heart if not yet her sexual parts, prompting her boyfriend to give him a beating that he survives to end up healing in New Jersey. But love-mad, he quixotically returns and this time, after sexually scoring at last, manages to get himself killed in the name of love.

This plot is embedded in an anthology of stories about Oscar's sister and mother and explanations of Dominican sexual obsessions and superstitions written on the same pages on which an extensive footnote recounts Trujillo-era Dominican history. While Oscar is a personage of the 90s, the novel's chronological setting is ahistorical, on a Latino plane of indifference to history. The background during the era of dictator Rafael Leónidas Trujillo, who died in 1961, suggests that either Oscar's family arrived from the D.R. as outliers or as part of a fifties immigration that did not yet exist. In either case, no Affirmative Action or financial aid programs existed to make it possible for Oscar to attend Rutgers University as those minority benefits were achieved by late-sixties and seventies Puerto Ricans.

Puerto Rican and Mexican American participation in the civil rights struggle created opportunities that in the post-sixties prompted the immigration of Dominicans, who in this novel exist in a bubble with no contact with other Latinos or *latinos* or connection to that history. Nevertheless, nineties Oscar flies south not just to the D.R. but back in time to the fifties of the Trujillo era while throughout the novel there are citations of seventies and eighties comic books, science fiction, and arcade games on which he grew up, characterizing him as American of his generation. But while he is informed by post-sixties culture and he is the educational product of post-sixties civil rights gains, he is not informed by the racial consciousness of the American sixties.

Consistent with Latino's evoking youth and making youth a model, even after Oscar graduated from Rutgers and became a teacher and a writer, he exhibits greater knowledge of generations of comics and science fiction and passes hours at arcade games. His impulse to travel to the Dominican Republic is not the consequence of his having read anything about the place, whose history he gets orally from Yunior. Oscar is a kind of child-like Quixote obsessed with fantasy and science fiction and whose American education left him not knowing or caring about his own history to read about it, including the perils of Trujillo. All he knows about his Dominican world is it's having exported their sexual excesses and *fukú* superstitions, among them a curse that Trujillo put on his family.

Oscar's limited Latino is saved by the narrating *latino* voice of Yunior, redeployed from Díaz's previous work. Yunior as omniscient consciousness narrates narrates Oscar's life, even his thoughts. He also provides the fifties Dominican history in a footnote that makes up much of the novel, filling in the reader on the horrors of island life under Trujillo in the same voice of his having lived that history even though Yunior too is a post-sixties contemporary of Oscar. In other words, *latino* Yunior fills in what Latino Oscar lacks, a historical consciousness, a connection to his Spanish-speaking heritage, having presumably read up on it. The only history that Oscar traces is Trujillo's curse on his family. From the perspective of *latino*, Trujillo was the curse on Dominican and Latin American history, inspiring the 2010 Nobel Laureate in Literature, Peruvian Mario Vargas Llosa, to write the novel *La Fiesta del Chivo*.[46]

Yunior's knowledge reminds that as *latino* he also contemplates ideas. Not ironically, *The San Franciso Chronicle*'s reviewer underscored Yunior's having ideas: "...Díaz's novel is also full of ideas, [the narrator's] brilliant talking...."[47] This ideation connects Yunior to a history by which he is defined, as he constantly reminds Oscar, and impresses on the reader that despite his college education, Oscar never gave any thought to the past except as a family thing. Oscar was killed by a history that for him as Latino, was literally a remote footnote that came back to haunt him when he crossed over into *latino* by returning to the Dominican Republic.

Seen another way, Yunior and something inside Oscar spared his taking Latino to its possible extreme, not just shutting out history but more specifically

---

[46] *The Feast of the Goat*, 2000.

[47] Oscar Villalon, "In 'The Brief Wondrous Life of Oscar Wao' a New America Emerges," *SFGATE*, September 20, 2007, https://www.sfgate.com/books/article/In-The-Brief-Wondrous-Life-of-Oscar-Wao-a-new-2501543.php

cultivating a conscious patriotic American ignorance of the past to obliterate it, a way of one's also being spared having to confront dysfunctional Dominican origins demoted in prestige in American culture. To be or not to be American; to remember or forget being Dominican. Undecided at that crossroad was how Oscar started out when Yunior intervened with his essential inner Dominican voice. Oscar's death, a deus ex-machina, resolves that quandary for author Díaz. We had encountered the same deus ex machina in Oscar Hijuelos' *The Mambo Kings.*

In sum, Oscar and Yunior serve as metaphors of the defining contrast between Latino and *latino*, the latter filling in the former's nonexistent historical consciousness. Yunior narrates a political history as product of a cultural history whereas Latino evolved from the seventies premise that politics defines culture, an axiom of seventies-popular Marxist economic determinism. Oscar's embodying an emphasis on personal experience as paradigms of social "issues" and not having felt the need to study his cultural history is Latino, so his conflict of needing to have sex like a true Dominican is his Latino "issue." What Yunior reveals in the broader *latino* context of essential Dominican themes teaches Oscar that his present issues have deeper roots.

Díaz's Oscar finesses one fundamental challenge as Dominican American: his place as American as determined by the Dominicans studied here and is now a Miami-based. Oscar, as earlier noted, was very much Latino in feeling reassured of not needing to know history, whether Dominican or American history. And he was representative in his having attended Rutgers in the nineties and expressed a thin consciousness of roots, but he was unrepresentative in having no racial consciousness, for Latinos usually the epitome of what one has to know about American culture, its racist history.

Latino presentism encourages anti-intellectualism not solely toward Latino's Hispanic history, but as well encourages a naïve dismissal of more dimensions to American history than its being racist. This limited perception produces the irony that those Latinos who do invest in learning American cultural history and not just its racial history discover that while some Latinos may broadcast boilerplate about disconnecting with Hispanic conquerors as white supremacists, as Americans it is impossible to cancel Hispanic, a formidable historical root of *American* heritage, from which Latinos as Americans descend.

For that reason, Latino efforts to define itself apart from Hispanic fall on deaf American ears, and in American diction Latino continues to remain simply a popular variant of generic Hispanic. Latinos may believe that tensions with white America are in fact racial because of American popular culture's racialization of Latino as brown, but the tension with Latino also derives from an American history of confrontation with Hispanic culture and not just over turfs as in *West Side Story* but over threats to the national identity. So, from a white American perspective the quibbling over Latino and Hispanic means nothing because of the two epithets formal English defaults to Hispanic as evocative of a cultural history. Americans may use Latino or Latinx, to reiterate, not for all the distinctions Latinos advocate but as a variant of Hispanic.

We saw this semantic feature at work in the late conservative Washington advisor Samuel P. Huntington's last book *Who Are We? Challenges to America's National Identity*,[48] in which Huntington identified Hispanization as one of the great threats to America's traditional identity.

By 2004 Latino had been strongly trending but Huntington didn't have to state the obvious: he had to label his targets Hispanic and Hispanization and not Latino and Latinization because, aside from its multicultural consciousness, Latino evokes no historical or cultural threat, and Latinization would have sounded like a plague of excessively flowery language, not the historically known threat to the national identity.

Huntington underlined that Hispanics are embodiments of a threatening history because Hispanics, represented by his pet peeve, Mexican Americans, are the only group in U.S. history that has asserted or could assert a historical claim to the U.S.:

> Almost all of Texas, New Mexico, Arizona, California, Nevada, and Utah was part of Mexico until Mexico lost them as a result of the Texan War of Independence in 1835-1836 and the Mexican-American War of 1846-1848. Mexico is the only country that the United States has invaded, occupied its capital placing the Marines in the "halls of Montezuma" and then annexed half its territory. Mexicans do not forget these events. Quite understandably, they feel that they have special rights in these territories.[49]

Huntington also confirmed that Hispanics represent a "cultural assault," not a racial one, warning of an inherent dysfunctional difference, such as the presumed lack of a work ethic or interest in getting an education, a dysfunctional "difference" that would adulterate American society. And "Hispanic" was also necessary because Latino does not evoke the greatest threat, which Huntington demurs from making explicit: that "Hispanics" are the only major minority group with a root in Western Culture.

Latino's lack of a historical consciousness and its semantic association with youth intertwine in "The Problem With Latinidad," published in the September

---

[48] Samuel P. Huntington, *Who Are We? Challenges to America's National Identity* (New York: Simon and Shuster, 2004).

[49] Huntington, *Who Are We? Challenges to America's National Identity*, 229

16, 2019 issue of *The Nation*, by Miguel Salazar. A transcript of an interview with a panel that represented "a growing community of young, black, and indigenous people … questioning the very identity underpinning Hispanic Heritage Month." (Can there be a Latino Heritage Month?) As that hooking summary describes, even though the panelists' profiles reveal that they are four journalists, an organizer, an academic and a cultural critic, they are being consulted on their authority of being young.[50] Salazar's use of "people" and not Latinos foreshadows an issue with epithets among the interviewees, who according to the description given are all "black and indigenous," none a white Hispanic or Latino. So, the "problem with Latinidad" in question is chiefly racial.

The panelists all decry being stuck with epithets with which they generationally do not identify, the conundrum expressed in one answer: "As a journalist, I cover Latino issues, specifically Afro-Latinx issues and Dominican issues, so I still rely on the term even if I don't want to identify with it." The problem is that all the available epithets are rooted in a Latinidad, which the panelists interpret as a default white consciousness and a motive for white passing:

1. "… usually white-passing Latino, Latina, Latinx people…"

2. "Those who can identify with Hispanic or Latinx are those who benefit from power because of language, race and religion."

3. "Latinidad is an academic term that failed because it erases away race."

[The speakers never read Vasconcelos *La Raza Cósmica*.]

Never once citing a journalist, scholar or writer, no interviewee evinces any awareness of the previous generation's giving the same racial reasons for replacing Hispanic with Latino and the discussion recycles the previous generation's boilerplate on Latino as if wholly original, each panelist his or her own authority to say even bombast:

1. Latinidad in general doesn't make room to talk about US imperialism, …

   [Latino was spun from Retamar's call for the epithet *latinoamericano* over *hispanoamericano*, which memorialized imperial Spain, making *latinidad* the original response to imperialism.]

2. If you're not interrogating Latinidad in smart ways, you're celebrating colonialism in a way. [*Latinidad* has always been interrogated in smart ways; there's a body of Latin American literature on the subject. English Latinidad, as the statement confirms, has not been.]

---

[50] Recall the same authority conceded by Morales to the "young folk" advocating the epithet Latinx.

This interview intended to communicate the insight of youth more disappointingly epitomizes Latino's having handed down to another generation its semantic chaos and the assumption of its being a pop culture subject, not one of serious study or intellectual discussion, so the panelists appear to believe that their just being Latinos makes them as authoritative as they need to be. In other words, each's respective education or profession does not appear to add nuance to their discussion, which is fundamentally populist, so subtextual throughout the interview is a younger generation's having inherited the Latino tribal notion that racial purity supersedes impure, transracial culture.

The interview skirts the question of what epithet does identify them satisfactorily, which if it is not any of the Hispanic-heritaged variety that they dismiss then suggests the shedding of "Latin" altogether, the assimilation into alternate America that Ed Morales had ascribed to Latinx.

The panelists' profiles do not include any subcultural identities. Except for the journalist who mentioned a specialty in the Dominican experience, one cannot tell whether the discussion was intentionally limited to a nonwhite second generation of the Latin American immigration,[51] which would explain their disconnect with the earlier generation's Latino introspection, of which a native Latino would more likely be informed. Instead, this conversation was subtextually driven by an immigrant *latino*'s ambition to assimilate, preferring the traditional shedding of the past, a shedding of *latino*'s default white as also suggested by Latinx.

I am extrapolating from their seeing no difference in any epithet just reiterations of the default white of *latino*, never actually addressing Latino. For even though in transcribing this interview Salazar wrote "Latino," the interviewees consistently addressed *latino*, indeed by default white, which coupled with their generational disregard or ignorance of the previous generation's having racialized Latino as brown, results in their racial rejection of *latino*. The confusion provides yet another illustration of the consequence of using Latino and *latino* interchangeably.

In fact, of course, the two epithets diverge in their respective racial preconceptions as well as in evoking discrete cultural contexts, each raising particular cultural questions that merit a more detailed dissection of the semantics of each separately. We should start with *latino*, the seed of Latino, understanding that its semantic relationship to Latino is constantly shifting according to the growth of Americanized generations and the continuing influence of immigration. Readers years from now can refine from this present that I chronicle.

---

[51] As I discuss subsequently in greater detail, the windows to an American identity are different for an *afrolatino*.

LIVING LA VIDA *LATINO*

Upon the spiking of Latin American immigration, Univisión and Telemundo made the homonymic Latino/*latino* their preferred epithet, obviously affording the advantage of addressing the combined demographic as a single media market. Their advertising addressed a *latino* middle class, which upgraded popular evocations of Latino by emulating the way that Latin Americans were used to seeing themselves in advertising in home countries. One saw fewer black or too indigenous-looking actors in Spanish-language ads, whether because in home countries media the default is white or because in the U.S. under the threat of racialization, the product would endanger customer support. In the U.S., this practice of addressing white middle class *latinos* is considered addressing "High Latino," the term revealed to me by a publicist.

One can oversimplify and reduce this practice to racial preference for white Hispanic while an implicitly Low Latino may include rhetorically "of color" but actually poorer white Hispanics even though what is considered white among *latinos* does not always coincide with Anglo America's idea of white. At the extreme political right of *latino*, assimilating means adopting racially adopting white American racial standards and attitudes including toward Latinos resulting in the oxymoron of *latino* racists against racialized Latinos. And so we see Latinos (really *latinos*) for Trump, and even Latino (*latino*) leaders of white supremacists groups. But those extremes distract with oversimplification the average white *latinos'* American experience. The reduction to simply "white passing" focuses on how they are treated by white America and not, what interests here, how they perceive themselves as Americans. Latin American immigrants arrive mainly knowing the U.S. for popular consumption, its global, more attractive facade. That is the American they want to be.

Over dinner at her daughter's apartment in Madrid, a retired, blond Argentine woman of Northern Spanish descent recalled how pleasant were the people and her life on Long Island in a town called Farmingville, the town that lent its name to the documentary on hate crimes perpetrated on Mexican day laborers. That topic, of course, I never raised. Her America was a peaceful, welcoming place. Whatever happened to those Mexicans obviously had nothing to do with her, who benefitted from the twin buffers of her Argentine proclivity to dissociate herself from other Latin Americans and by her town's pleasant reception of a blond lady.

Being treated as High Latino indeed does offer comfort if one can perpetuate the enchantment unaffected for the rest of one's life, preferably assuming a new identity. But if one continues to identify as *latino*, one is not so easily out of the woods in American culture after one is introduced under comforting delusion. White *latinos* may not personally feel alluded to in racial discussion on Latino but that discussion is really also cultural, soliciting a cultural allegiance to white Anglo perspectives on Hispanic culture that invariably tests respect for one's own cultural heritage, which encompasses also Latinos.

Latino experience, in other words, is comparable to Italo-Americans from the north of Italy, who however they may condescend to Southern Italians could not dissociate themselves completely from the hostility that killed Sacco and Vanzetti. My former Rhode Island fiancée from a fine Florentine family, informed me of their having moved to their new house after the first burned down for reasons nobody ever discussed. I intuitively never pressed the subject. One day she did volunteer having once applied for a job at a small dress shop in Boston, where she was studying. The very respectful woman owner never lost her pleasantness in informing her that "I don't hire Italians," which for my fiancée was understandable if she meant a Neapolitan. But that lady didn't even want to hire someone obviously of fair, fine Florentine stock that did not identify with Neapolitans, what her family would refer to as "real Italian."

That shop owner's attitude has been the American Way toward Mediterraneans in the past, and today many *latinos*, to prove their patriotism, perform that mimicking role toward darker *latinos* or stigmatized Latinos. Unfortunately, with Trumpism on the rise, history repeats itself even for *latinos* whose America is the land of Disney, where that history of conflict with Mediterranean cultures is redacted. But outside of Disneyland awaits Realityland.

There white *latinos* are preferred over rambunctiously race-conscious Latinos, which although not obvious, is the beginning of the *latino's* problems even while benefitting from that comparison, *latinos* confusing that social comparison with equal acceptance. For in time, it does become evident that the deficiency presumed of Latino intersects with perceptions of them, however subtler, that awareness becoming the test of their patriotic loyalty to continue tolerating the hypocrisy. For some, at some point there is only so much humiliation one will accept and then one wavers, and suddenly one is not as white American as one thought.

Before that breaking point, of course, white *latino* is a useful token. For white Americans befriending a white *latino* bespeaks of an absence of bias as presumably race is not in play, giving importance to a greater respect for a better social class. But that finessing is subject to the authenticity of individuals, who must suspend an older traditional heritage of Anglophone fickleness toward Romanic cultures. Americans have historically viewed things Latin fluctuating between an educated view and a pop cultural one. Latinate words swing between being accepted as respectable formality to being ridiculed as ludicrous, over-the-top floridness. *Latino* emotional expression and sensuality can be a pop culture ticket or an intellectual humbling, a shaming. A stroll down New York's Upper East Side shows evidence of the high esteem given to Italian and French design, architecture and food, a prestige contradicted by stereotypes of Italians as mafiosi and Jersey-Shore crass and the American running joke of the French being supercilious and arrogant bores.

Two public radio interviews reminded me of American bias leveled at the French. The program host interviewed an expert on product imagery who discussed the manufacturers of the BIC pen's suppressing its French origins because Americans did not associate the production of hardware and technology with France. On the same radio show, the French inventor of the credit-card chip security, on being asked why the United States held out as the last to implement a globally-proven invention, quipped in his accent that Americans resisted science from the "estupide French."

In that long tradition of condescending to "Latin," white *latinos* can start out proudly miming their American peers and can get comfortable while subsurface tensions seep until, after about a decade, they eventually fume–or none of this happens because the assimilation is complete. But before that decade is up, being white *latino* enjoys a better reception as a relief from Latino, and so the Teutonic Argentine woman completely aloof from the ugly happenings in Farmingville is safe. But the brown Mexican or black Dominican or any nonwhite *latino* is less so in a more characteristic scenario no different than what occurs when an African-American tech millionaire, however finely attired, can't hail down a cab.

Latino's evolving at counter racial purposes with Latino is epitomized in the cultural consciousness sown by the sixties Cuban *exilio* in Florida, which not just identifies as white Americans but as well with a white perspective on other Hispanics/Latinos. One illustration of that contradiction was Senator Marco Rubio's response to the plight of Central American children separated from their parents at the border, Rubio was not nationally loud in condemning it. Before Univisión's and Telemundo's cameras he spoke in Spanish in a tone of sympathy while clinging to his party's rationalizations.

Rubio's supporting Trump's policy to satisfy a political bloc that advocates a physical wall that would protect the country from more Hispanics/ *latinos* was either proof of great delusion or a strategic Cubanness. Long before the border crisis not just Rubio but the predominantly conservative *exilio* community had protected its class and race distinction from the downgrading *marielitos*, using its white image as political leverage in the Republican party. That same community therefore remained silent on the efforts of other Cubans– surely more of the *marielito* ilk, quintessentially Latino stuff– who because the policy of immediate exile after escaping from Communism was no longer in force, had joined Central Americans to seek asylum at the border.

Rubio's more aggressively self-loathing colleague Texas Senator Rafael "Ted" Cruz, staunchly identifies as a white American cleansed of Latino adulteration. The border crisis provided an opportunity for him to exhibit that he had absolutely no heart for those lesser, browner *latinos* seeking asylum as he was not one of them. He was, of course, no longer one but only as a consequence of his having been one. Still, his vestige *latino* dogs him.

In Cristian Farias' Feb 14, 2016 *Huffington Post* report "Ted Cruz Tried To Show Off His Español To Marco Rubio, But He Fell Flat"[52] we glimpse his linguistic condition: "In a back-and-forth over who's more extreme on immigration, Sen. Marco Rubio (R-Fla.) challenged Ted Cruz's ability to speak Spanish at the Republican debate on Saturday, and the Texas senator took him up on it. The result was rather disappointing. Or as Spanish-speaking Latino viewers might say, *decepcionante*." In 2012 Cruz refused to participate in a debate in Spanish with Texas' Lieutenant Governor, David Dewhurst because, to his patriotic credit, Cruz admitted to news reporters that he couldn't speak Spanish. Spanglish at best.

A graduate of Princeton University and Harvard Law School, Ted Cruz was described by his law professor Allan Dershowitz thusly: "Without a doubt he is among the smartest students I've ever had... I've had great students but he has to be at the top of anyone's short list, in terms of raw brain power."[53] So his inability to speak Spanish having heard it all his life was not a sociological study in socioeconomic circumstance; rather, he deemed it his patriotic duty not to learn Spanish that would have discredited his American worthiness.

True American signifies patriotic ignorance, according to the script advanced by Harvard's late scholar Samuel P. Huntington, who advocated selective patriotic ignorance of other cultures and languages. True Americanization begins with repudiating one's parents' language and being "embarrassed by their inability to communicate in English":

> If the second generation does not reject Spanish outright, the third generation is also likely to be bilingual, and fluency in both languages is likely to become institutionalized ....A persuasive case can be made that, in a shrinking world, all Americans should know at least one important foreign language...so as to understand a foreign culture and communicate with its people. It is quite different to argue that Americans should know

[52] Cristina Farias, "Ted Cruz Tried To Show Off His Español To Marco Rubio, But He Fell Flat," *Huffpost,* February 14, 2016, https://www.huffpost.com/entry/ted-cruz-spanish_n_56c0f58ae4b08ffac125b341

[53] "Alan Dershowitz Talks About Ted Cruz," *The Last Refuge,* May 10, 2013, https://theconservativetreehouse.com/blog/2013/05/10/alan-dershowitz-talks-about-ted-cruz-without-a-doubt-he-is-among-the-smartest-students-ive-ever-had/

a non-English language in order to communicate with their fellow citizens.[54]

Spanish, of course, was the first language of Cruz's fundamentalist preacher father and role model, Rafael Bienvenido Cruz, who by the time he had Ted in 1970 had dropped Hispanic Catholicism for proper American Protestantism.

From early on, pre-Mariel *exilio* Cubans exhibited their perfect confidence as *latinos* in expanding as a Spanish-speaking community while not inserting themselves as leftist, racialized Latinos although as part of their American commitment, they became an aggressively bilingual community. More like Mexican Americans who did not immigrate but belonged to the southwest, Cubans embraced southern Florida and the Miami culture they created became not just their new American identity generically. The Miami culture that they created became a space in which a white Spanish-speaking community discovered it could be the political and socioeconomic equal of white America without making traditional cultural concessions.

While the Cold War provided a packaging for their conservatism, actually their mindset descends from a history that precedes Castro's revolution, being the venting in our time of Cuban class and racial consciousness with a history of solidarity with the American South going back to the Civil War. According to the project "Cuban and Other Hispanic, and Minorities - Confederate Soldiers" 6,175 Cubans fought for the Confederacy:

> It is estimated that approximately 3,500 Hispanics, mostly Mexican-Americans, Puerto Ricans and Cubans (Puerto Rico and Cuba were Spanish colonies) living in the United States joined the war: 2,500 for the Confederacy and 1,000 for the Union. This number increased to 10,000 by the end of the war.[55]

Among the Cubans was the Confederate Colonel Ambrosio José Gonzalez who "At the age of 30, ...joined the Havana Club, a group that wished to have Cuba annexed by the United States as a way to escape what they saw as tyrannical Spanish rule and the threat of Spain abolishing slavery."[56]

---

[54] Samuel P. Huntington, "The Hispanic Challenge," *Foreign Policy*, October 28, 2009, https://foreignpolicy.com/2009/10/28/the-hispanic-challenge/

[55] "Cuban and Other Hispanic, and Minorities - Confederate Soldiers," *Geni*, https://www.geni.com/projects/Cuban-and-Other-Hispanic-and-Minorities-Confederate-Soldiers/24842

[56] Billy Moncure, "The Cuban Confederate Colonel," *War History On-Line*, July 17, 2018, https://www.warhistoryonline.com/history/cuban-confederate-colonel.html?firefox=1&Exc_D_LessThanPoint002_p1=1

Also illustrating historical Cuban ties with the South, Loreta Janeta Velázquez (1842-1923), a Havana-born American, wrote a memoir—albeit today believed as fiction— of her masquerading as a Confederate soldier to fight for the Southern cause, *The Woman in Battle: The Civil War Narrative of Loreta Janeta Velazquez, Cuban Woman and Confederate Soldier* (1842).

And it was to Cuba, envisioned as part of an independent Confederacy, where many defeated Southerners left in exile with their slaves, Cuba a focal point in the preservation of the institution of slavery:

> President Grant was disturbed by the existence of slavery in Cuba, but what bothered him the most was the possibility that citizens of the United States were large holders of 'what is there claimed as property', meaning black slaves. It is quite likely that President Grant heard about this from abolitionists like Henry Highland Garnet and others who formed the Cuban Anti-slavery Committee. Beginning in 1887, Cuba had erupted in a civil war with Cuban insurgents pitted against Spanish colonial forces. They fought not only for independence but also the abolition of Cuban slavery.[57]

In other words, the confidence of white Cubans on a par with white Americans has a very long history, a lineage that gives sense to an intuitive resistance to identifying with self-racializing Latinos, who in the sixties and seventies emerged admiring the Cuban Revolution's dismantling of privileged Cubans' traditional racial compartmentalization. The epithet Latino itself, recall, came from the emphasis given to *latino* as anti-imperialist and presumably anti-racist by the Communist Retamar.

The powerbase that Cubans have built on the American right has inspired other immigrant groups to build self-sustaining communities culturally extensions of their own countries, notably Argentines and Venezuelans. These communities too provide evidence of succeeding by harmonizing with white America as white *latinos*. But while being treated as High Latino does offer political comfort, it is naive of High Latinos to believe that they are out of the woods in American culture.

For notwithstanding Cuban loyalty to traditional American white hegemony and a shared fervent Westernism that would inspire many second-generation Cuban Americans to align with the right, in *Who Are We: Challenges to America's National Identity*, Samuel P. Huntington cited the successful Cuban economic

---

[57] Dennis Wagner, "Ulysses S. Grant 1872 - American Slaveholders in Cuba," *State of the Union History*, July 2, 2020, http://www.stateoftheunionhistory.com/2020/07/ulysses-s-grant-1872-american.html

restoration of Miami and South Florida as one example of how much has gained the "cultural assault" of "Hispanization." Huntington lamented somewhat hyperbolically that "Until the appearance of large concentrations of Spanish-speaking immigrants in Miami and the Southwest, America was unique as a huge country of more than 200 million people virtually all speaking the same language."[58]

In his subchapter "Hispanization of Miami," Huntington describes the Cuban success story and the consequences of the immigration of a well-off group that keeps the privilege that they had historically known. Huntington underscores that Cubans were not traditional immigrants:

> The Cubans did not, in the traditional pattern, create an enclave immigrant neighborhood in Miami. They brought into existence an enclave city with its own cultural community and economy, in which assimilation and Americanization were unnecessary and, in some measure, undesired.[59]

In 2020 Vice President Mike Pence's press secretary Kate Miller, the wife of Steve Miller who devised the anti-Hispanic border policies, in the course of being interviewed by MSNBC's Jacob Soboroff for his book *Separated: Inside an American Tragedy* (2020) mentioned her lack of feelings, even after being sent by the Department of Homeland Security to witness for herself, toward the children separated from their parents. "It didn't work."

Incredulous, Soboroff inquired if she was a white supremacist: "'No, but I believe if you come to America, you should assimilate," Miller responded, ... "Why do we need to have 'Little Havana?'"[60] The correlation between white supremacy and looking askance at a "Little Havana" is an American tell for white *latinos* to decipher for themselves at the American poker game. And yet, the casual bigotry expressed toward "Latinos" seeking asylum during the Trump administration did not affect significantly "Latinos (really *Latinos*) for Trump," who forgive white American bigotry, even if it targets their fellow Latinos/*latinos*, thus preserving their psychological equilibrium as white Americans.

[58] Samuel P. Huntington, *Who Are We? Challenges to America's National Identity* (New York: Simon and Schuster, 2004), 60.

[59] Huntington, *Who Are We? Challenges to America's National Identity*, 249.

[60] Igor Derysh, "Pence aide Katie Miller admits she was unaffected by seeing family separations: 'It didn't work,'" *Salon*, July 7, 2020, https://www.salon.com/2020/07/07/pence-aide-katie-miller-admits-she-was-unaffected-by-seeing-family-separations-it-didnt-work/

Florida Cubans are paradigmatic but not exclusive, so during the Trump era, in addition to counting on Cuban-American support, other *latinos* joined that chorus, such as "Latino" presidential advisor Steve Cortes, whose father is Colombian, whom Trump praised by pointing out in a rally that he was "as white as a WASP." Then there was the example of the Spanish-descended CEO of Goya Foods, Robert Unanue, about whom I created this graphic that I posted on Facebook:

"...I will never get the Hispanic vote. Like the blacks, they're too stupid to vote for Trump...."
–President Donald Trump
"We're all truly blessed... to have a leader like President Trump,..."
– Robert Unanue, CEO, Goya Foods

Figure 1.1 Goya Small White Beans. Graphic made by the author.

In the eighties, a Puerto Rican migration of the post-industrial island's middle-class, consciously dissociated from the New York Rican diaspora, found a haven in Orlando, eventually growing to comprise that city's largest Hispanic population, a community that increased with the island's 2016 post-María meltdown. Among them prevails a sense of their having never left Puerto Rico.

Like the Cubans, these island-centric Puerto Ricans patently want to be Americans as *puertorriqueños* but not as Latinos, esteeming themselves the Spanish-speaking, middle-class equal and duplicate of *americanos*– that mythos giving credibility to the fantasy of a possible future Spanish-speaking *Jíbaro* island state. Along with *cubanos*, those *puertorriqueños* are also eminently conscious of being *latinos* as Latin Americans, and of course, except to receive what benefits may be earmarked for all Latino/*latino* citizens, socially have no need of a Latino identity that homogenizes them with postwar mainland Puerto Ricans, their *marielitos*. In other words, island Puerto Ricans discovered the peculiarly Florida *latino* culture to which other like-minded Latin Americans have immigrated.

This *latino* Florida does not receive *large-scale* immigration of poorer Central Americans and Mexicans that for class and racial reasons do merge with and identify with brown Latino. Many white immigrants do, of course, struggle with rising rents and inflation, but not without the resources to survive those challenges because Florida's *latino*-welcoming climate has foremost received the skilled and better-off of Venezuela, Brazil, Colombia, and Argentina, to which one must also add the more modestly yet also skilled Dominican and Haitian communities.

These immigrations were ignited by economic crises back home and fueled by a period of plummeting housing prices in South Florida's *latino*-driven economy originally sown by the Cuban *exilio*'s financial build-up of a then-declining Miami and, in the eighties, pumped up by Colombian drug cartel money laundered in construction. TV's 1984 *Miami Vice* was fiction inspired by fact; the 2015 series *Narcos* was more documentary and introduces that history as background to the series.

Into the millennium, the spike in immigration that also transferred hemispheric wealth north prompted new construction being built specifically for this burgeoning market. More well-heeled Argentines were especially wooed, on the internet and in Buenos Aires, their visible presence and economic clout in North Miami now paralleling the Cuban presence in Miami proper. Well-off Venezuelans have built up the city of Doral. Reminiscent of Paz's observation of Mexican American culture floating in the air but not exactly blending, newly created South American communities make up outer provinces of their respective home countries, a virtual reality propped up by cell phones, the internet and international cable television. On a Buenos Aires public wall, a diptych mural fuses a view of that city and of Miami.

In this South Florida *latino* bubble another unique feature is the discovery that racialization in the American psyche can be played in two directions, so even of-color *latinos* can identify with or rationalize being culturally white. This transformation appears to be a concatenation of Anglo and Latin American racial attitudes. For Anglo Americans, one is of color with a drop of colored blood, no matter one's social status although money does modify in a presumably classless society. In Latin America, race can be more effectively altered by social and economic status, so excluding oligarchical racially higher standards of pedigree in their respective home countries, immigrant *latinos* feel free to introduce the value of socially-determined shades of white and discover that in this America not just "money whitens," as happens back home, but also politics.

Consequently, if in Anglo America *latinos* can be racialized even when they are white, upwardly mobile of-color *latinos,* who associate race with social status, arrive to this country's thinner demarcations of class providing the ability, if financially successful, to racialize themselves in reverse as white by taking advantage of this perk of culture war and adopting white politics. Such is the case, under the guise of anti-Communism, of the Cuban right, from whose third generation emerged the Afro-Cuban American Enrique Tarrio, leader of the white supremacist paramilitary organization The Proud Boys. Patently not identifying as a racialized brown Latino, Tarrio does not have to deny being *afrolatino* because as his advocacy of white supremacy (what he calls "Western chauvinism") redeems him as a white American.

During Donald Trump's October 15, 2020 Town Hall on NBC, in the background sat a black woman observer who distracted an entire nation by her exaggerated nodding approval of every sentence that Trump uttered. The morning after, she became the subject of discussion as much as the fly that, during his debate with Kamala Harris the week before, had parked on Mike Pence's white hair. That Trump cheerleader was Mayra Joli, an ex-beauty queen who had immigrated from the Dominican Republic, who like many Dominicans studied here and is now a Miami-based immigration lawyer.

When interviewed the day after the Town Hall, she expressed her support of Trump for "the good of the country." Trying to appreciate what Trump had done for the good of the country that could benefit her or her fellow Dominicans, 30,000 of whom were in danger of deportation owing to a Trump directive, one can only conclude that somewhere in the recesses of her psyche Joyli's identifying with Trump gave her a sense of psychological accomplishment, of truly belonging as an American.

From conversations with other *latinos* who support Trump, one infers that this political position against the option of identifying with minority Americans harkens to an anger over being secondary in race and class in their home countries. The American Dream is not just material but an ascent in class that is also tacitly racial, passing from socially nonwhite to psychologically white. Not ironically, therefore, among *latinos* in Florida, except in referring to African Americans one rarely hears discussions about race; they are all tacitly white. South Florida has an air of being a white Latin American haven free of the class and race tensions in respective home countries in part because, as noted earlier, Latin America's desperately poor do not come in great numbers to this state.

While I waited at a traffic light on Biscayne Boulevard, the driver of a black, late-model higher end BMW to my left lowered his darkly-tinted passenger-side window as he honked to get my attention. His passenger was a young boy. The driver signaled with his hand that I lower my window. He asked in a Venezuelan Spanish if he could cut ahead of my car because he found himself on a lane that required his making a left turn to a causeway. That he spoke Spanish first was normal in South Florida. He could have rented the Beemer or purchased more than he could afford. But he could have also been living successfully in Florida's *latino* culture without minimal reliance on English and, one deduces, no need to identify as a Latino. If idealistic Puerto Ricans believed a *Jíbaro* State was possible, its precedence is South Florida.

As Huntington noted of Cubans, in South Florida immigrant *latino* subgroups form economically and culturally self-sustaining communities. Although nationally all are considered "Latinos," they evince no intellectual or cultural connection to Latino as their American identity, preserving their origin histories over the unfolding of the history of the country they have adopted. This floating consciousness, as Paz described it, is shared with the general spectrum of South Florida *latino* immigrants at the opening stage of their Americanization. From the high-end cars so many drive, one extrapolates that, for now, being American is collectively understood as possessing such things, not an entry level American but a mainstream, complete American Dream.

Missing in this cultural phenomenon is a sense of a dramatic distance between where they are now and where they came from. This immigration's hallmark is not "huddled masses" but waves that arrive in our digital age already informed by hegemonic American culture and with a sense of privilege, landing on their feet in a Florida dissociated from the rest of America, each subgroup in its own space, each thinking itself wholly self-made.

In reality, of course, they all landed onto the history that preceded them, protected by civil rights legislation, equality that provides for equal access to housing, programs to start small businesses, educational opportunities, and Affirmative Action in employment.[61] Whether as permanent residents or citizens, they raise their children who will apply for scholarships and other assistance with a provenance in the sixties originally intended to benefit Mexican Americans and Puerto Ricans who fought for them. Of course, their children's American education will not include any of that history.

Most significant still, increasingly one witnesses a resentment and competition with that history, with immigrant groups of white *latinos* finding the omission of a "Latino" historicity politically advantageous. One agenda of that *latino* consciousness is to dodge history by adopting the shibboleth of Hispanic's being an immigrant culture, in other words, pledging allegiance to the traditional country preserved in the conservative imagination. Those *latinos* well know that Hispanic culture in the territorial U.S. dates back to the Conquest, a fact whose incursion into the national consciousness Anglo American purists are committed to wall out.

But populist patriotism cannot contain American intelligentsia, which is compelled to recognize that since the Revolution Hispanic culture has been the counterweight to measure the country's Americanness against its English heritage.[62] Nor could that patriotism overlook that America had historically made the existential choice of greater wealth at the cost of multiracial and multicultural impurity that has required more adamant racism and systematic mythmaking to keep from adulterating the country of the American Story. From that impure, multicultural American history, of which Hispanic culture is a

---

[61] Although the argument can be made that in a demographic of self-sustaining *latino* subgroups, equality precedes any need for civil enforcement.

[62] Starting with the "Columbians," those who wanted to name the country Columbia.

major tributary, descend today's Latinos who paved the arrival of recent Latin American immigrants.

Unfortunately, Latin American immigration began during a decade during which Latino consciousness was still gestating, when historically-conflicted Latinos were not equipped to invoke their own history. As a result, immigrants who knew even less of that history proceeded imagining that they landed on blank pages of American history on which they can freely write. Now, when informed of that history already written, Latino becomes an imposition on their envisioned destiny, seen as a political tactic of the Left, because acknowledging a native Latino seniority was a clause not highlighted in the contract they signed to commit to being just other white Americans. I am describing in summary conversations with South Florida immigrant *latinos* with whom the whiff of a disposition to giving credence to Latinos as connected to their American journey has threatened what had been a very pleasant and cordial relationship.

That disassociation with Latino and the historical struggles of minorities also comes from a sense of being a wholly different kind of immigrant, consistent with the era. For not just Latin Americans, in the late twentieth century, no matter from what part of the world, immigrants started "coming to America" already informed by the Information Age and already Americanized by American global hegemony. Every Latin American may not have had access to the same level of technology, but our world is structured and functions according to the dictates of the same technology, whether that involves a home tv set, a cellular phone, the sole computer in a small town's only café or those available at a school or at the home of a neighbor.

In our Digital Age, then, unless one comes from an Amazonian tribe cut off from civilization or an exceptionally impoverished sector, whether poor or better off the *latino* (or any other) immigrant who can afford to come legally doesn't experience a culture shock in "coming to America," nor feel particularly humbled with the need to prove that one is as modern and as technologically hip. For decades before Latin Americans started immigrating, they had enjoyed American music and movies. Well before emigrating, impending Latin American immigrants kept tabs on and learned what resources were available in their future country.

Many arrive, to repeat, with a sense of privilege and evincing little uncertainty of being in a new country. Hours away on the speed of jets is their home country, and with access to the internet and international cable television, they continue to receive the cultural sustenance missing here, and one doesn't have to be well-off to feel so empowered. Central American day laborers and Mexican farm laborers on Long Island call their families in their home countries on cell phones or use public library computers to Skype them, as they used to do from back home to speak to family members who had already emigrated.

Mexicans and Central Americans, of course, redirect the discussion to the issue of race, reminding that although I was discussing South Florida *latino* as semantically synonymous with default white, it is actually a transracial epithet, encompassing also *afrolatinos*. As African Americans, *afrolatinos* discover that race offers a different portal of entry into American culture, an entry that liberates from the racial limitations of home cultures and provides a comparatively empowering range of social participation in an alternate America that acknowledges its African-descended people as pillars in the country's creation.

Moreover, African Americans do not have a history of excluding *afrolatinos* that white Americans do toward white *latinos*. In fact, African Americans have demonstrated being strongly bonded to Latin America's African lineage, not seeing it as threat but as an enrichment to their identity as Americans. In other words, the personal redemption ever being offered to *latino* is not just to white *latinos* and the same cultural crossroads of either adapting *afrohispano* to their American identity or shedding that heritage completely is also ever before *afrolatinos*.

Finally, the *afrolatino* raises another distinction between Latino and *latino* in that the former invokes race as understood in American culture and the latter invokes *latino* notions of race. As noted earlier, and here again I cite Tannenbaum, Anglo Protestants have a history of struggling to accept the humanity of the African, and in order to rationalize slavery, turned being African into a metaphysical damnation. In *The Negro Christianized* (1706), Cotton Mather argued that blacks descended from Ham whom God had punished, so their inferior treatment was providential. American racial attitudes inherit that presumption of existential inferiority not changed by the Other's demonstrated intelligence or material success. The reversing of that inheritance is promised by the alternate America idealized by Latino and especially Latinx.

On the other hand, again invoking Tannenbaum's distinction, Catholic versus Anglo Protestant racial attitudes, *latino* has no history of demonizing African existentially. Catholicism acknowledged African humanity early in the history of slavery. Blackness did become a social stigma, an association with a lower station in life from which material success could, in effect, whiten. "El dinero blanquea." In contemplating the post-civil-rights Latino's canceling of Hispanic as essentially supremacist and white, one perforce also must reflect on older generations of *afrolatinos* who have clung to being *hispanos* not in blindness to the concomitant social racism.

One discerns that, less idealistic than the youthful Latino consciousness, those *afrolatinos* know more keenly about the impurity of social competition, so even if race were not a factor, social competition always exists based on additional class standards, but patently overriding the racial social stigma is the more valuable humanism of being *latino* understood as *hispano*.

In summary, for the *afrolatino* the options are between an Anglo Protestant culture historically racially conflicted over whether to concede human equality to its black members, and a *latino* culture that, despite a class challenge, intuitively presumes the humanity of its black members. These are not hard options for politically racialized Latinos, who as rhetorically brown, can and often do racially bail out.

LATINO (NOT *LATINO*) IN CULTURAL EXPRESSION

Latino has semantic usages most distinct from its homonymic function with *latino* in the contexts when it most emphatically operates to identify an American identity although not totally divorced from its heritage source. Still the speaker can be subverted by its semantics whose amorphousness makes unruly controlling what one intends to communicate, transmitting unintended nuances, evocations and even meanings. I am not a social scientist nor concerned with exact statistics on every possible instance of this occurrence; my emphasis is in proving that it is a chronic semantic circumstance that reveals itself as intellectual consequences at critical moments of cultural introspection. In this section, I offer four discrete (although linguistically related) reflections on the semantic problems raised by Latino and Latinx in a range of cultural expressions.

1. CORRECTION BY NOMENCLATURE

As noted earlier, Latino as more politically correct than Hispanic descends from the post-sixties' liberation by nomenclature –girl to woman, Indian to Native American, Negro to Black–as applied by the Cuban writer Roberto Fernández Retamar. His advancing that *latinoamérica* was more politically correct than *hispanoamérica* was picked up by U.S. Hispanics, who quickly adopted *latino*, soon transliterated as Latino, which in the southwest was further refined to convey an indigenous purity, racialized to become the color brown. But if that switch from Hispanic to Latino was influenced by and appeared to imitate exactly the post-sixties' liberation by nomenclature performed by other minorities, it actually wasn't, starting out of step with English in several ways.

For example, while mainstream America was racializing Hispanic to evoke brown, chiefly in academe and in the southwest racialized Latino was affirming of-color pride against Hispanic that was being racialized as white. As an identity refinement of "U.S. Hispanic," it did not take place in the sixties and early seventies; Latino was politically planted in the late seventies, gestated in the eighties, and got real legs with the Latin American immigration in the nineties. Finally, if Native American from Indian, Black from Negro, and woman from girl corrected a downgrading in American history, the change to Latino rejected the imposition of white Western supremacy in Latin American history.

Latino was also coined out of synch with its original role model, *latino* as a part of Latin America. By the millennium, when Latino really took hold, Latin America had evolved from its seventies revolutionary fervor more to cultural introspection. Meanwhile Latinos were no longer emulating Latin America but preserving its seventies consciousness that kept Latino more a socially activist than a cultural emblem. One expression of that consciousness was the disowning of its Hispanic history as racist and sexist, which led to correcting the Spanish gender deficiencies of "Latino," the "issue" to which I had promised to return in greater detail, whose history I pick up here.

Latinos' grammatical gender consciousness had really begun where it should, challenging the semantic gender values of Spanish, in which terminal -o is designated masculine and terminal -a feminine, with the default primacy given to the masculine -o form that also expresses gender neutrality. Woke Spanish speakers first advocated replacing the -o of a word like *amigo* with *amigue*, *amigos* with *amigues*. Whether or not this project survives in Spanish is not up to any one person to determine, and I am not addressing what is taking place in Spanish. I am focusing on the application of that Spanish correction to English, not a Latinate language.

The old joke applies to the doctor who, if you can't afford the operation, touches up the X-ray. Correcting Spanish grammatical gender by using English Latino amounts to touching up the Spanish in an English X-ray. That bilingual proclivity to pronounce Latino as an embedding of the Spanish *latino* in spoken English, whether out of habit or as an affectation, is actually done at the expense of linguistic and semantic sense. To repeat, the emphasis is on the terminal -o, presumably masculine. But except to differentiate between singular and plural, English does not communicate by inflection (changing endings), and does not distinguish between masculine and feminine grammatical gender. Because English has no masculine form, *masculine* is not the default operating in a gender-neutral word that ends in -o. *Bingo, photo, tobacco* are not masculine words. In other words, the Latino gender controversy overlooks that Latino is an English word; it is not *latino*.

Latino word-tinkering began with changing the modifier Latino to Latino/a, pronounced as "Latino/Latina," a practice not extended to other ethnic modifiers in English that don't end in -o. Gender was never a factor when the popular epithet was "Latin." There was no urgency to invent a feminine form for *American, African, Russian, French, Israeli*. English speakers didn't need to be reminded that some Russians are women by saying he-Russian/she-Russian. Neither is the Latinate Italian word *italiano* embedded to describe someone who is Italian. To spice up the sentence with the actual Italian modifier, we might say "She's *Italiana*," histrionically pronounced, but not routinely, knowing that is playful English and that *Italiana* is not a feminine adjective, which does not exist in English. A feminine gender form of the modifier Latino is invented in English or speakers are deluded into thinking that when saying "She's Latina," even though using Latino as adjective should produce, strictly speaking, "She's Latino," not "She's Latina." The workaround that we hear, "She's Latina," is actually using a noun as modifier, which English allows to shorten: "She's a Latina" is what "She's Latina" is grammatically saying.

That workaround causes semantic problems that are excused by the latitude given oral idiosyncrasies, "you know what I mean," but that can cause problems in written communication. For example, in using the double modifier Latino/a (pronounced as "Latino/Latina") two words are used when English "Latino" had already signified neutrally, semantically making the second either redundant or suggestive of additional meaning. "Latino/a culture" signifies in "you know what I mean" oral communication the same as "Latino culture." The added "/Latina" is redundancy that primarily flaunts the speaker's gender consciousness but that, if strictly read, also describes a particularly "Latina culture."

That over-refinement might not disrupt if one wants to float a sense of a distinct femininist cultural perspective but is not as felicitous when modifying other nouns, such as "Latino/a religious practices" or "Latino/a film studies." Should we understand that "Latino/a demographics" means the separate count of males and females or a different way of counting when it comes to counting Latinas: Latina demographics? The answer "we know what we mean" is oral communication and the acknowledgment of Latino as an oral consciousness. But literacy proscribes ambiguity.

Orally, even the most lettered Americans are prone to saying ungrammatically "There's a million things to consider." Orally, ebonics is respected as are foreign accents and grammatical errors peculiar to speakers of certain accents owing to linguistic interference. But oral convention and oral tolerance does not apply to non-creative, formal, written English. Read literally, therefore, "Latino/a demographics" can be interpreted as the discrete national count or a discrete method of counting Hispanic-heritaged males separate from females. "Latino demographics" may evoke a gender bias to a gender-conscious Spanish-speaker's ear who hears *latino*, but "Latino" is gender neutral to the native English speaker.

Moreover, fixating on the -o as masculine bias is not only linguistic interference, it doesn't even address the real masculine bias, which in English prevails even in words that don't end in -o. For, as feminism has demonstrated, a male default is built into all Western languages, including non-Latinate languages without a preponderance of words ending in -o and -a. The feminist remedy was to change the cultural consciousness, which eliminated the male default evocations in words like *doctor, nurse, pilot, cab driver* and even *soldier*.

Surely that more profound change of consciousness was the aspiration of advocating "Latino/a" but its short trending suggested either that it didn't make the gender case convincingly or it weighed with redundant usage. For whatever reason, it was tweaked to become the much cooler and high-tech-looking graphic or logo Latin@, still pronounced "Latino/a." While visually distinctive, Latin@ lacked the semantic and emotional resonance of the actual words on which it presumably improved. Attempt to extract emotion from reading the following sentence: "Marc Anthony sang with such Latin@ feeling." Can Marc Anthony sing with Latina feeling? Latin@ deferred to Latinx.

The gender consciousness of Latinx emulated a follow-up Spanish-speakers' tweaking, this time replacing the -o with an -x. In Spanish blogging one came across modifiers that replaced *mexicano, venezolano, americano* with *mexicanx, venezuelanx, americanx*. This textual change may work as a visual statement but phonetically the x in Spanish only exists either as an aspirated intervocalic *j* (English h) as in *México (Méjico)* or as the indigenous sounds, predominantly initial, /ts/ or /sh/, as in the woman's Aztec name Xóchitl or the application to the more indigenously spelled version of Chicano, Xcano. Spanish phonetics would make the terminal -x a mouthful if pronounced properly, as in "*venezolan-equis*." Instead advocates resort to English phonetics, "venezolan-ex."

Treating without regard to euphony, usage, and evocations is a self-subversion however woke the intention, and applying that terminal -x in English introduces a couple of semantic self-subversions. In English, X doesn't only cross something out, it is also a powerful phonetic negative. Elijah Muhammad, founder of the Nation of Islam, popularly called the Black Muslims, turned X into a symbol of defiance by requiring that converts strip that last vestige of slavery, surnames inherited from masters, and adopt the surname X. Hence Malcolm Little became Malcolm X. Latinx carries around the same moralistic weight, a scarlet X for male chauvinists to wear. One may choose to suspend judgment but euphony does intervene: "She's dating a Latinx" just doesn't sound like a pleasurable experience nor clarify if she's LGTBQ+.

Latinx's other phonetic problem is that while presumably changed was Latino's last vowel, the solution effectively affixed an -x to Latin, raising the volume on Latin because in English since The Great Vowel Shift, opening syllables predominate and terminal sounds tend to diminish in importance or become mute. Hence the silent "-e" in "come." Thus, by adding an x to Latin, which has an established semantic history in English, x sounds secondary and Latin is loudest. Latin's being gender neutral makes it the most commonsensical compromise, the -x instantly becomes redundant in neutralizing an already gender-neutral word. Who will remember that Latinx replaced Latino?[63]

Ironically, in general usage, Latinx's qualified popularity has stemmed from mainstream American solidarity with gender equality. Overnight public and media outlets signed up. News reporters frequently use Latinx, and publishers now have acquisition editors of "Latinx writing," and many organizations renamed to update to Latinx. Many college catalogs promptly changed their Latino Studies formal titles to be up to date. But returning to the reality of actual usage, Latinx is so exclusively English, diverging from a demographic that uses *latino* to pronounce Latino, the chances are not great of Latinx's becoming that successful as intuitive substitute for Latino usage in speech. Latinx remains more of an advocacy than a cultural fact. I don't anticipate watching the Latinx Grammys awarded for best Latinx music, and it is unlikely that two diehard "Latinx women" will be discussing "Latinx men" or chatting about the pressure to get married from their "Latinx mothers" unless they are being interviewed on National Public Radio.[64]

In other word's, Latinx's popularity among liberal white Americans as vehicle of gender consciousness seems to fuel its visibility more than the enthusiasm of Latinos. That discrepancy piques the curiosity of the mainstream press, which regularly finds a story on its usefulness and actual usage. Here's Wikipedia's summary of the stats in 2023: "Surveys of Hispanic and Latino Americans have found that the vast majority prefer other terms such as Hispanic and Latina/Latino to describe themselves, and that only 2–3% use Latinx."[65]

To reiterate my hypothesis: gender tweaks have been ways of expressing dissatisfaction with Latino's dysfunctional amorphousness, a complication displaced in expressing the more simply solved masculine gender bias. Latinx, however, is notably different among the nomenclature tweaks. They all express a frustration with Latino, but Latinx evolved to question that dysfunction even though its solution is as dysfunctional, evincing the Latino presentism of a newer generation disconnected from history, including the immediate history of the prior generation. In applying critical thought to the semantic amorphousness of Latino as their American identity, Latinx advocates see the solution in

---

[63] Of late one does hear Latin used, such as the name of the aforementioned website *The Latin Post*. On the other hand, in the semantic Wild West where Latino refinements collide, an up-to-date Spanish-language Facebook posting "tengo tantxs amig@s" reads as if on a parchment discovered on an asteroid.

[64] I limit discussion on Latinx here to its semantic features as nomenclature, reserving for the next section further discussion on its more recent implementation as identity epithet that signifies differently from Latino.

[65] "Latinx," *Wikipedia*, last modified June 22, 2023, https://en.wikipedia.org/wiki/Latinx

embracing its "elasticity," of not having to choose between established identities.

This new application of Latinx did not arise spontaneously from communal usage; rather, it was the creation of academic tinkering that later picked up advocates. By applying the semantic creativity feature of Latino, those Morales called "the younger folk" coopted Latinx, dismissing its original gender-correcting function and applying their generational questioning of binary identities to interpret Latinx as an undefined consciousness, what Morales called the "X factor," which allows for "crossing boundaries" of racial, cultural or gender identities. But read closely:

"Latinx allows one to cross boundaries more easily and construct identities or self-images that include a wide variety of racial, national, and even gender identifications."[66]

"Latinx allows one..." For those individuals who must forge possibilities because fed up with the binary racial and sexual identity constraint of *latinidad,* Latinx affords the freedom of gender, social, cultural nonconformity promised by alternate America. But is Latinx invoked for its "X-factor" addressing a collective consciousness or demographic? Are all presumably former Latinos fed up with binary identities and in need of crossing identity boundaries so now the entire demographic should call itself Latinx? If the dismantling of binary identities actually does overhaul known civilization, as Morales claimed of the "X factor," then a future conversation will be in order.

For the present, outside of its flashy promotion as the next great thing to hit the Latino consciousness, the relation of binary to nonbinary on the planet is still a work-in-progress, and so long as Latinos cling to its homonym *latino* to sustain some modicum of cultural sense, Latinx as an nonidentity identity shows no evidence of being a substantive replacement of Latino, a flawed but still evocative American identity. In wider usage, if Latinx is used, it will likely be to replace the terminal -o, not to replace the idea of an identity no matter how many testimonials appear of individuals being saved of binary identity restrictions by adopting Latinx.

The fact that this youngest generation has made the world aware of the potential for oppression of binary identities does not mean that binary will cease to exist. "Younger folks" who picked up the academic identity-stretching of Latinx as their remedy for identity confusion are not representative of actual usage. The low percentage of users of Latinx only indicates a collective intuitive

---

[66] Morales, *Latinx: The New Force in American Politics and Culture,* 4-5.

appreciation of redundancy, of Latinx's offering no great improvement on Latino. Latino is mainly used because of its phonetic ambiguity with *latino* as synonymous with *hispano*. Where does Latinx's questioning of conventional identity fit into the bigger cultural picture being at least subtextually preserved by Latino when Latinx more aggressively seeks to shed Latin? Why should it then continue to be part of this conversation?

Moreover, Latinx is not as new as it looks. Except for its function as gender corrective (and, of course, its "X-factor") Latinx is a recycling of Latino never understood intellectually in the first place. Latino had already intimated a passive assimilation to American woke as a liberation from presumably racist and sexist Hispanic; it already was, as Morales implied of Latinx, a walking away "after generations of Latin." Latinx only more aggressively erases that vestige of a *latino* historical consciousness, starting with a phonological divorce. No different than Latino, otherwise, Latinx essentially relieves a younger generation of being burdened with having to learn Spanish or study a history, and even allow circumventing Latino's racialization, rationalizing an identity in a nonplace by invoking the trendier liberation of disposing binary oppression.

In the end, the small percentage of users of Latinx are proselytizing its usage disconnected from the core Latino dilemma: yes, Latinos do want to assimilate "after years of Latin," and are not satisfied having to accept either an Anglo or a Latino idea of white or black, but they also don't want to assimilate absolutely, not left in cultural uncertainty, and so still passively cling to roots in *latino*. Of the small percentage that even uses Latinx, an even smaller of academically-conscious users use Latinx thinking of it as a "queering" or dismantling of binary identities. Individuals certainly may, but not in numbers that will change either Spanish or English usage, in other words, not in numbers that should distract from our focus on Latino as the labyrinth of multitude.

2. LATINO/X AS MODIFIER OF ART

The murky cultural substance of Latino and Latinx comes into question when used in phrases modifying art and writing. Not a problem in music. As noted earlier, Latino music is not a translation of *música latina,* and we must get creative to figure out the possible meaning of the phrase Latinx music. *Música latina* signifies not just music produced by *latinos* but a style, a musical genre. Unless one knows that the speaker means to translate *música latina,* Latino or Latinx as modifiers of music may convey that its creators are Hispanic-heritaged and that the speaker is referring to *música latina* or Latin music but neither Latino nor Latinx evoke a musical style. *I love dancing to Latinx music?* What's an example of Latin music? Of course, *musica latina* or Latin Music predates Latino and are laden with a musical history and generations of artists and styles. In contrast, art and writing produced by Latinos are still relatively nascent and modified by words whose meanings are amorphous and in flux. Because "art" and "writing" invoke culture, Latino and Latinx as modifiers are intended to underscore culture so notably "Latino" is used understanding *latino.*

Noteworthy too, before art and writing Latinx takes on a third semantic function. First had been as a gender corrective of Latino and second was to announce what Morales called the "X-factor." As modifier of art and writing, however, Latinx isolates from the broader Latino/*latino*/Latinx to mean specifically "U.S. Latinx." But the semantics of Latino and Latinx is different in each case, Latino/x art and Latino/x writing. Let us begin with the peculiarities of Latino/x as modifier of art.

Art described as Latino or Latinx points to the artist's origins, the Hispanic-heritaged world, caught in the intersection of Latino and *latino.* But Latino provides more latitude. American websites frequently understand "Latino art" as a composite of U.S.-based and Latin American art. Latin American-centered websites rarely use the epithet Latino (or *latino*) nor include U.S Latino art as Latin American. "Latino art" at one point implicitly denoted only U.S. art that was Latino, implying as well a less sophisticated work, the prejudice that operated early in Latino writing.[67] As Latino art established legitimacy, affording more opportunities for it to be exhibited, and therefore for others to be exhibited alongside, the epithet's possibilities expanded to signify also *latino* or Latin American art, from which practice the epithet Latino became more generic, prompting the need for a more U.S-specific epithet, which is sometimes conveyed as "U.S. Latinx" or simply Latinx. But more semantic amorphousness can come into play.

Here is a definition of Latinx from the "C& America Latina" website: "The term Latinx' is an update of traditional labels such as 'Hispanic' or 'Latin' which emerged around the mid-twentieth century to describe Latin American migrant communities in the US." Actually, both epithets are way much older. Another questionable claim: Latinx is simply "an update of traditional labels"– so much for Morales' X-factor–and describes "Latin American migrant communities." While "migrant communities" is intended to commit to the art's being specifically U.S.-based, encompassing by implication immigrant Latin American communities, the statement excludes the idea of Latino as native and not migrant, adopting the shibboleth of Hispanic as an immigrant culture, that

---

[67] Oscar Hijuelos complained over drinks that, even after receiving the Pulitzer Prize, he sensed a resistance to acknowledging him as simply a writer, Latino implying a narrower range.

statement a paradigm of Latino's semantic amorphousness that can be used however the art market wants to exploit it.

One way is to deprive the recognition due art that is "U.S. Latinx," argues Arlene Dávila in *Latinx Art: Artists, Markets, Politics*,[68] in whose diction Latinx isolates U.S. Latino from the art world's "Latino art" (implicitly generic *latino* or Latin American). Dávila uses Latinx as a gender corrective of Latino without the consciousness of Morales' "X-factor," defining Latinx art as work by "artists from Latin American backgrounds in the U.S., whether they are first generation or have a longer history here, who work primarily in the United States and identify with the U.S. Latinx experience."[69]

I read that sentence thinking back to Ed Morales' words: "...the race narrative of Latin America, which is transmitted through the social mores of Latinx that emigrate to the United States," recalling back then that the sentence jarred after his book's announcing that Latinx was "a new force in American politics and culture." Does not "Latinx that emigrate" signify that Latinx can also have origins in Latin America? Then I re-read Dávila's requirement that to be Latinx the artist must "identify with the U.S. Latinx experience." The "U.S." modifier suggests another kind of Latinx experience, perhaps Morales' "Latinx that emigrate"?

And if artists can be Latinx before emigrating, then at what point do they stop being Latin American and become "U.S. Latinx" artists. And at what point does that X-factor kick in among "Latinx that emigrate," "after years of Latin...," and therefore at what point do U.S. Latinx artists become American artists? And what about their work would make it Latinx and distinct as American art or distinct from American art?

Dávila admits to Latinx's being a problematic identity even for Latinx artists because the modifier narrows their work's importance to being representative of a marginalized culture and not expressive of the universal advancement of art. This crossroad Dávila illustrated with the example of Basquiat, whom the art world markets as an African-American or Haitian American artist, not acknowledging him or his work as Latinx.

Dávila argues that Basquiat was Latinx "because Haitians are also Latinx. Basquiat's mother was Puerto Rican, and he was immersed in Nuyorican art worlds and incorporated Spanish words in many of his works."[70] Here Dávila extends to Latinx the semantic feature of Latino's reclaiming Hispanic on call:

---

[68] Arlene Dávila, *Latinx Art: Artists, Markets, Politics*, (Duke University Press, 2020).

[69] Dávila, *Latinx Art: Artists, Markets, Politics*, 18.

[70] Dávila, *Latinx Art: Artists, Markets, Politics*, 18.

"incorporated Spanish words in many of his works" (so much for being done with Latin.) Morales had referred to emigrating Latin Americans as also Latinx and Dávila does the same in arguing that Haitians, as French speakers, are also Latinx.

But Basquiat's mother's being Puerto Rican also makes him Latinx, and then there's his having worked "immersed" in the Nuyorican art world, "immersed" a word that suggests his complying with her requirement for being a Latinx artist: those "who work primarily in the United States and identify with the U.S. Latinx experience." Basquiat can be said to meet Dávila's requirements of what makes a Latinx artist although he also achieved being seen exactly how Dávila explained many Latinx artists wanted to be seen and not narrowed into a set of expectations.

Basquiat's addressing and actually having worked more immersed in a broader audience would seem to explain why, having myself lived immersed in the Nuyorican experience, including its art scene, I have no recollection of Basquiat as one of its artists to say that I saw evidence that he "identified with the U.S. Latinx experience." But did he have to, given his other Latinx credentials? Could his work be Latinx despite his not identifying with "a U.S. Latinx experience" and never having publicly promoted himself as a Latinx artist? Does his being a Latinx artist depend entirely on the art world's giving him that recognition?

As I noted above, in the U.S. "Latino art" is understood generically, closer to *latino*, encompassing both Latin American and "U.S. Latinx" (while *latino* rarely modifies *arte* except as a Latino affectation in several art websites, such as *www.artelatino.com*). In general usage, while *latino* can and does identify Latin American cuisine in Spain, *arte latino* does not conventionally convey *arte latinoamericano*. On the other hand, I know Latin American artists who have spent the better part of their lives working in the U.S. and who never identified with the "U.S. Latinx experience."

But do they have to identify with the "U.S. Latinx experience" to be part of that total U.S. Latino/*latino* experience, which also produces "Latinx art"? Those Latin American artists work in this northern branch of Latin America populated by Latinos, and therefore possibly also Latinxs, whom some museums allow are also generically Latino/*latino* artists. There appears to operate a semantic border in art between Latino and Latinx art, but if Latinx can also be "Latinx that emigrate," can those Latin American artists be denied being also non-U.S. "Latinx"?

Another confusion in discussing Latinx as modifier of art is touched upon in Dávila's reference to the Spanish words in Basquiat's art, images of his biography as the son of a Puerto Rican mother. Dávila also acknowledged his

Latinx credentials as Haitian. If French words appear in his work, wouldn't that imagery also make his work Latinx? Dávila's citation of that Spanish-word imagery also raises the question of whether it is the artist's biography that makes a work Latinx and or something about the art. The biography seems to be the convention although Dávila also offered the imagery of the Spanish words. On the other hand, while Dávila's definition of Latinx spells out the requirement of identification with "the U.S. Latinx experience," the "C& America Latina" website called Latinx the artistic expression "of Latin American migrant communities" and the paradigmatic "U.S.-Latinx" experience is not predominantly migrant, with the larger numbers of Mexican-Americans native Hispanics.

And is a Latinx biography an absolute requirement? It isn't in music. Larry Harlow Kahn (born Larry Ira Kahn) was a great *música latina* artist, "el judio maravilloso," who played a particular genre of music called *salsa,* a form of *música latina.* Could Larry Harlow be a *latino* artist? He certainly identified with the "U.S. Latinx" music. Could Larry Harlow be considered a Latinx musician? In composing in the style of a Latino, adopting a Latino voice and Puerto Rican rhythms for *The Capeman,* did Paul Simon produce a Latinx musical? More on this to follow.

Neither Dávila nor America suggest that Latinx can be a style or an artistic movement that non-Latinx artists can adopt, and it is in the nature of art to begin with a blank canvas, with only preconceived aesthetic or thematic expectations of a particular artist's signature aesthetic orientation. Ideally, unless one is explicitly looking for propaganda or folk art that celebrates fixed iconography, in commissioning art that will presumably be Latinx, one might have to establish the Latinx authenticity of the artist but not on the assumption that his or her being Latinx will produce art of a predictable style peculiar to Latinx, something that does not exist.

3. LATINO/X AS MODIFIER OF WRITING

In contrast, when modifying writing, Latino and Latinx evoke a particular style and content. As in "Latino/x art," "Latinx writing" now conventionally isolates "U.S Latinx" but Latino can also be understood and is confused with generic *latino* or Latin American writing. Publishing houses are wont to assume that Latin American and Latino writing comprise the same market. On a *Huffington Post* web page titled "23 Books By Latinos That Might Just Change Your Life," Carolina Moreno offered this list: Julia Alvarez, Junot Díaz, Sandra Cisneros, Pablo Neruda, Gabriel García Márquez, Eduardo Galeano, Jorge Luis Borges, Isabel Allende, Isabel Cepeda, Paulo Coelho (Brazil), Rolando Hinojosa, Miguel

Piñero.[71] Moreno effectively showcased a publisher's list of Latino writing, which merges what in academe would more often be separate lists of Latino/x[72] and Latin American writing.

Liberal academics more likely include Latino/x writings among Latin American writing while stricter Latin Americanists rarely include Latino/x writing. Comparative feminist and queer Latino/x and Latin American writings may form a single syllabus reading list. And Latino/x writings can become extensions of the more socially-conscious branch of Latin American writings but have nothing to contribute in discussing Latin American literature's history of philosophical and aesthetic inquiry.

Moreno dispensed with academic distinctions in her publisher's list of an eclectic market, and while her list consisted of generically *latino* writings, not all are by any measure what we call Latino writing. I am not expressing a personal opinion; I am applying the standard set by the closest thing to a Latino/x literary culture, Latino Studies. Borges and García Márquez are on Moreno's list of Latino writers but their work does not qualify as Latino Studies' expectations of Latino writing, not alone because those two writers did not come from a "U.S. Latino/x" experience but because we read them to be enriched by the aesthetics and themes of their writings. Real Latino writing is not about aesthetic originality or about themes but about authentically documenting personal and social experience, not that experience translated into literary metaphors.

Interviewed in 2010 by Chloe Schama for *The Smithsonian*,[73] Ilán Stavans, editor of *The Norton Anthology of Latino Literature*, was asked: "Given that so much of the material included in the collection is political or historical and not necessarily what we think of as literature, how did the editors define literature?" Stavans' response: "The anthology understands literature in a very open-ended fashion, not only short stories and poetry and novels, but memoirs and nonfiction books, logs and letters and types of music ranging from *corridos* [traditional Mexican ballads] to pop songs, also cartoons, comic strips, and jokes. We ended up endorsing 'literature' as a written expression that conveys the search for identity."

---

[71] Carolina Moreno, "23 Books By Latinos That Might Just Change Your Life," *Huffpost*, November 19, 2015, https://www.huffpost.com/entry/23-books-by-latinos-that-might-just-change-your-life_n_564c11e0e4b045bf3df1b939

[72] "Literature" in course titles actually mean "literary history," which strictly speaking, Latino writing doesn't actually have after Latino's presentist disowning any connection to Hispanic.

[73] Ilán Stavans, "What Defines Latino Literature," in *The Smithsonian*, December 2, 2010

Stavans' Latin American anthology consists of conventional literary selections.[74] His separate standard for Latino is premised on an understanding that Latino writing does not engage in a literary conversation but primarily documents U.S. social and cultural experience. The best of that writing, according to that definition, produces moving and earnest documentation, not an intellectual contribution to be extrapolated from a crafted figurative language.

One consequence of this standard for Latino is the norm that during still-called Hispanic Heritage Month, outnumbering all others guest speakers are Latino authors on a lecture circuit as survivors of domestic abuse, addiction, gang life, threats of deportation, homophobia, etc., who have written in any genre, including journalism, all important chiefly as testimonials of having experienced injustice or a search for identity. Latino writing, to extrapolate from the definition of literature applied by Stavans for his Latino anthology, is not read to have, strictly speaking, a literary experience.

In other words, to reiterate, Latino writing is not meant to be read for ideas and metaphors outside of social and political allegory. Latino writing is presumed to not make thematic associations but aspires to create the genuine voice that is synecdochic of a cultural group and allegorical of an ethnic or racial experience. The writing is presumed to be a vehicle for a collective voice, a group in struggle. One can say that it is expressive of ideas to the extent that they are the social ideas of a documentary, and the writing is assumed to be realism even if fiction, not expressive of more creative ideation or figures of speech or of a philosophically broader consciousness of universal human experience. The writing is less important than the writer, to whose authenticity as voice traditional textual literary criticism threatens to be insensitive, literary exceptionalism having been demystified as no different than ordinary communication by postmodernism.

Postmodernism is never cited or acknowledged or in most cases even known as the philosophical underpinning of Latino writing. Postmodernism questioned objective truth as the imposition of ideology and dismissed the validation of hierarchies. Its powerful influence in the sixties and seventies is evident in the rethinking of America that led to the Civil Rights Movement's revision of what had been considered the country of The American Story of white Americans. In literary criticism, postmodernism scaled down the authority of literary language, equating written and oral expression, prompting the questioning of the traditional literary canon. The standard that the canon had referred to as "quality" was debunked as an arcane gimmick employed to justify excluding the marginalized.

---

[74] Ilán Stavans, *The FSG Book of Twentieth-Century Latin American Poetry: An Anthology* (New York: Farrar, Straus, and Giroux, 2012).

Postmodernism's breakdown of critical hierarchy empowered the formerly excluded to pressure textbook editors into being more representative. The argument was paradoxical, on the one hand asserting that a truer American canon should recognize mastery without bias toward the writer's gender, race or ethnicity while, on the other hand, making it imperative that textbook selections be representative according to gender, race, ethnicity on the assumption that the hierarchical gauging of language mastery was ethnocentric and subjective.

In principle, the idea of a multicultural canon implied that, owing to ethnocentric myopia, comparable "quality" or literary mastery among women and minority writers had been suppressed. But literary multiculturalism came to demand a rethinking of the traditional idea of literature, redefining literary importance not as a performance of exceptional language mastery to be enjoyed as its own experience and needed to be taught properly to be read. Instead, applying Stavan's editorial measure, the new literature comes from oral language, dispensing with "elitist" hurdles or preparation, but accessible to read for authenticity of Latino experience, which (given Latino as the cultural confusion discussed throughout this book) invariably defaults to a search for identity.

In this effort to democratize, multiculturalism politicized writing itself, disqualifying formal writing as less "representative" than oral or popular literacy. Too literary, William Carlos Williams stops being an antecedent to Latino writing; Langston Hughes is more truly the black poet than Robert Hayden. Coined in this philosophical milieu, the epithet Latino as modifier of writing now evokes being synonymous with oral writing or emulating its authenticity. I received numerous invitations to read as a recommended Latino writer from prospective hosts who, as they eventually revealed in further discussion, understood that I was a Nuyorican or performance poet.

Postmodernism's influence only makes Latino writing a product of its American time, that influence now standard in American literature survey textbooks, which to become multicultural mainly insert multicultural texts among traditional selections with minimal effort to connect the traditional and the multicultural selections with literary criticism. The editing does not acknowledge that the textbooks are also showcases of competing expectations of reading and writing, concatenating a postmodernist definition of literature and a traditional definition of literature, a design that can satisfy a national market, from which professors can customize their classes.

4. OTHER REFLECTIONS

In 1998 The Poetry Society of America organized a black-tie fundraiser that afforded a world premiere of the song of Paul Simon's forthcoming musical *The Capeman*, about a fifties sixteen-year-old Puerto Rican gang leader convicted of killing two white boys and later spared dying in the electric chair. The event was held at the theater of the City University of New York's John Jay College of Criminal Justice. Preparation for the play's premiere was clouded by constant picketing against a play that exonerated a killer of two boys for racial reasons. Meanwhile, discord between producers, directors, and Simon contributed to the musical's destiny of becoming one of Broadway's biggest flops.

Nevertheless, even its harshest reviewers consistently praised the music. In the August 8, 2010 issue of *The New York Post*, writing on a free revival to be performed in Central Park, drama critic Elisabeth Vincentelli briefly retold the musical's sad history but still concluded: "And yet 'The Capeman' had one thing going for it: A really, really good score."[75] But the Poetry Society of America was thinking by association when it chose to stress the Latino protagonist's biography and the musical's being about a Latino, and not stress the musical as Simon's artistic achievement when they planned the fundraiser at John Jay College of Criminal Justice.

Paul Simon composed assuming the voice of a fifties Puerto Rican, a score that included the songs of Puerto Rican folk sounds, mambo, as well as a mainland Rican kid's doo-wop. I appreciated his having taken on that artistic challenge, and his lyrics do capture an authentic *latino* consciousness, in lyrics enriched with an aesthetic sensibility not always found in Latino writing–a collaborator on the lyrics was the Nobel laureate poet Derek Walcott.

Simon's adopting a Latino voice and some reviewers' not getting it or feeling he had not succeeded seemed to be an additional reason for reviewer Anthony Decurtis to call the previewing CD "a mongrel project": "Simon himself, not the cast members, sings most, but not all, of these tunes — which makes it an odd preview of a musical...."[76] Stephen Thomas Erlewine's review in the AllMusic website panned the music that he described as "forced and labored": "...like he has to push the melodies into unnatural paths – and it never has the graceful, joyously organic spirit of doo-wop and Puerto Rican music, which is what he needed to capture in order for *The Capeman* to succeed. Instead, the project is

[75] Elisabeth Vicentelli, "'Cape' of Good Hope," *New York Post*, August 8, 2010, https://nypost.com/2010/08/08/cape-of-good-hope/

[76] Anthony Decurtis, "Songs from *The Capeman*," *The Rolling Stone*, November 14, 1997, https://www.rollingstone.com/music/music-album-reviews/songs-from-the-capeman -183895/

a cerebral exercise..."[77] Indeed, Simon took on a considerable challenge and sang those songs in that CD as a completion of his artwork, his writing not just about a Puerto Rican character but assuming the voice of his Puerto Rican character.

Simon has always written songs with touches of poetic effects more than rhyme, monologues that create a character. In 1965, for the album *Sounds of Silence,* he put to music Edward Arlington Robinson's 1897 poem "Richard Cory." His "Graceland" is ambiguously not just about Elvis' Graceland." Not as a conscious comment on Latino writing, in *The Capeman* Simon attempted Latino writing's ideal balance of art and social consciousness. This hypothesis prompted me to research, when I discovered a specifically Puerto Rican influence on Simon throughout his career: Puerto Rican bands alternated with his father's band at the Palladium (where my aunt went dancing every weekend), and Latin music was his original window to "World Music." His passage went from his 1963 recording (as Paul Kane) of "Carlos Dominguez"[78] to singing to Latin beats alongside "Julio down by the schoolyard" to composing as Salvador Agrón's consciousness in *The Capeman.*

This thematic thread was also influenced by the history of *West Side Story,* a musical that ended up being about the hostilities between a gang of youths descended from earlier immigrations and recently migrated Puerto Ricans but that was originally titled *East Side Story,* a "musical was about warring Jews and Catholics...altered to reflect a changing NYC."[79] Written by Jews who were going to tell an American Jewish story, in Puerto Ricans they found fresher metaphors for the Jewish experience. Simon also saw Puerto Ricans as metaphors of his own experience as a New Yorker.

In an interview with radio talk jockey Don Imus, addressing those picketing the production, he explained that he understood his musical to be about forgiveness "...I begin to ask, well what is enough, or is there an enough, because I don't think we're a society that believes in forgiveness..."[80] He was referring, of course, to society's forgiving Salvador Agrón, but Sal (ironically named for one who died for our sins) as metaphor extends that forgiveness to the people whom Sal represents, which since *West Side Story* have been

---

[77] Paul Simon, "Songs from *The Capeman* Review," *Allmusic,* https://www.allmusic.com/album/songs-from-the-capeman-mw0000596435

[78] "Paul Simon – Carlos Dominguez – Rare," Youtube, https://www.youtube.com/watch?v=JPju1YFCerQ

[79] Jordyn Haime, "Jews were behind the original 'West Side Story' and today's remake. Should they be?," *The Times of Israel,* December 12, 2921

[80] See http://rhhardin.home.mindspring/transcription.simon.txt

national metaphors of Otherness and who have never really been forgiven for committing the original sin of having transformed New York forever.

My research produced an essay that I submitted to a major Latino Studies journal. The submission was rejected for not being about an actual Latino writer. *The Capeman* was indeed a play about a Latino subject but my writing of Latino as influence on Simon was not germane to Latino Studies; Latino as a theme does not cut it in Latino Studies. I sent the essay to Simon's studio with no outcome in mine except thinking that Simon might find it of interest. Sometime later a message was left with my department's secretary from Paul Simon's studio. A week later Simon received me with the manuscript in hand, having found "fascinating" things I saw that he had not seen.

The journal's rejection invoked the literalness requirement of Latino/x writing, including critical writings. Years later, with the resounding 2015 success of *Hamilton*, I thought back to my experience with *The Capeman*. Lin-Manuel Miranda, Puerto Rican and generically a Latino, composed the book, music and lyrics for *Hamilton*. Does that make *Hamilton* Latino writing? Will that journal that rejected my essay on Simon's adopting a Latino voice to compose the music of *The Capeman* accept an essay on *Hamilton* even though the musical has nothing, strictly speaking, to do with Latino/x except in the casting as metaphor of inclusivity. For, ironically, while *Hamilton* is not about a Latino if by a Latino, it invokes a Latino literalness.

Casting the revolutionaries as multiracial does remind the white audience that the principles fought for also applied to other races; on the other hand, that casting also implies a dumbing down, an inability to extrapolate that, the actual American revolutionaries' all being white and far from perfect humans, are still metaphors of the principles they stood for, which we today daily rely on through the Constitution. When I witness the excitement of that historical moment interpreted for a younger generation so they can associate the American ideals because acted out by someone who looks like them and performed to their contemporary music, I wonder if that is as good a sign as the celebration of that spoon feeding suggests.

LATINO (*Latino*) STUDIES

Like all academic minority programs, Latino Studies owes its existence to the sixties civil-rights agenda of challenging university studies that were created to instill as patrimony Western Civilization primarily in young whites. Overlooked by that traditional education were descendants of non-European citizens, whom Americans call minorities, a slant that in the post-sixties prompted the corrective of providing higher-education studies of minority cultures. Intuitively, minority studies implied a questioning of Western ethnocentrism as white brainwashing, the position advocated by the most radical. The more moderate, who reread their Western education as an instrument of a liberation from the West's oppressive past, prevailed and ultimately minority studies settled into researching the relation of Westernized non-European peoples to their non-European heritages.

Minority Studies also began with the postmodernist idea of countering traditional hierarchical academe, of education as also being "about the people," open to the equal wisdom of surrounding communities. Originally Black Studies engaged in that partnership with the community, at times to be discredited for lowering college standards to pass unprepared students. From that origin, however, Black Studies scholarship evolved into intellectual maturity and became an academic imperative. Florida's Governor Ron DeSantis' recent diminution of the value of AP courses in African American Studies recycles that perception of those early days, since when he obviously has not opened his eyes to the national impact of African-American public intellectuals now consulted on nationwide media on a range of subjects and not strictly on matters of race.

Latino Studies, which came into being around the same time, is not there yet. Latino, in comparison, has produced leaders and spokespersons primarily on matters germane to Latino, the border crisis and voting trends. While African American public intellectuals can be invited to a news outlet because they have recently published a book, Latino spokespersons more likely lead an important project or are advisors to a campaign. Where one sees a collaboration of African American Studies with nonacademic public intellectuals, Latino Studies' only acknowledges Latino intellectuals that are scholars. Also contrasting, while African American Studies has universally become an academic imperative, Latino Studies is a southwestern imperative but throughout the rest of the country primarily functions as a college service to a particular student population, a service often carried out by other disciplines, programs or departments. In all cases, Latino Studies relies greatly on the political support of local communities, its mandate is not solely academic because Latino Studies started out steeped in ambiguity.

In the seventies specifically Mexican-American and Puerto Rican Studies programs were first created, the latter destined to be soon changed by increasing Latin American immigration and Latin American literature's replacing the historically Iberian legacy of departments of Romance Languages. Throughout the eighties, the national demographics projection that by the millennium Hispanics would become the largest minority made compelling the broadening of the academic commitment to disciplines related to Hispanic. Meanwhile, the effort to create Latino Studies required retooling faculty resources because doctorates did not exist in an area that would come to be called Latino Studies and faculty had to come from professors of related disciplines. The most germane, consistent with the broadening mandate of Latino and Latin American, were recent immigrants with higher degrees and a concentration in Latin America.

Budgetary restrictions came into play. Programs came into existence by cross-listing History, Political Science, Spanish, Sociology and other courses that might touch upon some Hispanic subjects. Only larger institutions had a Romance Languages or a specifically Spanish department. Many colleges that merged programs would create some variant if not exactly "Latin American and Latino Studies" or perform as such still called Latino Studies. In the majority of cases, the priority was teaching Latin America as social science research, no different than Latino. Learning about Latin America as a fount of ideas or literary expression remained the rarefied opportunity of students at larger universities or colleges with departments of Spanish or Romance Languages while Latino writing is not taught as a fount of ideas and more as graphic "representation" of social science research.

The physical possibilities of offering Latino Studies are indeed manifold, but consistent throughout Latino Studies as an area of concentration is the need to reconcile ambiguities inherent in "Latino" and its founding political premises. In focusing on "U.S. Latino," scholars work conscious of a commitment to be in solidarity with popular presentism. For literary, historical and intellectual discussion Latino Studies resorts to Latin American letters, *latino* Studies, a finessed crossing over from Latinidad to *latinidad* in a way that presumes a Hispanic past without actually naming it. A more recent challenge is the effect of Latino literalness on second-generation Latin American immigrants, who seek out the same literalness in Latino Studies, which understands that Mexican-American and Puerto Rican American histories are the paradigms, and therefore model metaphors of Latino/*latino* relations with Anglo America, metaphors from which recent immigrants should extrapolate their participation in that legacy. Instead, they feel left out. Let us review more problems us review the problems posed by Latino/x semantics in the scholarship.

In her preface to *Making Hispanics: How Activists, Bureaucrats, & Media Constructed a New American*[81] G. Cristina Mora explained why she chose Hispanic for her title: "So why, then, did I title this book *Making Hispanics* and not Making Latinos? Simply put, because this book is about history and I felt it necessary to use the labels that the actors and institutions in question favored."[82]

---

[81] G. Cristina Mora, *Making Hispanics: How Activists, Bureaucrats, & Media Constructed a New American* (Chicago: University of Chicago Press, 2014).

[82] Mora, *Making Hispanics: How Activists, Bureaucrats, & Media Constructed a New American*, 10.

Mora is right in that her book researches decades when Hispanic was the operative currency. But she could have also written because this book is about history and Latino does not evoke a history, for the same if unstated reason that, writing in 2004, Samuel P. Huntington chose Hispanic over Latino in *Who Are We?*

Mora expressed a measure of guilt for having given in to the historical semantic feature of Hispanic. Personally, she adds, she preferred "to be called Latina," explaining why by offering Latino boilerplate about Hispanic:

> For many in the community, the term Hispanic seems more conservative than Latino because the former seems to emphasize a cultural connection to Spain. Growing up, I for one cringed when some referred to me as Hispanic. I preferred to be called Latina because to me the term conveyed an alternative vision of pan-ethnicity based less on a cultural link to Spain and more on how the legacies of colonization have united persons south of the U.S.-Mexico border.[83]

Mora, of course, was invoking Retamar's original call now long forgotten and largely replaced by the primacy of solidarity with her generation that repeats Retamar's seventies view as their own insight. But Mora's solidarity impairs her appreciating her argument's contradiction. If she grew up with such a keen politically-correct consciousness that her anti-colonialism would make her "cringe" at the idea of being associated with Spain, given the history of Anglo southwestern conquest of oppressed indigenous peoples and Mexicans and given that she is writing in an imposed English, she might well have said that she also cringes no less at being called American.

Mora's recycling of Latino vis a vis Hispanic, a hallmark southwestern Latino grievance, is emblematic of how Latino Studies fails to address Latino as also the complicated product of American ethnocentrism and of an American education. What, in fact, is the source of Mora's anti-Hispanic feelings? Popular American culture is also anti-Hispanic, the bias Trump used to arouse his base. Meanwhile, American culture intellectually betrays Mora's anti-Hispanic feelings as think thanks acknowledge a Hispanic tributary in American history, why they perceive "Hispanics" as a challenging Western rival in a country that holds Western roots as justification for supremacy—think back again to Huntington.

---

[83] Mora, *Making Hispanics: How Activists, Bureaucrats, & Media Constructed a New American*, 11.

In *Latinos, Inc.: The Marketing and Making of a People*,[84] Arlene Dávila demonstrates that marketing forces created a rhetorical "people" composed of otherwise discrete Mexican Americans, Puerto Ricans, Latin American immigrants. Dávila begins by distinguishing between the bilingual "U.S.-centered Latinidad" distinct from a Spanish-dominant Latin American "Latinidad," the distinction that I label as Latino and *latino*.[85] But Dávila does not make clear when she is referring distinctly to either Latino or *latino*, at times suggesting that the distinctions she has established are insignificant.

That's what one deduces from an argument in her chapter "Language and Culture in the Media Battle Zone." Despite the difference that Dávila had originally established between an Anglophone "U.S.-centered Latinidad" and a Spanish-dominant Latin American *latinidad*, Univisión is criticized for not programming for Anglophone Latinos. Univisión should blur its cultural brand, a *latinidad* that addresses *latino*, with a Spanish-language requirement, to also encompass U.S. Latinidad, which has no language requirement, defaulting to English. At that moment Dávila, who had started out more scholarly objective in acknowledging "Latinidades," switches to the solidarity semantic function of Latino consciousness, political correctness that glosses over sense.

In *The Trouble with Unity: Latino Politics and the Creation of Identity*,[86] Cristina Beltrán studies the sixties alliance of Chicanos and Puerto Ricans as the original model interface with white America that all other subgroups will inevitably inherit as Latinos. The cohesion that created this alliance was "*Latinidad*," which Beltrán italicizes presumably to mean the idea underlying *latino* although she expresses her awareness that *Latinidad* is semantically amorphous. One definition Beltrán offers of *Latinidad* is "the sociohistoric process whereby various Latin American national-origin groups are understood as sharing a sense of collective identity..."[87] Another definition, not consistent with the italicizing, describes *Latinidad* as the conceptual essence of English Latino: "a historical practice constituted by homogenizing effects of racism

---

[84] Arlene Dávila, *Latinos, Inc.: The Marketing and Making of a People* (Berkeley and Los Angeles: University of California Press, 2001).

[85] My subject in this book, as noted earlier, is not original; its originality is in being written with the methods and from the perspective of the humanities as checks and balances of the primacy of the social sciences in Latino Studies.

[86] Cristina Beltrán, *The Trouble with Unity: Latino Politics and the Creation of Identity* (New York: Oxford University Press, 2010).

[87] Beltrán, *The Trouble with Unity: Latino Politics and the Creation of Identity*, 4.

experienced by Latinos and other people of color....," which provides "a shared history of racial struggle."[88]

As already seen in Dávila's discourse, academic convention allows one to establish a distinction between *latino* as cultural epithet and Latino as racial epithet while, deferring to solidarity, also retaining the license to use them interchangeably, and Beltrán invokes this academic ambiguity while struggling to make sense of that license. On the one hand, Beltrán notes that "*Latinidad* is a political concept,"[89] contrary to Spanish *latino's* being a heritage epithet. But then she cites Latino's semantic amorphousness, calling it "subjectivity," which allows it both to mean the same as *latino* and also evoke a "shared history of racial struggle," that fusion with Latino suggested in the morphology of *Latinidad*: English uppercase L and Spanish italicized *latinidad*.

As noted above, Latino Studies faced new challenges with the addition into the Latino demographic of the second generation of the Latin American immigration, notably its displeasure with and disconnect from the Latino American history that Cristina Beltrán argued was the original model of interface with American culture. Having also inherited the established Latino allowance of creativity as critical thought, this second generation employs that creativity to criticize or disengage from Latino to find its own space, in the end only further obfuscating Latino. Two elaborate examples are books by Claudia Milian, who in her first book wrote as an "Afro-Salvadorean."

In *Latining America: Black-Brown Passages and the Coloring of Latino/a Studies*,[90] Milian writes on parallel tracks. On one track *Latining America* emulates sixties personal race testimonials and on the other track she seeks scholarly legitimacy. Ironically, on a personal track race is not her issue. Instead, Milian voices a Salvadorean exclusion and competition with Chicanos and the "Hispanophone Caribbean" in Latino Studies.

Race is her subject on an academic track. Latinidad is defined as the bonding agent of "a Latin, Latin American, Latino and Latina triangulation"[91] that, she argues, are bonded in a way that both Latino and *latino* camouflage as cultural but is actually racial, an echoing of Salazar's panelists. This thesis is not followed by a fully developed argument; it is simply stated as a truism that presumably behooves her inventing an epithet that more explicitly addresses that racial bonding, the transliteration "Latinity." If *latinidad* signifies being

---

[88] Beltrán, *The Trouble with Unity: Latino Politics and the Creation of Identity*, 7.

[89] Beltrán, *The Trouble with Unity: Latino Politics and the Creation of Identity*, 110.

[90] Claudia Milian, *Latining America: Black-Brown Passages and the Coloring of Latino/a Studies* (Atlanta: University of Georgia Press, 2013).

[91] Milian, *Latining America: Black-Brown Passages and the Coloring of Latino/a Studies*, 1.

informed by cultural inheritance, "Latinity" is a consciousness of being "shaped" by what she calls "an ethnoracial logic."[92]

And because "Latinity" means being racially marginalized, then other racial minorities experience it, including African Americans, who become "Latin participants." Latino Studies, whose focus is on Mexican-American and the "Hispanophone Caribbean," should therefore broaden its color spectrum to encompass more than white and brown—obviating that Hispanophone Caribbean includes Afro-Caribbean—and should include Afro-Latinities of "other migrations," the shibboleth of Hispanic as an immigrant culture.

Milian's fundamental grievance springs from two other Latino semantic features, its being literal and non-ideational. The Mexican American and Hispanophone Caribbean that Beltrán had identified as paradigms and foundations of Latino American history that subsequent immigrants inherit is not germane to Milian because as Latino she does not interpret metaphors as actual communication. Her Latino purview is strictly literal, so identifying as "Afro-Salvadorean" she does not see that her being American ideationally connects her to Mexican Americans and Puerto Ricans as collectively Latino Americans.

Carlos Fuentes, who certainly merited receiving the Nobel prize, never did, but responded, on García Márquez's being so honored, that as a Latin American he felt as if he had received it. Where traditionalist German and Italian and Swedish Americans and, however subtler, even African Americans, adopt the ideational lineage of descending from the Founding Fathers on becoming Americans, Milian cannot because the American revolutionaries did not include Afro-Salvadoreans. On the other hand, being a quintessentially race-conscious Latino, Milian does identify with the single idea of racial exclusion, and that racial history she invokes throughout her book with global African as core metaphor.

In her second book, Milian's drops race as a basis of identity and interprets her sense of exclusion from Latino Studies as the consequence of being *Latinx*.[93] Writing this time not as an "Afro-Salvadorean" but as a "Salvadorean" and "Central American," Milian vents that as Central American she feels treated as "secondary Hispanic status" in Latino Studies. So much for the prior generation's tempest in a teapot over being Latino and not Hispanic and so much for her racial "Latinity." Rather, this book is the stage on which Milian enacts a persona for whom Ed Morales's *Latinx* served as script, an invitation

---

[92] Milian, *Latining America: Black-Brown Passages and the Coloring of Latino/a Studies*, 3.

[93] Claudia Milian, *Latinx* (Minneapolis: University of Minnesota Press, 2019).

to creativity to which Milian responded, starting with celebrating Latinx's lack of definition, what Morales called its "elasticity" obliterating conventional expectations of identity.

This semantic feature of Latinx, really because it's the same elasticity of Latino, Milian evidently interprets as a license to write of Latinx not as scholar but as social victim free to express feelings however imprecise, preciseness an expectation that, one infers, she considers retrograde. Latinx is a cauldron of undefined possibilities, and Milian is fine with its imprecision, fed up with the strict demarcations that have excluded her. Of course, while this imprecision may seem okay in chatting about Latinx, it doesn't work when writing about it, especially when she veers from Latino literalness to reaching for metaphors, creative writing the only option when one opens with this admission: "I am not particularly confident what Latinx is."[94]

Nevertheless, Milian proceeds to discover that her personal experience "was an early articulation of LatinX": "The X as one that is falling through the Latin cracks, the spaces between the o's and the a's, between the conventional understandings of what it means to be Latino or Latina."[95] The metaphor of cracks between "the o's and the a's" and "between the conventional understandings of what it means to be Latino or Latina" suggests a gender issue that is never discussed. That metaphor is all we get, relying on the oral reasoning of "you know what I mean," which outside of referring to finding oneself in a vague Nowhere, Milian does not articulate any clearer.

Despite the trappings of this being an academic book, published after all by a university press, like *Latining America*, *Latinx* reads like pretend scholarship to justify a memoir on her feelings, a personal statement that performs all the pitfalls of oral Latino and Latinx, incurring into the kind of creative writing that is not her forte. In her introduction, for example, she attempts to define Latinx by comparing her Latinx marginalization to her being from New Jersey:

> Latino has hardly functioned as an equivalent for nationality in my uprooted world of the Garden State, which has stood for Manhattan's margins, an epicenter of the hemisphere's deracinated entities. For years, it has provided the City that Never Sleeps with surplus Latin labor, moving underground, in Manhattan's subways, in a space of unknowability, of transitions, of crossings: the ultimate X.[96]

---

[94] Milian, *Latinx*, 1.

[95] Milian, *Latining America: Black-Brown Passages and the Coloring of Latino/a Studies*, 11.

[96] Milian, *Latinx*, 2.

Outside of really vintage pop English that speaks of one's origin culture as "nationality," Latino had never been thought of as a "nationality" that functioned anywhere else. New Jersey may be in Manhattan's shadow on the intellectual level of New York jokes about Jersey drivers, but not in formal discussion. New Jersey writers include Junot Díaz, Joyce Carol Oates, Norman Mailer, and Allen Ginsberg, for whom being from New Jersey was just being from another American place.

William Carlos Williams was from New Jersey. Williams' metaphor of marginality was of the truer American country's existing in the shadows of New England's foundational myth about the Puritans, who Williams argued had "nothing to do" with America. Occasionally Williams felt personally marginalized by the New York intelligentsia but not because he was from New Jersey. Williams' *Paterson*, one of the great American epic poems, celebrates that city as an American microcosm.

In literary argument one exploits the language's already established metaphors or, in true literary performance, elevates images to metaphors. Milian may have personally felt in Manhattan's shadow, and her private feeling of being seen as less owing to her coming from the Garden State can produce empathy but extracting empathy does not produce critical argument. Moreover, New Jersey's being the butt of New Yorkers' jokes does not make it the metaphor she thinks it is in formal English. But her reliance on oral humor is consistent with her treatment of Latinx as an oral culture for personal chat that counts on Latino solidarity, free from the expectation of a critical response.

The publicist's copy that describes Milian's *Latinx* on the Amazon site makes the claim that "Latinx is the most powerful conceptual tool of the Latino/a present,"[97] suggesting that Latinx was like *latino* in having a past when, except for making a gender statement as a revamp of Latino, Latinx recycles Latino's presentism. The publicist's copy, then, returns us to the Latino Studies dilemma, sustaining solidarity with Latino without losing sight of *latino* as history.

One novel attempt at resolving that dilemma is the anthology *The Latino Nineteenth Century: Archival Encounters in American Literary History*, edited by Rodrigo Lazo and Jesse Alemán.[98] This otherwise valuable anthology provides critical essays on nineteenth-century texts certainly antecedents of today's Latino writing, what its editors describe as a "Spanish-language

---

[97] A citation that I couldn't find in a search of the text. Milian did write the less comprehensible, "Latinx is the most powerful conceptual point of our moment, a matrix offering a way to tinker with the unfathomable and the unfamiliar."

[98] Rodrigo Lazo and Jesse Alemán, *The Latino Nineteenth Century: Archival Encounters in American Literary History* (New York: New York University Press, 2019).

heritaged literary tradition in American letters," writings that they choose to call Latino.

One example of the latitude of this treatment is the essay by Kirsten Silva Gruez, "The Errant Latino: Irisarri, Central Americanness, and Migration's Intentions," on the Guatemalan Antonio José de Irisarri's *El Cristiano Errante* (*The Wandering Christian*, a play on *The Wandering Jew*, *cristiano* a synonym here for *hispano*). In this fictionalized autobiography of its author's travels through Latin America in search of a Guatemalan identity, Silva Gruez reads an errancy antecedent of today's Guatemalans who migrate north, as depicted in the film *El Norte* (1983).

De Irisarri traveled throughout Latin America and Europe. *El Cristiano Errante* was published in Colombia. But if Irisarri's novel has an identity theme (Irisarri is a nom de plume) that included finding himself as Guatemalan, strictly speaking, migrants to *El Norte* are not in search of their Guatemalan or Latin American identity– in most cases finding themselves unfortunately having to flee from a rawer sense of their identity.

Irrisari, who ironically did die in New York while on a diplomatic mission, does offer a metaphor of a quest. But his *El Cristiano Errante* does not convincingly read as early or antecedent Latino or even as antecedent of today's Central American errancy. Picasso rendered homage to the baroque Góngora as inspiration for Cubism but understood that Góngora was a baroque, not a Cubist artist. Silva Gruez was more credible with labeling antecedents in her own seminal *Ambassadors of Culture: The Transamerican Origins of Latino Writing* (2002).

Robert Mckee Irwin, another contributor to this anthology, questions its premise, making clear he can only offer nineteenth-century antecedents to Latino, not Latino in the nineteenth century. Irwin opens his essay "Almost-Latino Literature: Approaching Truncated Latinidades" with a caveat that Lazo and Alemán should have heeded:

> How to talk about "Latino" literature in a period that predates the general usage of the term as a category of cultural production and identity. If there's likely going to be a general consensus on whether a given literary text might be categorized as Latino in the early twenty-first century, applying this category in another historical context is in itself an exercise that calls for definition.[99]

---

[99] Lazo and Alemán, *The Latino Nineteenth Century: Archival Encounters in American Literary History*, 110.

After offering a catalog of "almost Latino," Irwin provides the Anglophone definition of Latino as a "U.S.-based" consciousness, in other words, an American identity.

Defending the anthology's premise, co-editor Rodrigo Lazo's Preface opens with a citation of Ramón de Contador y Muñiz's description of the newspaper he founded in San Francisco in 1878 as an organ to serve "la latine raza." Contador y Muñiz used the French phrase from where Spanish and English respectively got *América Latina* and Latin America. Having cited "la latine raza," Lazo tweaks it as evidence: "In the nineteenth century appeared throughout the Americas, not only to name America Latina but also to posit a people, 'la raza Latina,' with the latter claiming a European antecedent that went back to Rome."[100]

Indeed, the epithet *latino* was known that far back, but this link, which by itself would have made Contador's newspaper an antecedent of today's Latino writing, did not satisfy Lazlo's need to see the morphologically English "Latino" physically planted. That zeal appears to explain his translating "la latine raza" as "la raza Latina," a linguistic interference that would not have appeared in any century because in Spanish national and cultural modifiers are written in lower case. So while it is true that *latino* is not an anachronism in the nineteenth century, Lazlo's Latino is a hybrid, the Spanish word with the uppercase L making it English Latino. This merger of the ambiguous Latino/ *latino* homonym, to paraphrase Irwin, concatenates two modifiers that do not mean or evoke identically.

Lazo's litigation of a nineteenth-century "Latino" is just another illustration of the fact that Latino Studies can be linguistically, semantically, and literally all over the map, adding to the already Latino/*latino* ambiguity having to make geographic mental adjustments when referring to Latino Studies. Southwestern Latino Studies intuitively means Mexican American/Chicano Studies or Southwestern Studies and indigenous roots concomitant with the understanding that in nationally discussing a Latino consciousness, the southwest defers to the bilingual ambiguity of Latino/*latino*. Meanwhile, in parts of the country that more likely received immigration from noncontiguous Latin America, the national operative ambiguity is the norm, with Latino also phonetically alternating with *latino*, the ambiguity sometimes encompassing funding justification for Latin American Studies.

Surely Latino Studies finds itself in a tricky situation. More radical Anglophone Latino advocates a racialized American identity against Hispanic as an agency

---

[100] Lazo and Alemán, *The Latino Nineteenth Century: Archival Encounters in American Literary History*, 2.

of whiteness while Spanish *latino* remains a synonym of *hispano*, the sum of a Hispanic heritage and history, whose inherent transracialism threatens Anglo racial attitudes but which is by default white. A post-immigration generation competes with a native Latino history invoking the ignorance of history, the shibboleth of Hispanic as an immigrant culture. There is much to contemplate collectively to make sense of Latino America and, ultimately, as much to make sense of Latino Studies. For the present Latino Studies remains stuck between scholarship and solidarity, Latino and *latino*, and Latin American and Anglo-American cultural histories.

CONCLUSIONS

In a television ad for the Ancestry genetic testing company, a middle-aged, brown-complexioned southwestern-looking and -sounding woman tells us that all her life she has identified as Hispanic but that after she had her DNA tested, she discovered that she was a mixture whose highest percentage was Native American. This obviously Americas woman had to have her DNA tested to learn that she has Native American genes–only three percent more than Iberian, by the way.

Of course, her having more Native American genes than any other does not change one iota her culturally being Hispanic. Any Latin American or Latino is keenly aware of being an amalgam of racial and cultural heritages, of descending from some discrete subgroup version of Hispanic combined with some discrete version of non-European roots, African or Native American. In what used to be northern Mexico, that Ancestry spokeswoman's non-European inheritance would more preponderantly be Native American.

But this ad was written for an actor to perform the stereotype of the American myth of one's having shed the past, a nuance also of Latino/x especially in the southwest, a past now to be rediscovered through DNA. The woman spoke as if not having ever before in her life expressed any curiosity about her origins about which parents, aunts, uncles, or grandparents would have been the proper oracles. According to the traditional immigration formula, her past would be left back in the Old Country, so she had to rely on her genes, DNA testing. And so the ad's mythic Americanizing continues by tacitly racializing Hispanic, juxtaposing her vague Native American genes to her equally vague Iberian genes, which she identified as Hispanic but could also be Portuguese, Basque, or Catalan.

A culture is a system of ideas, values, and mores that can be adopted or imposed transracially, meaning also trans-genetically, what occurred in the Americas, in which Western cultures were imposed on Native and African peoples. So now that this woman has discovered her genetic composition, we are being shilled to believe that her world has changed. In reality, she will still go around identifying as Hispanic because she certainly couldn't believe that discovering that she had three percent more Native American genes meant anything to make her any different than who she was before she learned it, especially since Ancestry didn't provide what specific Native American nation.

She always identified as Hispanic because that was what she felt she was, that admixture of heritages that we call *hispano* or *latino*, which in Spanish also encompasses Native American and African heritages, not exclusively white as many Latinos mythologize about Hispanic. When I meet Mexicans or Guatemalans as kindred *latinos* or *hispanos*, I don't pause to think about how Native American they look. How would they otherwise be Mexican or Guatemalan? Yet a more purely indigenous Guatemalan can converse with a more purely white Guatemalan and know from cultural manners and linguistic markers that he or she can't be anything but Guatemalan.

The ad also reminds that semantically Latino and even Latinx lose out to Hispanic as the historical umbrella of collective memories over discrete subgroups that resulted from the Spanish Conquest. Hispanic is still the dominant umbrella for the same reason that it served this Ancestry ad, because ads exploit the viewpoint of the language: Hispanic is an identity that evokes a history, while Latino evokes a social circumstance. Hispanic is dominant because it has a history in the English usage, so when Latinos speak of refusing to identify with Hispanic, realistically it has no bearing on English, in which Hispanic is an important component of English' social and cultural history. For that reason, despite almost a decade of media adoption of Latino and recent sporadic, journalistic deference to Latinx, Latino and Latinx still have not replaced Hispanic, which continues to be preferred in more formal contexts, and is used to define Latino.

In 2018, when Latinx was the new latest thing, *The New York Times* published an opinion column titled "El Espace," a random Spanglish coining, in which Latinx was described as the epithet of choice among presumably Latinx contributors. That novelty and the column did not last long. Four years later, a July 20, 2022 *New York Times* piece reported on Argentina's banning the use of gender-neutral Spanish, which ironically Argentines call not *español* but *castellano*.

In reviewing that debate internationally, reporter Ana Lankes cited the example of gender-neutral Latinx in the U.S. But even among Hispanics, many have not heard of the term Latinx and few, mainly young college-educated women use it, according to a survey in 2019 by the Pew Research Center cited by Lankes. In other words, as of 2019, according to Lankes, the gender correction from Latino to Latinx in Spanish had not taken hold. As important for us to note, her reporting used "Hispanic" as the superset in "Hispanic people" under which come Latinos, with Latinx being an even smaller subset that would not sustain being synonymous with the breadth of "Hispanic people."

The Ancestry ad also underscores a real problem for Latino or Latinx as a racial correction of Hispanic based on the argument that Hispanic is a historically-imposed whitening. Any serious contemplation of an identity that includes an Americas gene pool begins with the impure, historically ignoble fact of Western conquest, a fact from which one is neither redeemed nor liberated by using ironically using Western erudition and language to reinvent oneself as if original to the time before that conquest. There is no such purity ever possible again no matter how creative the radical claim to it. We, like anybody of our time, descend from flawed forebears who were products of their time yet today we ride their conquering and racist descendants' cars and elevators. Wearing a feathered headdress can be a reminder. On the other hand, idealizing in English a Latino stripped of its Hispanic history on racial grounds bestows the forgiveness of the past on Anglo-American conquest not treated as imposed like Latino's Hispanic heritage.

Latino, as I already underscored, does not constitute a culturally communicative community so that my writing of the advocacy of canceling Hispanic as an influential trend in one region of Latino may sound to another region as a gross exaggeration. As I earlier differentiated, Eastern Latino is less passionate about that agenda than nationally hegemonic Mexican Americans coming to terms with their discrete history that goes back to Cortés. But their understandable indictment requires more nuanced and less idealistic rethinking because while talking of canceling Hispanic might pay for drinks, de facto that cancelling does not really happen anymore than legally changing one's name erases memories of a previous life. It becomes a perpetual reconciliation with a denial of reality. This conundrum notwithstanding, the southwest's providing the largest demographic interest in Latino Studies compels all Latino Studies to be sensitive to that enduring resentment.

Outside of academe, however, since breaking with monolithic Spanish to emerge as its own civilization, Latino's original role model Latin America has come to distinguish between the errors of Spain's imperial past and the breadth of the Hispanic culture that produced Latin America. Ironically, if in the seventies the Cuban writer Retamar advocated retiring the label *Hispanoamérica,* four decades earlier the Cuban poet Nicolás Guillén had come to terms with the Caribbean's compromised reality in "West Indies, Ltd." (1934):

gente sencilla y tierna, descendiente de esclavos
y de aquella chusma incivil
de variadísima calaña,
que en el nombre de España
cedió Colón a Indias con ademán gentil....

Aquí hay blancos y negros y chinos y mulatos.
Desde luego, se trata de colores baratos,
pues a través de tratos y contratos
se han corrido los tintes y no hay un tono estable.[101]

[A simple tender people, descendants of slaves
and of that uncivil riff-raff
of a every kind of ilk,
that in the name of Spain
Columbus, posing-genteel, bestowed on the Indies....

Here are whites, blacks, Chinese and mulattos.
Colors, of course, of little value
as contracting and interacting
has run colors to no fixed tone.]

The American Founding Fathers owned slaves. Freeing their descendants cost the greatest number of war deaths this country ever tallied. If some Spaniards enslaved Native Americans and their descendants enslaved Africans, others saw the sinful mistake and corrected it by invoking Spanish Catholic humanistic values. A form of liberalism but still racism. Indeed, contradiction of another time. On the other hand, in order to allow slavery, Texas was wrenched from Mexico, which had outlawed it. Some Cubans fought for independence from Spain to preserve slavery. If some Hispanics only married other Hispanics, sufficient others married Native Americans and Africans. Hispanic racial attitudes toward the Other had matured since the conquest, and however still racist according to our contemporary measure, constantly undermined enslavement based on human equality. Vasconcelos described the resulting Hispanic mélange as the procreation of a Cosmic Race, however romanticizing a portrayal.

That checkered, impure history that descends from Latin America is what Latinos/*latinos* carry into their equally checkered, impure Anglo-American experience, whose history also ironically owes its beginning to Hispanic roots. As William Carlos Williams noted, no matter how much Americans redact history to favor their ethnocentricity, the entire hemispheric America descends from the multicultural/multiracial "mingling spirit" that was originally sown in this hemisphere by Hispanic culture. But Latinos, educated in American historical amnesia, believe that their eyes were opened by progressive America that redeems them from their simplistically summarized Hispanic past.

---

[101] Nicolás Guillén, *Songoro Cosongo* (Madrid: Libresa, 1997), 117.

A final linguistic consideration is that the Latino American discussion bandies about Latino as if a term solely for usage as American diction, another consequence of an American education. Latino cannot semantically divorce itself from *latino*, which evokes the same in every Western language. We hear news of Middle Eastern and Africans trying to enter Europe through Spain and Italy but no such drama is reported in the insulated U.S. about international *latino* immigration, of which emigrating to the U.S. was one option. In the same eighties and nineties that Latin Americans emigrated to the U.S., other Latin Americans started new lives in Canada and Spain and Italy, and in the last two discovered that Mediterranean *latino* is what they had already been.

Not ironically, therefore, today Spain, Italy, and Latin America share *música latina* not just at the Latin Grammy awards but overflowing in the streets and shops in Spain and Italy. One can listen to a *latino*-only radio station in Madrid and come upon a block party dancing to *música latina*, and even hear of Spanish youth identifying with *latino*. Eating pizza in Napoli to Celia Cruz and riding a train toward Sorrento to a duo playing "Despacito" on accordions was just normal; drinking wine before a beach sunset in Salerno to a CD of *bachata* played by a bar for the public to enjoy spoke volumes.

Neapolitans know what *latino* means as distinct from the less *latino* and more *tedesco* northern Italy. Recall the taxi driver who observed, that after all *Tutti siamo latini* and he wouldn't live north of Rome, which is "not Italy." When Napoli-- forever grateful for the Argentine soccer genius Maradona, today virtually a god in Napoli—won Italian League championships in 1987 and 1990, some Northern Italians were said to have remarked that Africa had won the Italian championship. Of course, certain Castilians feel that way about *gitanos* just as New Englanders expressed hostility toward immigrant Italians.

Still, in Spanish, as noted earlier, *hispano* and *latino* are synonymous, just as in Europe Mediterranean and *latino* are synonymous, both evocative of a Catholic humanism that extends through Spain and Southern Italy. That humanism, working against the Conquest, ultimately produced the Latin American multicultural and multiracial countries that continued to self-acknowledge as products of the better angels of Spanish Catholic nature, producing *Hispanoamérica*, which later asserted itself as *Latinoamérica*.

Oligarchies work to preserve differences of class and race, reclaiming purist white origins of *latino* just as conservative America interprets the country as not the one bestowed by the Founding Fathers but the patrimony of Anglo-Protestant founding settlers. Such are the hemispheric American dynamics, and while one speaks any inherited European language, in a predominantly white society white will always be the default. So, to reject any epithet for being default white implies a desire for a purity that can only be achieved by adopting a non-Western language, with nonwhite defaults. Rejecting in default white

English the default white of Hispanic or *latino* is to perform a naïve intellectual joke.

For racialized or not, white, black, and brown *latino* is now also Western, of white origin then customized by multicultural and multiracial influences. There will be no Reversal of the Conquest but there has been a reconquest of history and the product is the impure, multiracial, multicultural Americas. The Mexican Catholic was never exactly a Roman Catholic when absorbing indigenous worship. Celia Cruz, Basquiat, and Pelé were all African-heritaged *latinos*, which only meant they were *latinos*. Without that complete, nuanced, complicated history as culturally *hispanos* who are *latinos*, Latino is just empty solidarity cant.

That history now includes Latino's most recent history, its origins in post-sixties revolutionary fervor from whose purer simplistic objectives of rebellion that generation of Latinos cannot seem able to get past and confront a more intellectually and existentially challenging impure reality. A product of the Digital Age, of postmodernism, of an American education, Latino is also now "woke" in eliminating "elitist" ideation, invoking a racial or tribal identity.

In "The True Left is Not Woke,"[102] Susan Neiman points out where sixties liberalism and subsequent generations of wokeness split off, the latter becoming (I add, consistent with Latino), more populist and anti-intellectual, clinging to the literal and the present. Neiman notes that liberalism had begun with a "commitment to universalism over tribalism, a firm distinction between justice and power and a belief in the possibility of progress."

Woke branched out of liberalism, but what began as a "concern for marginalized persons, …ends by reducing each to the prism of [self-]marginalization." And more sharply to the great dysfunction of Latino: "Woke demands that nations and peoples face up to their criminal histories. In the process it often concludes that all history is criminal." Including, of course, Latino's only, Hispanic history.

Finally, the idea of Latino as a youthful search for identity starts to get risible as the original Latino generation begins to collect Social Security. At some point, Latino must begin to make intellectual sense in the broadest context of humanities erudition, and the measure of the state of Latino should cease to be the next generation's idea of it but what that generation has inherited from antecedents, their brief Latino history. For that to happen, however, Latino must recover a historical and heritage consciousness, including an appreciation of *latino* in Western culture, not just as an American word to flaunt as political

---

[102] Susan Neiman, "The true Left is not woke," *UnHerd,* March 18, 2023, https://unherd.com/2023/03/the-true-left-is-not-woke/

correctness but as a consciousness that spans continents across a global spectrum.

We also don't need new nomenclature nor more tinkering with nomenclature. We have all the epithets we need. What we need now is intellectual maturity, meaning Latinos living in the same world as *latinos*, immigrant *latinos* and Latin America, as adults who must take their cultural complexity as intellectually serious as any other identity, expecting not the bullet-proofing of solidarity or a tacit adolescent protection against critique but the expectation of intellectual consequences to unfounded declarations and lax language usage.

Latinos/xs, if they need to purge themselves of Latin, should make that decision without inventing something that pretends to be a refinement of the Latin they leave behind. If one is done with Latin, that should end that conversation, not begin a movement to convert everybody else, not be the start of a career blaming Latin for not having accommodated one's personal grievances, performing that cultural criticism from the perspective of woke Anglo America.

Culture is a narrative in which one either sees oneself cast or one doesn't and its always a distorting narrative that one is compelled to change. But one must do so *within* the narrative, not with one foot in another narrative, a presumably superior Anglo-American narrative, an expression of colonialism. If Anglo-American superiority preached by Anglo Americans has not proved convincing to Latinos/ *latinos/hispanos*, it is unlikely that its delivery in the form of Latinx will be more convincing. Consequently, the Latino consciousness *not* done with Latin must assume the stature of a true cultural tributary destined to inform future American culture and, despite the compromises imposed by political reality, not accept the role of a ward culture.

Maturity also means understanding that the process of defining an identity is always impure and imperfect, leaving no tribe or society pure or innocent because victimized. The process of identifying and defining identity promises an answer that in fact is talked to death, always intuited as possible but never perfectly visualized until maturity reveals that identity signifies *being informed by the urgency to define the identity*. In the end, there is no badge or perfect answer, the reward being a fuller if incomplete sense, feeling within oneself a historical dimension to wearing an identity-proud T-shirt, to dancing to *música latina* and to picketing at the border.

It is probable that Latino will never create an actual community, that as consciousness it will replicate Latin America's model and preserve subgroup discreteness. But one hopes it will move toward a more functional confederation that is not only political, exchanging as well intellectual, literary, artistic and musical expression in the way that Latin American nations do without being a single nation. That would still leave Latino as a public mask of unity over a labyrinth of multitude, not a bonding that would create such a community, which to make reality would come at the cost of losing discrete subcultures, the African-American model.

For the present that harsher choice is not on the horizon as Latino remains a "knot of contradictions" bonding by sociopolitical issues, an American identity ostensibly stripped of *latino* yet not feeling compelled to adopt American culture beyond popular symbols while still subtly weaning from *latino*. Latino will continue to seek understanding as a unique consciousness although it is difficult to see how that happens without its continuing to tacitly claim *latino* and work to better articulate Latino's relationship to *latino*. But, owing to Latino's being a "knot of contradictions," the undertow of *latino* with its Spanish language requirement and intellectual baggage continues being Latino's political agenda to keep at bay, Hispanic heritage and history to be invoked only tacitly, on an as-needed basis and in denial, the equivalent of convincing oneself of keeping house while playing dolls.

As I write MSBNC is running a trailer promoting a new documentary series on Latinos hosted by the actor John Leguizamo. His excited voice promises that his series will cover "every kind of Latino you could name." Or was that "Every kind of *latino* you could name"? For the phrase made me think, "Latino" popularly evokes only one kind while "*latino*" connotes the multitude of subcultures. Consistent with that multitudinous *latino* consciousness, this trailer runs to the music of what Milian called the Hispanophone Caribbean and images are flashed of major Latino/*latino* sites, Chicago, Miami, Los Angeles, D.C., New York, San Juan.

Leguizamo then proceeds to explain that his ambition was to produce a series that would inspire those who watch the series to say "I wanna be Latino," which one hears pronounced to actually say "I wanna be *latino*." The trailer promises cultural diversity and yet a public official is cited saying, "We are one Latin family." Formally, the series is titled *Doing America*. Obviously, not MAGA's traditional America but the multicultural alternate America that Latino and Latinx await to make sense. But even in an alternate America, we must return to Octavio Paz's observation about the *pachuco,* applicable to all Latinos/*latinos*: our American condition will always be a "knot of contradictions."

Undoing that knot could come at an existential loss. Managing it requires closer attention to its complexity, and so I have tried to articulate the state of things and the semantic and conceptual obstacles that, for the present, hamper our appreciating our true complexity. Hopefully, out of our labyrinth of multitude will emerge a collectively-defined, more functional Latino American consciousness that could serve not alone as political unifier but as well as a substantive cultural and intellectual foundation in either an alternate or traditional America.

2.

HARVARD PATROLS THE BORDER

> The university must accommodate itself promptly to significant changes in
> the character of the people for whom it exists.
>
> –Charles William Eliot, at his inauguration as president of
> Harvard on October 19, 1869

1

The most radical American revolutionaries called themselves "Columbians," reinventing their origin away from England and inspired and reborn in Spain's visionary marriage of Columbus and Queen Isabela, the figurative mother of "Columbia."[1] That Isabela was herself a monarch was overlooked; her being a woman made her a victim of oppression under Ferdinand. Moreover, in 1776 Spain's King Carlos III provided the military aid that, according to historians, made possible the American republic. This alliance also explains a Hispanophilia that runs through early American literature and extends into the next, Romantic century, revived by the Transcendentalists' opposition to the American grab of Northern Mexico.

In the spring of 1917, I found myself taking part in that little-taught tradition of Anglo and Hispanic convergence in American culture, having accepted an invitation to teach a semester at Harvard, taking a leave of absence from an English department to join the same Department of Romance Languages where Washington Irving, James Russell Lowell, and Henry Wadsworth Longfellow were once professors of Spanish. I was invited as the author of *The Spanish American Roots of William Carlos Williams*, which extrapolates a literary influence from Williams' Hispanic roots through his Caribbean-raised English-born father and his mother from Spanish-colony Puerto Rico.

Not an unearthing after deep excavation, I simply read Williams without the canonical ethnocentrism that had selected from Williams' true complexity to showcase only the textbook Bill persona, which in fact, competed with a Carlos persona, who argued that the source of his truer American spirit was the hemisphere's Hispanic heritage. Not despite that heritage but thanks to it,

---

[1] This metaphor of Isabela comes up again in nineteenth-century feminist writing, also countering the anti-Hispanic imperialism represented by the war with Mexico.

Williams believed that he was the more genuine American poet. I especially got a kick out of bringing Carlos to Harvard as Williams would have liked, by way of Romance Languages, the home of the Spanish poets Quevedo and Góngora, the Baroque patriarchs of Williams' "line"– an ambiguity he always highlighted with quotation marks.

I began writing *The Spanish American Roots* in the early eighties, between writing poetry and completing doctoral work. The book was published in 1994, and by the time I went to Cambridge the epithet "Hispanic," which I also reference in my book by way of "Spanish," had given way in popular usage to "Latino," which had gained an academic foothold as "Latino Studies." This epithet-refining was part of a post-Civil Rights generational preference for a less ethnic European Hispanic identity and a more Americas identity congruent with the millennial prospect of a multicultural America.

At Harvard one expression of multiculturalism's influence was the course "Bilingual Aesthetics," taught by Professor Doris Sommer, who extended the invitation that I teach at Harvard, requesting that, in addition to my also teaching an undergraduate course (I chose Latin American Colonial Literature) and giving a lecture on Williams, I design a graduate course on Latino Writing. Privately I understood that final request as addressing my purview as writer because my book on Williams wasn't written from a perspective that one would call Latino, whose literary consciousness did not acknowledge Williams, and which by then as an area of study I had come to contemplate more critically, realizing that my book and what "Latino" meant in English worked at cross purposes.

Williams appreciated history as literature and literature as a special kind of history; in both he saw himself descended from his Spanish-language "'line.'" Williams understood literature as building from a consciousness of a past, a constant procreation from antecedents, a documented history of voices. Latino focused on the present by default, with Latino constituencies discounting Hispanic history as well as traditionally understood literature. Where it is taught, Latino Writing is likely to be given a practical, socially-conscious reading, as lively sociology that affirms, allegorizes and illustrates but rarely questions its own consciousness and, of course, too busy with important sociopolitical stuff to consider aesthetic authority. In colleges, therefore, the one constant– whether formal or tacit– is that "Latino" writing belongs to a "learning community," applying it to some area of the social sciences. A personal survey that I took of Latino Studies programs on the internet reveals that few have a literature component save, of course, as *latino* or Latin American or as assignments embedded in social science classes.

This convention chiefly draws students who expect Latino Writing to affirm politically correct insights they already have, with no expectation of having to read unknown historical settings or to decipher literary tropes. Such previous experiences with Latino students in literature courses discouraged me from teaching an entire course on Latino writings, but now we were talking Harvard; if at any place one could discuss this writing as literary, Harvard had to be that place. I was disappointed.

Harvard enjoys conflicting reputations. To liberals it symbolizes New England's WASP tradition –Williams hated having to read there– while conservatives paint it politically pink all over even though its largest undergraduate department, Economics, places it to the right. I was invited to teach Williams as part of a Latino Studies package although I knew that Harvard has long resisted acknowledging "Latino Studies." I deduced, therefore, that I would be visiting one of several Harvards, one where I might find a transient haven, not traditional Harvard. But that safe possibility wasn't enough to trump my gut feeling before I got there that in every corner of the campus Latino and Harvard in the same breadth were foils for reasons so transparent that didn't require my giving the matter much thought. When I got to Cambridge, however, that juxtaposition imposed considerable, disturbing thought.

One would expect that Harvard would be educating its Latino students to address in intellectual depth the question that the very existence of Harvard and New England should raise: how do Hispanics/Latinos address the range of complexities, challenges, and responsibilities that come with their also being Americans? But at Harvard I discovered that encouraging those students to arrive at intellectual maturity as Hispanics or Latinos does not appear to be a priority as much as molding that consciousness to conform with Harvard's own venerable, prepared answer.

Hispanic/Latino Americans are, of course, hardly a blip on the huge screen of Harvard's vast enterprise and national role. In fact, an important component of its cultural agenda would appear to be perfecting the indifference it gives to Hispanic Americans as academic subject–or rather perfecting the indifference it only appears to cultivate. For in the twenty-first century, in an era of multicultural debate and demographic change, when Hispanics/Latinos comprise the largest minority demographic, to a university that is a national think tank, that spiking demographic is a highly-charged minor matter–as Harvard's distinguished professor Samuel P. Huntington let the country know in his *Who Are We: Challenges to America's National Identity* (2005).

At Harvard "Latino" did not appear in a course title but in the name of a student club. Addressing Latino unheralded as motive, The David Rockefeller Center for Latin American Studies occasionally invited writers and artists, sometimes—although not in my case– in collaboration with Romance Languages. But one also discerned a tailored marginality, intended to camouflage that Hispanic/Latino American, as both population and consciousness, does pose a threat. Not just to the national identity as Huntington warned but to Harvard as university because ultimately, in the same way that Huntington felt the need to confess in his introduction to having struggled between patriotism and objectivity, Hispanics are a test of Harvard's commitment to *Veritas* over traditionalist cultural politics before those who embody a competing account of America's hemispheric history.

2

The inner city or urban bicultural minority youth that Latino first evokes wasn't highly visible on campus and didn't gravitate to Harvard's Department of Romance Languages, a homing phenomenon common at other colleges. More cosmopolitan, Harvard's Romance Languages majors were predominantly *latinos* from other countries and from higher social classes, with a surprising number of legacy students from Puerto Rico's upper crust. Exactly where Latino resided on campus was mystifying. My visit was not formally announced to any Latino group that might have cared. Nor did Latinos noticeably show up to departmental activities to become so informed. A flier announced an event sponsored by "Fuerza Latina": a night of Flamenco dancers.

The week before the start of classes I was already surfboarding the semantic undulations of Latino. A graduate Latino Writing course must have sounded like an advanced idea but in practice afforded vague profit to students preparing to become professional scholars of Spanish-language texts. Opening the course to undergraduates gave it more hope because those students chose electives less conscious of professional relevance. Then the week before the first class I was asked to lecture–on a syllabus of English-language texts– in Spanish, this last-minute request, I was told, in response to an objection raised by the English Department that Romance Languages already offered too many literature courses in English.

Ironically it was at an English Department-sponsored poetry reading that another nuance of Latino came to mind. Thirty years earlier, the then young poet James Tate taught one of the poetry-writing workshops that I took as an M.F.A. student at Columbia University's Graduate Writing Program. That was over a decade before Latino emerged to inform me that I had attended Columbia to write for cultural studies, correcting my delusion that I really wanted to write as masterfully as my favorite writers. I greeted Tate, into his seventies as I was then sixty-one, and remembered my youth in his workshop, when I didn't think that my being Puerto Rican or Hispanic would determine what or in what style I should choose to write, as Latino would tacitly do.

The reading took place in a large salon full to capacity, and in the audience was a contingent of Romance Languages graduate students from both Spain and Latin America well-read in contemporary American poetry. I looked around to identify any student who might be Latino (although markers are elusive) but didn't stumble on any face that I might have risked counting as one. Then it occurred to me that this was not a Latino venue because it was foremost a literary event and Latino in relation to writing implied not ideas or masterful writing but performance, cultural documentation, and political commitment. James Tate as poet would not have been a draw.

This was one example of the mainly semantic divergence, if sometimes convergence, of Latino and *latino*, of which Harvard offered examples, such as a group identifying as Latino and offering a Flamenco show. A doctoral candidate from Spain was writing a dissertation comparing several *latina* (Latin American) writers, including Latina writers in English, while what Latino/Hispanic majors in Spanish existed did not come forth to show any interest in Latino Writing. In a Latin American literature class that I visited, a few Latino students sat among newer immigrant *latinos*, kindred but one sensed not on the same cultural page, an impression confirmed by an overheard casual observation made by a *latina* about her Latina classmate's thinking herself different, presumably better, and ultimately apart. A fledgling Ph.D. from Puerto Rico shared her relief with me that she had secured a tenure-track job for the fall semester. Congratulations were in order, but one couldn't help wondering how she was going to fare on an east coast campus where she would be teaching a sizeable population of mainland Puerto Ricans, a demographic that would inevitably conscript her into Latino when she also haughtily made a point of making it plain to me that she did not identify with mainland Puerto Ricans.

Finally, also illustrative of amorphous Latino at Harvard was the status of Cuban Americans. Latino consciousness was born of seventies liberal and left-wing post-modernism, in other words a child of today's Humanities that investigates social injustice as cultural artifact, so Latino Studies advances social change implicitly from the left. Consequently, although generically *latino*, Cuban Americans do not participate as Latinos nationally and didn't at Harvard. Cuban-Americans come together in separate organizations and engage in discrete activities implicitly in a broader Latin American context although, judging from their website, to the political right of other Latinos and most other *latinos*. The yearly Latino student talent show–to which I shall return– did not include any moments of Cuban music and dance.

Given the existence of The David Rockefeller Center for Latin American Studies and a Department of Romance Languages that showcases Latin America, with Latino as an occasional side specialty in both, *latino* is an intuitive academic imperative but not so Latino to the extent that it behooves Harvard's having to address Latino Studies as a discrete academic area of study.

Whether or not that approach to Latino sits well with students, given that other colleges do offer programs focused on Latino, is an argument for another time because from all indicators at present that policy does seem to coincide with their Latino student population's perception of Latino, which arguably could also reflect a lesson that Harvard itself instills: as subject of academic study the Harvard Latino student expresses ambivalence about Latino, which is mainly perceived as a motive for advocacy and social bonding.

3

Harvard's Latino students offered two illustrations of their advocacy in *The Journal for Hispanic Policy*, on political and socioeconomic issues and statistics, and *The Latino Law Review*. A student-organized yearly conference consists of guest speakers from among the students themselves, whose topics are also social and political. This practice is consistent with Latino Studies convention throughout academe: if to understand Latin America one is compelled to read García Márquez and Jorge Luis Borges and Carlos Fuentes, Latino doesn't compel one to read any Latino writings, which except for Romanic-consciousness gender injustices otherwise document without reflecting critically on Latino. Reading is not required or expected because generally among university students, including at Harvard, Latino is understood as an oral culture, and when not invoked as a fount of social righteousness, the default vehicles of cultural expression are music and dance.

The annual talent show, put on by Fuerza Latina,[2] was a spring event that coincides with recruitment, evidently scheduled and funded for this purpose of welcoming potential new students and therefore was titled to propagandize for Harvard's admissions office against any doubts that Latinos exist at Cambridge: "Presencia Latina." In the theater lobby, before curtain, I mingled amid a linguistic range, from Spanish-dominant, to bilingual, to English dominant. I, of course, was anonymous, as no formal effort was made to connect me to those students.

The event opened with a voice-over reading of lines from Pedro Pietri's late sixties poem (published in 1971) "Puerto Rican Obituary," which urged Puerto Ricans to resist assimilation. Puerto Ricans, including those from the island, also enter the world as American citizens and therefore the post-WWII diaspora made them *cultural* immigrants not actual immigrants, not like the majority of students present in the audience, either the children of or themselves from

---

[2] The name of this group, Fuerza Latina, a rallying cry, does not evoke the self-assured agenda or commitment of an "organization" or "association."

recent Latin American immigrations. But the script assumed the same identity problem for all.

Each performance consisted of a song and dance representative of the students' varied Latin American background followed by a mimed interlude narrated by an amplified voice. Every interlude dramatized a moment of cultural self-doubt and concluded with the narrator's sharing the wisdom that identity doubts are resolved by "turning off thought" and "listening to one's music." Theatrical segue and musical truth but unfortunately not artistic hyperbole, reaffirming that Latino culturally expresses itself foremost in music and dance, not words, ironically undermining Pietri's recited lines.

Sadly, there was no danger that students would reflect at all on that contradiction nor read much about their Latino situation if one gauged by the gift handed out for purchasing a ticket to the show, a book titled *La Vida: A Guide to Latino Life at Harvard and Beyond*, a paperback compendium of local "Latino Life" that documented the impression that at Cambridge "Latino" was indeed a floating world. Contents: Some student scuttlebutt on their campus social life, tips on where Hispanic foods could be found nearby, a reprint of an old *Harvard Crimson* interview of Professor Doris Sommer (who had no knowledge of its being reprinted), a section on "Latino Arts" that showcased three dance clubs, but no other art form. No mention of the Mexican American and Colombian artists who had been invited by the Rockefeller Center that semester and, disappointingly, no student creative or expository writings. No mention of my lecturing on Williams. I was reminded that I had not seen a Latino newspaper or newsletter or literary journal; letters and thought appeared to have no specifically "Latino" venues.

La Vida had a lighter purpose, of course, but one couldn't avoid being troubled that at Harvard, the university that produces leaders in many disciplines, these students merely echo their Latino generation in less prestigious colleges in still not seeing the need for an intelligentsia and a critical literary consciousness. Even more troubling, Harvard doesn't seem to have a problem with that product. Of course, those students and their cultural needs are not Harvard's special responsibility although Harvard's catering to their low expectations of themselves does bespeak of a cultural agenda: preserving mainstream or white tradition.

For one item in Harvard's liberal/conservative inner conflict is its reconciling tradition, presumably committed to *Veritas* as classic Western truth against a multiculturalism that threatens to alter the national identity. Ostensibly adhering to the principle articulated by Charles Eliot Norton, Harvard has embraced change, as exemplified in its distinguished Department of African American and Africana Studies and newer programs in Women's and Queer Studies. But other evidence indicates a qualified response. For example, while

American cultural complexity is surely taught in diverse humanities departments, at the time of this writing the great symbol of American academe does not have a Department of American Studies, today usually a hotbed of multiculturalism, and one possible home for Latino Studies.

Actually, because throughout academe Latino is mainly curated by the social sciences and fluctuates between Anglo and Hispanic cultural studies, lacking a discourse of its own, it belongs to the rhetoric that claims it. Consequently, one can deduce that at Harvard, where Humanities disciplines are rooted in a pedigree and Hispanic/Latino Americans do not fit in the traditional American Story or the traditional story of immigration, outside of multicultural American Studies, Latino Studies would not easily find an unproblematic place. The Department of Romance Languages itself seemed far from unanimous about my visit. Latino students come to Harvard to learn that, if they want to be taken seriously, their sophistication arrives with learning that their particular identity is too simplistic and banal to invest important hours of their education.

4

Nobody thought of that cultural barrier back when my generation mobilized to open more doors of the best colleges to minority students. And, indeed, Harvard must be credited with providing its superlative education to a greater number of Latino/*latino* students than were admitted before the late sixties. That education affords the opportunity to acquire far more insight into the Latino American experience that should enrich an area called Latino Studies. But this area is not acknowledged at Harvard and what discussion on Latino takes place is not at the level of Harvard.

If African American Studies is represented by nationally prominent scholars and thinkers at Harvard, for the most part, Hispanic/Latino students are on their own, and at the yearly conference, they speak to themselves. Latino does not evoke intellectual authority and Harvard has no interest in seeing that it matures. My visiting professorship felt fine-tuned to acknowledge the revealed multicultural importance of Williams, with me as the one credited with the discovery but not as having authored it as part of a broader literary discourse of which I am also an authority.

On the other hand, why should Harvard layer such problematic gravitas on students whose only interest in their cultural backgrounds is folkloric, in its music and dance? In other words, it is logical that Harvard doesn't take Latino seriously because their Latino students don't as a consequence of their American education. Despite the Harvard education that they were getting, the Latino students that I met did not seem tooled to contemplate more rigorously their own Hispanic history as Americans nor saw any important relevance to them whatever that I had written on Williams as literary antecedent to their own American experience.

In Robert DeNiro's 2007 film *The Good Shepherd*, the Harvard alumnus and now CIA Branch Head (Matt Dillon), is a church-going, bespeckled father of a quintessential American family. During his work hours, he tortures potential threats to America, and so protects his country at any cost. In one scene, an Italo-American mafia connection (Joe Pesci) who performed a secret task for the CIA has just picked up cash but pauses to resolve something that he couldn't figure out. He observes that other American groups each have a unique personality. "Even the niggers have their music, but you guys, what do you have?" The answer comes from an agent whose career gestated in a pedigreed Harvard fraternity: "We have the United States of America. All of you are just visiting." Like that agent, Harvard too patrols a clearly defined cultural border, an agenda consistent with its being the academic home of Samuel P. Huntington.

The late chairman of the Academy for International and Area Studies, Huntington embodied traditional WASP ethnocentrism. If Harvard is a bastion of tradition, Huntington was its grenadier attacking Hispanics, whom he perceived as cultural assailants who undermine the traditional national identity. In the March 2004 issue of *Foreign Policy*,[3] he published as advance publicity the provocative "The Hispanic Challenge,"[4] a chapter of his then-forthcoming *Who Are We? Cultural Challenges to America's National Identity*, a diatribe disguised in the tweed with elbow pads of scholarship. In this book, Huntington traced the national culture not to the Founding Fathers but to the founding "settlers," arguing that the country is a patrimony that Anglo Protestants have been willing to share with others but that Hispanics want to culturally change, making them "The Hispanic Challenge."

Huntington was not Harvard's spokesperson but articulated and defended the traditions preserved in Harvard's evident choices and structures. Harvard's welcoming of Latino students parallels Harvard's speaking of America as welcoming of immigrants: Latino students are accepted to Harvard to partake in its cultural vision in the same way that immigrants have traditionally been welcomed to adopt the culture. But just as Huntington detailed cultural conditions for that acceptance, Harvard's generosity also comes with conditions taught in subtle lessons that Latino students give every impression of taking.

---

[3] Huntington, "The Hispanic Challenge."

[4] Huntington's use of "Hispanic" might appear to be merely old-guard, but the challenge to the nation's identity is best conveyed by "Hispanic" and not "Latino," which does not immediately evoke a historic rivalry with Anglo-Saxon culture, presenting no real challenge to the traditional identity.

For, as the narrator at the talent show proposed, "Latino" is to be understood as shutting down thought and not making any intellectual investment.

This posture may sound like rebellion against bourgeois intellectualism but it is really a circumvention of the difficulty of reconciling an uncertain identity– not completely Hispanic and not exclusively Anglo American [5] – and the consequences of that hybrid condition to upward mobility, Harvard's promised reward. That American Dream, implicitly inevitable after an education of Harvard's caliber, grounds Latino/*latino* students in pragmatism. Consequently, Harvard is a crucible where idealized "Latino" semantically melts down, a place where, despite activities and talk of its actually being a topic of intellectual discussion, it is only an extracurricular pastime. In fact, if there was a unifying factor among Harvard's diverse Latino/*latino* students, it was their intuition about not taking too seriously this lightweight Latino thing, that uncertainty affecting the outcome of the Latino Writing course I was asked to create.

Twelve students attended the first "shopping" session, five of them Latinos. As part of the introductory discussion, to give context to writings produced in murky cultural weather, I brought up Huntington. All said they had read "The Hispanic Challenge." I suggested that they also read Huntington's book, not foreseeing that my suggestion would strip me of credibility. The five Latino students [6] responded with dismissive smiles and shaking of heads in disappointment. Knowing that Huntington was anti-Hispanic was all they needed to know, which made me wonder why, knowing that summary wisdom, they would have actually bothered to read the essay– or were they just familiar with it from the public outrage and therefore believed they essentially knew what he said.

"The Hispanic Challenge" was edited, I explained, to make Huntington and Anglo-Protestant culture sound surer of itself than it comes off in his book, which was written in a tone of a besieged New Englander. His book identifies a Hispanic threat to Anglo-Protestant culture, "challenges" producing an in-progress Anglo-Protestant decline that he wanted to stop. That sense of loss overtakes his reasoned argument, which even he admits at the outset at times sacrificed scholarship for patriotism, essentially admitting to writing a jeremiad. They should read the book, I argued, because Huntington's poor argument epitomizes the desperate state of the traditionalist discourse. His

---

[5] This is the "knot of contradiction" that Octavio Paz observed of the *pachuco* as Mexican American.

[6] The non-Hispanic students seemed to be unaware of the controversy or had no interest in the course subject or themes, like the student who explained that he had only considered the course "to practice Spanish."

writing itself was the best evidence of Anglo-Protestant decline, no longer paradigms of higher standards, including critical thinking. But I had summarized my thesis to blank faces not interested in the subject.

At first I believed that they saw me as off-the-wall because I bothered to pay such close attention to Huntington. But on reflection I realized that, while they might have believed that they were laughing off Huntington's bigotry and my suggesting that they read his book, they were laughing at my taking this Latino subject way too seriously: I had made the mistake of not first reaffirming their dislike of Huntington in mindless, Latino solidarity, using racial diction perhaps. It was the first signal that I couldn't presume to make a real literature class of "Latino Writing." None of those five Latino students chose to stay in the course, which dwindled to a seminar of two graduate students, from Spain and Mexico.

I would have hoped that more than Harvard hubris had rubbed off on those Latino students who departed, but unfortunately neither Harvard nor the conventions of Latino impart that being an educated Latino also comes with intellectual, not just political responsibilities. One major irony is that Huntington contemplated Hispanic Americans in more depth than Harvard offers its students for study. Huntington asked the questions that those students should be taught to ask of their American identity but aren't—except maybe by an occasional visiting professor, whose pretentious ideas students have already been persuaded to hear as a false prophecy. Instead, Harvard provided a prestigious, permanent academic forum for Huntington's sophistic answers.

Another major irony about Huntington is that in portraying Hispanics as resistant to adopting American culture he uses a Latino Studies convention. Despite the outrage over Huntington's bigotry, Latino Studies has inadvertently long collaborated by not cultivating letters and critical thought, promoting Latino Writing as a populist experience or earnest representation of social science insight, reserving sophisticated contemplation, including of Latino, to writers and intellectuals from Latin America.

Huntington, to cite an intellectual, in the chapter "The Hispanic Challenge" quoted the Mexican novelist Carlos Fuentes on the cultural "difference" between Hispanic and Anglo cultures. Then, to demonstrate how other Hispanic Americans themselves have written on their "difference," he cites the self-promoting autobiography of a successful Mexican-American businessman, who uses "difference" as code referring to Hispanics as less ambitious. Huntington finally recruits "author Robert Kaplan," who interviewed a young, "third-generation Mexican American in Tucson" named Alex Villa, who bragged that he didn't "buy into America" and who said that he knew "almost no one in the

Mexican community of South Tucson who believes in 'education and hard work.'"[7]

Huntington's scholarship, in effect, employs the equivalent of Jay Leno's Streetwalking skit to portray the values of an entire community, documenting with a conservative businessman who condescends to his Mexican origins and, as representative of dysfunctional "Hispanics," a street *vato* who boasts of not having bought into America.

Huntington's personal peeve is with Mexican Americans but his target is "Hispanic," which he understood as a civilization and a history but knew that his readers saw it as racialized and synonymous with Latino, evocative foremost of social condition. And who would speak best on that subject than a successful businessman who overcame the dysfunction he critiqued in his kind and Alex, a man of the people. In sum, in the question of letters and thought, both Huntington and Latino Studies associate Hispanic/Latino with coming-of-age narrative and social science documentation, while, for intellectual substance, drawing from Latin America.

5

At the Hollis Library counter, a pair of male and a female work-study students conversed as they checked out the books I was returning. In a southwestern lilt, the brown, Chicano-sounding male asked the female if she had looked into joining Fuerza Latina and whether she had spoken with the club's woman president. To him she sounded "pretty hardcore." I resisted asking exactly what he meant but interpreted from his demeanor and native English that the club president was more culturally separatist, more *latino* and Spanish-dominant, and probably more politically left than he considered himself. He apparently felt Latino but not that *latino*, culturally or politically.

I couldn't help asking myself yet again what Latino means if not Hispanic in some visceral, "hardcore" way? Can Latinos/*latinos* enjoy the historical rite of European immigrants of reinventing themselves as distant from an Old Country if the Old Country is hemispheric America, psychological border being English, which as this English-speaking student demonstrates, does a poor job as he still continues to search for Latino at Harvard.

Of course, whiter Latino students have the freedom to assimilate and not have to stigmatize themselves while brown and black students must identify as separately ethnic American, as that apparently monolingual Chicano student seemed to have already decided. On the other hand, that student's

---

[7] Huntington, *Foreign Policy*.

disappointment with the "hard core" also illustrated a reaction to taking Latino too seriously, an understanding of Latino as a motive for socializing with others of the same background but nothing to get "hardcore" about. In other words, he was reacting as traditional American culture expects of a second or third generation Latino American looking to simplify his ethnic past.

That Chicano student also reminded me of Richard Rodriguez, Huntington's perfect model for Mexican-American citizenry but whom, in his book, he doesn't mention– perhaps because Rodriguez would have contradicted Huntington's determinist portrait of Mexicans as not assimilable. Rodriguez had made a career of publicly purging his life of Spanish and its speakers. In his debut memoir, *Hunger of Memory,* he called that assimilation his "education," which began with Catholic school nuns that taught him not to learn Spanish nor continue his parents' culture. It is the fundamental paradox of an American education: learning that celebrates a customized, patriotic ignorance.

How many Latino students, I wondered, came to Harvard to refine an American identity founded on not-knowing, not getting "hardcore," and Harvard's protecting that American identity from too much thought. Senator Ted Cruz attended Princeton and then Harvard Law, throughout determined not to recover his father's Spanish. Until that moment when I heard that Chicano student, I had presumed that Harvard acted by omission. But it acted by commission by teaching structurally; giving no academic standing to Latino Studies, actively fostering a customized ignorance and inculcating in Latino students the understanding that their background is not significant enough to include in their educated examination of their lives as Americans. In the course of Harvard Latinos' good education, they are never taught to contemplate more rigorously than popular discourse on being a Latino American, a subject that Huntington thought important enough to publish an essay about in a major policy journal and to devote a core concern in a nationally-discussed book.

Consider the distinction and platform Harvard bestowed on Huntington, who criticized Hispanics as poor candidates for a true American identity because of their "Spanish retention." According to Huntington, to become real Americans Hispanics should unlearn or refuse to become fluent in a language taught in the Department of Romance Languages, implicitly making unimportant what is taught in that language, its history and every form of its expression. This was the wisdom followed by Ted Cruz. Of course, what is ultimately feared is the retention of an American hemispheric memory that contradicts the Anglo Protestant one, the rise of an intellectual challenge to the American Story, to American racial attitudes. But from every indication, whether or not they retain their Spanish, Harvard's Latino students as yet did not pose that threat.

Consequently, even though they partook in ceremonies of righteous anger over Huntington's bigotry and marched in favor of immigration reform, their satisfaction with the quality of their *presencia* also confirms their taking well the university's lesson that they are a softcore subject, not worth rigorous effort, at best an extracurricular activity. One would hope that their Americanization was less conciliatory, more self-aware of what they can bring to enhance American culture, not only music and dance and food but as well an intellectual presence. Patently, Latino as stalwartly populist provided the intellectual vacuum in which Huntington felt empowered.

Meanwhile Harvard reconciles with this successful stasis: it rewarded Huntington for his hardcore ethnocentrism and compensates Latinos for their inconsequential *presencia* with funds for softcore cultural activities, such as the guide *La Vida*, the talent show, and transient visiting professorships that, in retrospect I should not have been surprised, suggested softcore expectations. Logically, a non-Hispanic woman undergraduate came to my office to express her interest in staying in the Latino Writing course but lamented that she couldn't devote the time to write what was actually a standard course term paper. Similarly, the "shopping" Hispanic students looking for relief from real coursework deemed neither valuable nor intriguing that they could read William Carlos Williams and George Santayana as literary legacy.

A month later I recognized one "shopping" woman student's face among the campus-wide chorus chanting as part of an immigration-reform rally. In her chant I heard my generation also rallying. Amid our seventies emergence of Latin American roots–an explosion of world-class writers and intellectuals–we had envisioned a future, comparable Hispanic American emergence and advocated equal opportunity so that Hispanic students could attend superior universities like Harvard. But that was a different American time, and my generation was naive in interpreting what Harvard understood by *Veritas*. Now the number of Hispanic students fills a Harvard theater, and they too march for righteous causes but fail to see the politics of being taught and effectively learning to accept themselves as lacking complex humanistic dimensions, as stick figures of political boilerplate and social science statistics.

Postscript #1: After the talent show, on a rainy night I opened an umbrella to walk off-campus and a man who had just come from the theater asked me for directions to the street where he had parked his car. We had both parked on the same street, and on the way we chatted. He was a Mexican immigrant who now made his home in San Diego and had accompanied his daughter to Cambridge. She had been invited to the talent show that weekend to get to know Harvard, one of three other Ivies that had accepted her. He enjoyed the talent show, and after asking me what I did at Harvard, he was curious about my visitor's impressions. I could only confirm that Harvard indeed offered incomparable opportunities for his daughter to grow and do great things.

Postscript #2 (seven months later): I was a new member of the Parents Advisory Council of an organization that seeks gifted minority students to place in private high schools. At a Christmas party for its scholars, I was introduced to a young Mexican American known to be considering a major in science or math. Harvard, among other universities, had just accepted him, but he was still undecided. He asked for my impressions of Harvard. Understanding that his major would be in science or math, I apologized that I could tell him little that would help him to decide because I was mainly invited owing to my writing a book on Williams. He remembered being told that I write and asked to know what else I had published. I told him that except for that academic book, I mainly wrote poetry and fiction, why I was also asked to teach a course on Latino Writing.

I thought that the conversation had run its course, but he grabbed a napkin and asked to write the titles of my books. Jotting them down, he added, "I might study math, but I'm also interested in other things, maybe writing." I feared that my having mentioned the Latino Writing course and my lecture on Williams led him to believe that much more of that was waiting for him at Cambridge. I advised that Harvard indeed is Harvard, but that if he was genuinely interested in writing, he would avoid disappointment if he went there to explore writing on his own and attend Harvard to major in science or math.

3.

THE NATIONAL MUSEUM OF WHAAAT?

In April 1993, Robert McCormick Adams, Jr., Secretary of the Smithsonian Institution appointed a 15-member task force to study the focus on Latinos in the Smithsonian collections and exhibits, governance, personnel policies, and programs. On May 10, 1994, the Smithsonian's in-house report *Willful Neglect* acknowledged a disregard for Latinos in its exhibits, staffing, and programs.

In 2003, Representative Xavier Becerra introduced legislation to establish a commission to study the possibility of creating a museum on Latino Americans. In 2008 Congress created a Commission to Study the Potential Creation of the National Museum of the American Latino, to be affiliated with the Smithsonian, twenty-three members appointed by President G.W. Bush and the House and Senate leadership.

But the legislation faced opposition. Here's *The New York Times* Kate Taylor's report published on April 20, 2011:

> Though the creation of such an institution has support from members of Congress, Interior Secretary Ken Salazar and celebrities like Eva Longoria, building it faces significant obstacles, including budget pressures and a feeling among some in Washington that the Smithsonian should stop spinning off new specialty museums and concentrate on improving the ones it already has.
>
> "I don't want a situation," said Representative Jim Moran, a Democrat from Virginia, "where whites go to the original museum, African-Americans go to the African-American museum, Indians go to the Indian museum, Hispanics go to the Latino American museum. That's not America."[1]

An additional opposition, also cited in that *Times* piece came from sectors who wanted to save the National Mall from overcrowding:

> But any construction on the Mall can be controversial. Judy Scott Feldman, the president of the National Coalition to Save Our Mall, said her group

---

[1] Kate Taylor, "National Latino Museum Plan Faces Fight," *The New York Times*, April 20, 2011, https://www.nytimes.com/2011/04/21/arts/design/proposed-smithsonian-latino -museum-faces-hurdles.html

opposes any construction on the mall until a new master plan is created
to guide development.[2]

When advocates finally agreed on a plan to designate the Smithsonian's Arts
and Industries Building, and legislation was introduced by its congressional
backers, opponents proposed a National Museum of the American People,
which would look at how all ethnic or national groups came here.

In November, 2011 *The New York Times* reported on the project's bleak outlook:

> When the Latino commission started its work in 2009, supporters
> predicted the museum might be up and running in a decade. Today Mr.
> [Estuardo] Rodriguez, the lobbyist, said, the path looks longer. He said
> he hoped to persuade politicians with large Latino constituencies of the
> merits of the proposal and build from that.
>
> "I was in a conversation with a colleague of mine the other day," Mr.
> Rodriguez said. "I said, 'You know, the African-American museum was
> in process for some 25 years,' and they said, 'No, actually, 75 years.'"
> Mr. Rodriguez paused in his recollection, and added, "We don't want to
> get to that position."[3]

Congress sat on the project and the obvious was reported on October, 2014
by Elizabeth Llorente on the Latino Fox News website: that the National Latino
museum remained "in indefinite limbo because of congressional gridlock...."
The same was reported a few days later by Scharon Harding on the website by
Scharon Harding in *The Latin Post*: "Bills Approving Smithsonian Site for a National
American Latino Museum Continue to Wait in House of Representatives,
Senate." In December 2020, along with a proposal to create an American
Women's History Museum, legislation was re-introduced for a Latino
museum and both proposals were blocked by Utah Republican Senator Mike
Lee: "The last thing we need is to further divide an already divided nation."[4]

The above news thread traces a straightforward American melodrama: a
minority group wrangling to achieve national recognition in the form of a
museum and coming up against traditional ethnocentric opposition. But in
this case much more funny business is going on in the name of "Latino," the
exploiting of the overlapping of the English and Spanish homonyms Latino/*latino*.

---

[2] Kate Taylor, "National Latino Museum Plan Faces Fight."

[3] Kate Taylor, "National Latino Museum Plan Faces Fight."

[4] Suzanne Gamboa, "National Latino museum vote blocked by Utah GOP Sen. Mike Lee,"
NBC News, https://www.nbcnews.com/news/latino/national-latino-museum-vote-blocked
-utah-gop-sen-mike-lee-n1250819.

The differences between the two are illustrated in the respective language of the museum's two most prominent advocates.

Estuardo Rodriguez, president/CEO of Friends of the National Museum of the American Latino defends "Latino" as a political agenda, and is therefore given to general, politically correct boilerplate responses. To the proposed American People Museum that would presumably make a Latino museum unnecessary: "I think it mixes the messages, ...I think there's going to be a challenge, as it relates to educating (Congress) and the supporters we need about the distinctions and differences between these efforts."[5] To Senator Mike Lee's stonewalling: "a sad commentary based on fears around the diversity of our nation. [Lee] fails to understand that by highlighting the diversity that has helped build our nation, we are able to better understand each other and come together."[6]

In contrast, the bill's co-sponsor, New Jersey Senator Bob Menendez, enters impassioned and historically detailed, thinking of *latino* and Hispanic as culture and history: "We Latinos are not invaders. ...We have been here from the beginning...We have been systemically excluded. We, who founded the oldest city in America before there was a United States of America. We, who were ultimately used as farm workers and discriminated against in the Bracero program. We, who were discriminated against when we voluntarily joined the Armed Forces of the United States to defend the nation."

Menendez's more sharply-delineated expectation represents what most Latinos presume of a museum about them, understanding Latino to convey the same as *latino*, which is Hispanic, and so presumably he expects a museum that will educate on Hispanic/Latino as also American history and heritage against the traditional foreignizing and ghosting of it. But that clarity doesn't jump out on reading from the Friends of the National Museum website that whips up solidarity with familiar speak that invokes popular assumptions of Latino. The website also reminds that for the present "Latino" remains a semantic hologram, the public mask of an actually fragmented and competing multitude of subgroups, and the American identity of a demographic not yet a community.

Appreciating that fragile semantic foundation of Latino/*latino* to promote this museum is important because even though its cause is overall noble, the rhetoric and public relations used to campaign for its creation raise questions

---

[5] "National Museum Of The American Latino Could Be Threatened By Immigrant Museum," *Huffington Post,* December 5, 2013, https://www.huffpost.com/entry/national-museum-of-the-american-latino_n_4063100

[6] Suzanne Gamboa, "National Latino museum vote blocked by Utah GOP Sen. Mike Lee."

about its "mission and purpose" and of its understanding of "Latino" as consciousness. Troubling indications bespeak of a questionable agenda being smuggled into the broad support it seeks in the name of Latino solidarity. Red flags first stood out for me when I read the composition of the commission's original members.

Six were Mexican Americans, the number representative of the largest Latino subgroup. But the remaining seventeen require deciphering. Five were born and raised in Cuba while three Puerto Ricans were raised and educated in Puerto Rico, no mainland Puerto Ricans, no native Floridian Cuban. One New York-bred commissioner who represented Northeast Puerto Ricans lives in California while no commissioner was from the Northeast where Puerto Ricans are almost double in number than on the island.

One commissioner from a Central American background, Nicaraguan born and raised, had as Latino American connection his employment with ExxonMobil Nicaragua. Another commissioner, born in Argentina and raised in Chile, worked out of Nevada, not known for its South American Cone population. The single black commission member was an African-American immigration lawyer, among three other white non-Latino immigration lawyers. The remaining commissioners were arts administrators and businesspeople.

The commission also counted on the star quality of the actress Eva Longoria and the music producer Emilio Estefan. But no journalists, writers, or public intellectuals. No scholars in Latino Studies. The four academics were Cuban Americans, none a scholar on native Latino, an identity with which Cuban Americans demure from identifying, meaning that they understand their own being Latino to mean strictly *latino*.

By 2019 the commission had been adjusted in geographic and ethnic representation as well as personal and professional relevance to Latino, but still did not include journalists, writers, or public intellectuals, or Latino Studies scholars and what corrections may be made after I have written this essay will surely be cosmetic without changing the fundamental ideas that seem foundational to this project: no commission will undermine the original agenda of finding a way to represent "Latino" without the baggage of its automatic association with the political left or racialized Latino.

This agenda explained the choice of the original four Cuban American academics, who doubtless would not have identified with Latino particularly because it is inherently leftist. When they left the commission, they were not replaced with other academics, suggesting that scholarship was not their contribution to the original commission, so their removal didn't change the composite picture of the commission as politically moderate or right-leaning, eliminating that problem in Washington. For the Friends of the Museum, overcoming already established left-wing associations with Latino poses the challenge of contextually reinventing Latino in its promotion, using the creativity semantic feature of "Latino."

One indicator of the museum promoters' using Latino's semantic elasticity is the coining "the American Latino." The switched-syntax sounds insignificant, adding perhaps a nuance of formality, a raising of the volume on Americanness but also smacks of a bygone relationship with white America. In too many American minds "American Latinos" might be better off, along with "American Indians," on a reservation. "American Indian" works to identify geographic habitat[7] but offends when American as modifier implies a white overseer. That connotation was one motive for adopting Native American.

This derogatory quality becomes apparent when we change the names of other cultural epithets. A Museum of the American African is jarring. A Museum of the American Jew perilously approaches Nazi-speak. In sum, "American Latino" reveals a tone deafness to the sensibilities of the post-civil rights country and is patently the brainchild of someone not informed by the sixties, someone, strictly speaking, not Latino.

As reflected by the commission membership, the less prestigious minority Latino is downplayed, one deduces, in order to exert political advantage by perpetuating the shibboleth of Hispanic American culture as immigrant. But advocating for a museum bespeaks of a historical consciousness at work and tells us that behind this project is a *latino* consciousness because Latino, which ambiguously can represent a shedding of "Hispanic" consciousness that is its only history, has no functional historical semantic feature, and if one is to invoke a culture and a history in a museum, it makes more sense for the Latino in "American Latino" to mean *latino*.

This is the same tacit semantic shift already applied in Latino Studies, which as an area of scholarship and to survive as academic imperative cannot just address Latino as the more popularly promoted oral and pop culture with no historical Hispanic context but applies the ambiguity to also implicitly defer to solidarity. But a culture is a history, and while neither Latino nor *latino* is, strictly speaking, an actual culture, Latino identifies itself as one, implying a history while, as *latino*, it signifies a heritage, which presumes a history, the foundation of a museum.

The names of the other two Smithsonian ethnic museums contain the word "history." The National Museum of American Jewish History and The National Museum of African American History and Culture. The proposed name for this

---

[7] The rationale, it would seem, for preserving the title The National Museum of the American Indian, clearly a vestige of the year in which it was established, 1922.

museum, however, circumvents that issue by claiming to be about the ambiguity itself, not a museum of the culture nor of the history but of the cultural specimen, "the American Latino."

Because an ethnic museum implies a history and because ethnicity is conventionally associated with immigration, and because American myth traditionally assumes that Hispanics/Latinos are foreigners– the only scenario in which Latino Americans "came here"–congressional opponents to the "Latino Museum" countered with the idea of a National Museum of the American People, described as a showcasing of "how all ethnic or national groups came here." This response was practically invited by the museum proponents in their using Latino to mean *latino* as an immigrant ethnicity. In other words, purposely confusing Latino and *latino* invokes the shibboleth of native Hispanic/Latino's also being immigrant.

As I write in 2021, 173 years have passed since the 1848 Treaty of Guadalupe-Hidalgo ceded about half of Mexico and made Mexican culture a component of the longer years of American history. New Mexicans preserved their Hispanic consciousness, calling themselves *hispanos*. Puerto Rico became a booty of the Spanish-American War in 1898. To resolve legal issues of shipping between contiguous and noncontiguous ports, Puerto Ricans were extended/imposed citizenship in 1917. In other words, Mexican Americans/Chicanos, New Mexican *hispanos,* and Puerto Ricans lost their lands in the configuration of the present United States. None "came here."

Combined, those groups represent the largest Latino-American population and their story is the history that, whether or not immigrant *latinos* acknowledge it, they inherit upon arrival. Reinstating Hispanic/Latino as an immigrant culture returns us to the xenophobia that Ezra Pound wielded to humble William Carlos Williams as a "foreigner," implying that Hispanic/Latino is irrelevant to American culture, the patriotic myth that Williams worked to debunk. The matter is indeed complicated, and here is where the immigrant *latino*-conscious museum advocacy gets thrown the cultural curve ball.

In a country whose population better knows its shibboleths than its actual history, despite their true history Hispanics/Latinos have always been perceived as immigrants and, for most Americans, they arrived on planes at the airports of the national consciousness in the sixties. The Friends' strategy to highlight immigrant *latino*, therefore, inadvertently undermines their own claim to a right to a museum because as ground was being broken for an African-American museum centuries in the making, from all appearances, within forty years of gaining visibility, this pushy immigrant group is demanding its own museum.

Rodriguez's dilemma is that his "American Latino"– really *latino* – politically needs to piggyback on the imperative of a Latino American history that he also wants to deny, and at the same time he wants mainstream America to appreciate a fresh *latino* as distinct from a stereotypical Latino. (Compare Rodriguez's dignified responses above to Menendez's minority roar.) In other words, he hasn't won support for a museum that is actually intended to be about *latinos* because he has been unable to make credible the subtly stated truer mission of this museum, it's really not being strictly about Latinos.

Consider this statement that appears in the museum's Commission *Final Report* in a section on the importance of the visual arts: "Most institutions have rich collections in Mexican, Puerto Rican, and Cuban art, but there are many gaps that will need to be filled. A major task for the American Latino museum will be to identify, research, and collect materials from undocumented and/or underrepresented areas of Latino history and culture."

Mexicans, Puerto Ricans, and in select historical contexts, Cubans represent the Hispanic/Latino chapters of American history. What would be the "underrepresented areas of Latino American history and culture"? Unless the report is referring to Latino as *latino*, short for *Latinoamérica*. If that's the case, there is a great deal of underrepresentation. But which of the Smithsonian's missions should this museum serve, to document Latino as an American experience or in its anthropological focus to showcase world cultures, in this case Latin America. Is the language of the *Final Report* clever or shoddy ambiguity?

The report's ambiguity provides an explanation of why this museum is not affixed explicitly in either of the Smithsonian's missions and why the title appropriately announces its subject as the ambiguous "of the American Latino," making it sound as anthropological as "of the American Indian." Returning to the matter of the coining "American Latino," we realize that it is a translation of *latinoamericano*. Indeed, viewing Latino as Latin America, a world culture, circumvents the question of Hispanic/Latino's being a native American consciousness, deferring to the shibboleth of Hispanic/Latino as a "foreign" or immigrant culture, and does not disrupt the other myth of the U.S. as the uniquely white Western City on the Hill above barbarous, multiracial, non-Western Latin America.

It is doubtful that a museum commissioned to clearly establish that Hispanic is a native culture and that the country has always been multicultural, is a project of which the Smithsonian would be so supportive. Nor is Congress likely to endorse a museum that pretends to correct the centrality of traditional white hegemony. The proposed museum's only rational political option is to play along with traditional myths that Americans harbor at the expense of

Latino intellectual seriousness, why the Commission has no scholars or writers.

The museum website has a tab for those who want to take action. But before action, there needs to be more thought on its objective. One already reads between the lines of its proposed "vision and purpose," which is not about researching Latino. The museum offers a willingness to compromise on Latino with white America because the real prize is a museum that would celebrate newer *latino*, the presumably underrepresented in American culture, overriding the American historical authority of native Hispanic/Latino.

That this museum was proposed by *latinos* demonstrates once again immigration's enrichment of American society. New Peruvian, Dominican and Guatemalan citizens indeed are equally American and equally Hispanic/Latino Americans. But in attempting to make an end run to gain the leadership of the millennial "largest minority" over hegemonic Latino, the *latino* consciousness inversely parallels Latino's shortcoming of giving only activist importance to "the people" as political and not also cultural and intellectual entities. While youthful Latino is destined to gain from a more adult *latino* sophistication, as its experience in Congress is demonstrating, *latino* is also destined to trip over American cultural terrain about which Latino is more experienced.

One can say that Latinos already have a museum, the United States of America. Its prime exhibit is a Congress that doesn't know nor want to know the American cultural history to which Hispanic/Latino is a native tributary and in which a Latino consciousness is too conflicted over racial, anti-intellectual, and idealistic agendas to understand its actual range and depth in American culture. It is worth citing Senator Bob Menendez's definition of Latino: "We have been here from the beginning...."

In other words, if the proposed museum agenda is to take advantage of the semantic amorphousness and cultural dysfunction of Latino as a source of funds for a museum that, while generously showcasing native Hispanic/ Latinos as diversity tokens, is actually envisioned to celebrate *latino* as a world culture at the Smithsonian, then I see a "Latino Museum" as an exploitation of Hispanic/Latino American history. If this museum's true mission is to educate America on Hispanic/Latino as a protagonist American heritage that historically has informed the gestation of a more perfect multicultural union – "We, who founded the oldest city in America before there was a United States of America"– this museum is overdue.

4.

LATINO NOMADLAND: READING A JOB
ANNOUNCEMENT IN LATINO STUDIES

Latino Studies: Tenure track, Assistant Professor, Fall 2007.

Research and teaching in culturally-oriented social sciences or cultural studies, with possible focus on diaspora, transnational migrations, literary representations and performances of nationhood, creating Latinidad. Basic Qualifications: Applicants must possess a Ph.D. in American Studies or a closely related field. Ph.D. must be completed by June 15, 2007. Applicants must also show commitment to scholarly research as evidenced by publications in scholarly journals or work in progress and demonstrated teaching ability as indicated by teaching assessments.

–posted by a major eastern university
on the Jobs website of *The Chronicle of Higher Education*
in November 2006

What called my attention about this job announcement was its description of Latino Studies and the underlying definition of Latino.

The announcement opens by affirming the convention that Latino is a research area of the social sciences:[1] "*...culturally-oriented social sciences or cultural studies...*" The candidate is expected to do research and teach "with a possible focus on diaspora, transnational migrations, literary representations and performances of nationhood..." Whatever the candidate's focus from that catalog, if one follows the structure of the sentence, the objective of the research and teaching is "creating Latinidad."

This ambiguously-formulated objective appears to have to two functions. The job announcement cannot legally exclude possible non-Latino/*latino* candidates, and consistent with Latino's rejecting metaphorical or ideational associations that do not contain the word Latino, the applicant is described as someone whose ultimate academic responsibility is to create Latinidad. That description imposes on the candidate the qualification of possessing a

---

[1] It should be noted that this follows the convention also in Latin American Studies. In an informal survey I made of Latin American programs with very few exceptions, the cross-listed courses were in the social sciences, not in literature or art.

consciousness that is unteachable in any graduate course, a qualifying attribute that the possible candidate must naturally possess. In other words, the candidate should be a Latino or a Latina.

Its other function modifies the provided definition of literature, defined here as "literary representations" and as "performances of nationhood, creating Latinidad," presumably literary expressions of solidarity with Latinidad. "Representation" invokes a template of Latino writing, creating something predetermined and not a product of creative possibilities. If I am asked to demonstrate the most "representative" examples of my students' writings, they would be those that assemble socially-conscious clichés and rehash politically-correct diction. Based on representation, with no consideration for capturing the authentic and not simply recycling a catalog of social imagery makes the Pulitzer Prize winners no different than the equally representative, cliché-ridden student writings.

The possible foci suggest they are all applicable to "Latino" but two of the possible foci really address *latino*, "diaspora" and "transnational migrations." Chicano/Mexican Americans do not constitute a diaspora as they were absorbed in the U.S. acquisition of Northern Mexico and it is debatable even among Puerto Ricans if their diaspora is a transnational migration, so either the operative model "diaspora" seems to be the more recent Latin American immigration or a tacit invocation of the premise that Latino is by definition immigrant.

The announcement goes on to detail the best candidates' expected qualifications. Given that the announcement came from a department of American Studies, the ideal candidate would be a Ph.D. in American Studies who had the foresight to research and teach the stated possible foci. One intuits that the chances seem better for applicants from "a closely related field," Latin American Studies or Romance Languages or Cultural Studies, or minority American Studies, reflecting the Latino Studies' spectrum. That would be the intuited range, but the announcement's language suggests that the only real qualification is to be a social scientist in any field who possesses a Latino consciousness and published, not actually having devoted scholarship to Latino as a stated requirement: "Applicant must also show commitment to scholarly research as evidenced by publications in scholarly journals or work in progress and demonstrated teaching ability as indicated by teaching assessments." Presumably an in-progress recent commitment to research Latino in response to a job opening will qualify.

This flexibility is important because that would mean that Latino candidates who had never published anything directly touching upon Latino but with a fresh interest in applying their scholarship qualify as do scholars with a single publication that can be seen through the proper lens as touching upon Latino: Octavio Paz and the *pachuco*; Frieda Kahlo's influence on the Latina artist.

Whatever the candidate's academic provenance, for this position in a Department of American Studies, Latino as an American consciousness is not a primary focus and doesn't have to be a candidate's interest or expertise. Which begs the question. So what relation does Latino Studies have with that American Studies department? Whether owing to that university's budgetary circumstances or other departments' bias or administrative politics or this department's commitment to community outreach, Latino Studies is part of American Studies, but judging from the job announcement, with no scholarly connection to American Studies.

What does it signify that the announcement speaks about a "nationhood" that is clearly not American nationhood in the context of American Studies? Does this reflect the progressivism of this American Studies department to allow not just the academic freedom of individual professors to advance a nationhood but the agenda of an entire program to be about building a distinct Latino nationhood? Or is this wide latitude signaling that this program is intended to perform a service that is not seriously taken as academic whatever it advances, and in the administrative scheme of things, Latino Studies performs an important service of hosting Latino students who can be taught whatever.

Finally, one also takes away from the announcement that *Latinidad* is not a subject that should inspire students to inquire into what that means. The suggested foci and syllabi do not suggest an exercise in stimulating thought and wrestling with messy ideas so much as to reinforce a defined consciousness. At a time that American culture debates what it believed it was, what it is now, and what it will be, Latinos should be trying to make better sense of their American identity as well as inquire what being Latino means in the context of hemispheric *latinidad* with more dimensions than entertainments and being racialized victims. Most troubling about the job announcement is its demonstration that Latino Studies' disconnect to American Studies aptly mirrors the intellectual disconnect of Latino as consciousness with literate, non-pop American culture, which should inform Latinos to enrich but whose history of inculcating ethnocentrism now serves to rationalize the communal pretense of a liberation in a conscious ignorance of an American culture not summarized in racism.

LATINO WRITING AND AMERICAN LITERARY HISTORY: IMAGINING A SURVEY TEXTBOOK

Note: Latino (not latino) *writers write from their specific* latino *subcultural experiences (as nobody actually lives a literally Latino life), which portrayed reiterates, however ethnically-flavored, a shared minority experience, and thus Latino also signifies that the writing is American. In reflecting on Latino in American writing, one confronts that literature is a history of the culture and the language, in this case English, one reason why, from a traditionalist American perspective, an intuitive assumption is that Latino is a rootless flowering that converses only with recent multicultural writings. Ironically, from today's woke Latino perspective, both its presentism and ahistorical multiculturalism boast about the same disconnect with a presumably irrelevant canon primarily of dead white men. Consequently, Latino is read by all erroneously presuming an absence of literary discourse with American literature.*

In 1968, while I sat in an NYU graduate class on the History of the English Novel, my professor lectured on *Moll Flanders* as the first true Western novel, skipping over the never mentioned *Don Quixote.* He elaborated on the picaresque without mentioning *Lazarillo de Tormes.* As his omissions complicated my plan to write a term paper comparing the English with the Spanish picaresque, I visited him during office hours and asked why he circumvented those two seminal works. Elbows on his desk, his clasped hands covering his mouth, his only response was a "Yes, yes," punctuating each title with a backhand dismissal. Exactly what those yeses meant was unclear– *you may be right but those works are insignificant at least to me* –but he did make clear that he had no desire to explain his response or discuss the importance of those works or at least not with me. His silence with a look of, "Something else?" shut the door behind me.

If this encounter had taken place a few years later I could have cited from a two-volume study I had discovered, Stanley T. Williams' *The Spanish Background to American Literature*, published in 1951.[1] Williams was a traditionalist who wrote at a time when "Spanish" was still monolithic, spanning Iberia and Latin America. In other words, owing to the years during which it was written, Williams' "Spanish Background" also didn't acknowledge Latin American literature in its own right[2] and, of course, did not unearth a Hispanic or Latino American writing presumed not to exist. Rather, Williams was correcting the academic convention of denying an influence of monolithic "Spanish," whether Iberian or from the Americas, on American letters. His dated "Spanish" notwithstanding, this volume still provided a valuable rebuttal to the ethnocentrism that deemed Hispanic irrelevant to American letters, and so his book served as foundation for my personal rereading of American literary history.

And so, looking back, I still wish I had known about Williams' two volumes before I took that graduate course. I also occasionally laugh to myself imagining that professor's reaction if I had blurted out that I was an English major because I had pretensions of someday being a writer. Williams wrote his study to correct English's traditional resistance to accepting a "Spanish background" to American literature, a chronology that ranged from Cervantes to Neruda, so imagine a post-sixties conservative's view of scribblings then-called "U.S. Hispanic." My professor left little to imagine about his stand on the burgeoning minority consciousness in writing, surely dismissing it from someone like me who, for him, arrived on the banks of American letters in a basket of post-civil rights diversity. For in that tradition, one can easily assume that even more random and disconnected to the American past is today's Latino writing and conclude that it belongs at the American literary feast, as a saying goes in Spanish, like a cockroach at a hen's wedding.

I make this pronouncement quickly acknowledging the paradox that I became a writer gratefully as a consequence of assigned canonical readings before I had any thought of writing. This was before conscious multiculturalism, before mainland "Puerto Rican" was racialized. Nothing that I read in literature classes did I pass through today's politically correct filters, racial or cultural. Reading Shakespeare or John Keats or Emily Dickinson or Robert Frost touched a nondescript person in me no different than when I was taught by Irish Christian Brothers or attended mass and heard an Irish priest talk of a Middle

---

[1] Stanley T. Williams, *The Spanish Background to American Literature* (New Haven, Yale University Press, 1951).

[2] In her review of *The Spanish Background* poet Muna Lee, wife of Puerto Rico's first elected governor, critiqued Stanley Williams' not recognizing "the Puerto Rican poet" William Carlos Williams.

Eastern Jew who was born to be crucified and cleanse the world of its sins. Simply mastery of language fascinated me.

English mastery because I grew up studying in New York, but when a member of my family in Puerto Rico recited Spanish poems or I heard island folk songs based on seventeenth-century *décimas*, I felt the same excitement for rhythm, rhyme, especially baroque wordplay quintessential to a Hispanic Caribbean sense of humor. Years later I would identify with William Carlos Williams' crediting Góngora and Quevedo for sowing in him that love of baroque wit. Literary mastery, what I was instilled to enjoy in both languages, enthralled me.

I don't think that I would have been as excited about writing if I had not first been taught the poetry of those white male "masters"– in English or Spanish, which in fact included women. If I had been brought up on today's critique of that writing, I would have simply disregarded it and most likely wouldn't have been smitten with the possibility of writing because a diet of less masterful works, even if ethnically relevant to me, would not have been as inspiring. I would have most likely looked somewhere else to invest my talents. And when multiculturalism became a thing, I came to learn that what multiculturalism was dismissing about literature was really not the writings but how traditional critics and educators served them up reheated on platters of ethnocentrism, racism, and sexism. In other words, the woke literary debate confuses the power of criticism with the actual writing, which it fails to reread correctly.

Writing is writing; it becomes "literature" when defined by a critical audience that determines the canon. In America's case, writing is expected to narrate or expand upon the traditional The American Story of an immutable white male protagonist. Canonical works were also selected for being masterful writings, the criterion traditionally referred to as "quality." The criticism was assumed to be an infallible authority; the canon was premised on the patriotic assumption of the nonexistence of writings equally as masterful produced by marginal cultures and women.

In the post-Civil Rights Era, postmodernism intervened to take down social hierarchies of all kinds, including the authority of literary language, equating written and oral expression. This new democratizing philosophy immediately gave those excluded –who had interpreted the "quality" standard as a mere gimmick that justified excluding– the moral authority to demand that textbook editors be more inclusive. Moreover, as if being the revanche of students burdened with their English teacher's expecting them to extrapolate themes from complicated literary devices, multiculturalism questioned the traditional definition of literature.

Poetry epitomized this storming of the canon's hierarchical castle, with minority poetry first emerging as descending from American oral traditions:

African American poetry as descending from Negro song traditions, and more recent assaults on tradition; from Whitman's suggestion that readers put down their books and listen to their own breath as picked up by the Beats reading to jazz; from Whitman's celebration of spoken language as the natural American rhythms rather than the artificial iambic; from William Carlos Williams' rejection of the traditional emulation of Britain at the expense of the American Idiom, Williams another tributary to the Beat Movement, which symbiotically identified with minority writing oral traditions.

The Beats' influence, converging with the intervention of postmodernism, produced the performance poetry movement, whose paradigm in both Latino and mainstream writing was New York's Nuyorican Poetry Cafe. The exhilaration of liberation from tradition and especially the canon encouraged the thinking that past ideas of literary writing were bygone. At poetry slams the microphone was open to anyone who had an original poem to read. In the anthology *Aloud: Voices from the Nuyorican Poets Cafe* (1994), co-edited by Miguel Algarín and Bob Holman, Holman announced that the "page poem" was dead.

Reviewers of this book all cite Holman's description of the anthology as "a home for the tradition that has no home but your ear." Interviewed by Mark Silverberg for *Chicago Review*, Holman ascribed his oral poetics to the lessons of the Beats, notably Allen Ginsberg: "Ginsberg for me was the Bard. Whether wheezing away on the harmonium, backed up on Blake by the angelic chords…,"[3] adding "The job of the bard is to let meanings fly into the audience's ear." And the oral poem became a democratizing of poetry, what the Beats intended. Open mics and poetry slams made "literature" something one didn't have to learn in order to write. Interviewed on television after winning a national poetry slam, the reigning champion recounted how she had started writing after first attending a slam: "It's easy. Anybody can do it."

Teaching creative writing and American literature in that climate, in the classroom I had to reestablish the relevance of writing for the page, a connection once intuitive. Memorably, after my pointing out Frost's achieving another level of suggestiveness by making subtle changes to speech, a woman student did not express admiration for Frost's achievement, instead commenting dismissively, "I write poetry, but I don't put all that stuff in it." The trending of post-page poetry and the media attention focused on The Nuyorican Poets Café overshadowed the reality that there also existed "page" poets emerging from both Mexican American and Puerto Rican communities who, like me, also

---

[3] "Bardic Travels with Bob Holman (an interview with Mark Silverberg)," *Chicago Review*, August 13, 2021.

descended from a traditional literary education of readings of mostly dead white men.

While the leap to oral traditions appears to be a solution to what to do with that literary history presumably written solely by and for white people, it skirts that the oral poem and the more highly crafted page poem produce different art that, while politically proselytized as profoundly different, are rooted in the same language, in the same Western history of imagery. Consequently, as Jorge Luis Borges observed, all writing is essentially about writing and thus invokes precursors, which may come from a literature not even in the same language. The poet may profess willful ignorance of the formal poetry imposed in school, but orality does not escape the precursors that come with the language.

Similarly, Latino writing can have precursors that are both in Spanish and in English, rooted in both even if the poet is unaware of that lineage. Naively, then, like Oscar Wilde's Jack found in a leather bag in Victoria Station, many Latino writers begin with the arid foundation that most English teachers lay out for them of their really having nothing to inherit from the American literature being taught. That too is the broad assumption in the literary culture. But Latino writers who reread properly American literature can discover that, exactly like Jack, they only appear to lack a pedigree and arrive at a nobler surprise ending from a rehabilitated beginning.

To claim that heritage, however, Latinos must relearn to read metaphor, and give credence to ideational connections and not just to social, political, and biographical affirmation. A distinguished Latino scholarly journal turned down as not germane to Latino an essay that I wrote on Paul Simon's having assumed Latino personas throughout his work and ultimately composed as a Latino his musical *The Capeman*. Obviously, to the editors, relevant Latino Studies discussion must be about actual Latinos, not Latino as an idea, as metaphor. Literature is a history in which one preserves metaphors of the national identity. Consequently, to reread that literature Latino writers must also reinstate a historical consciousness, including of the Hispanic that some Latinos disavow, because most of Latino writing's American literary heritage is Hispanic.

By making those adjustments we can imagine a survey textbook composed of selections that provide Hispanic/Latino with roots in American literature, either inherited from direct Hispanic forebears, who are few, or, in the majority of cases, writings whose truly American vision foreshadowed multicultural inclusion, including the acknowledgment of Hispanic tributaries to the American cultural consciousness.

COLONIAL PERIOD

Like today's multicultural textbooks, our text would open with Spanish chronicles and letters (which, one colleague gingerly informed me, she routinely skips over), writings that make the Puritan's arrival a late chapter of early America's history up to that time written only in Spanish. In reading standard textbooks, students do not fully appreciate that Spanish-speaking America is over a century older than Anglo America.[4] Another notable absence from the standard text but included in ours is the acknowledgment of how much Anglo history in America owes to the publication of *A Short Account of the Destruction of the Indies* (1552), by the cleric Bartolomé de las Casas.

This indictment of the Conquest's atrocities and cruelty, was translated throughout Europe, providing the English propaganda to advertise themselves as the more civilized. That the original indictment came from a Spaniard was overlooked when the English and the Dutch, allied to combat their Spanish rulers, generated the Black Legend that essentially racialized Spanish civilization as savage in its treatment of the natives, a propaganda on which England promoted itself as the superior culture that vowed to settle humanely, the bias that we inherit today.

Bypassing de las Casas in the classroom also omits explaining the true origins of American slavery, the exporting of the slave trade practiced among African tribes to the New World was initially Spain's and Portugal's practice that the English adopted, the misguided handiwork of the Bartolomé de las Casas. Known as the Defender of the Indians, who were dying off owing to their being overworked and succumbing to foreign disease, de las Casas convinced Columbus to import Africans, which the Portuguese had started doing. In the ignorance of that time de las Casas would only later realize that Africans were humans too, as would the Church, which would be the first to condemn slavery and the continued importation of slaves.

By the end of the seventeenth century, European intrigues over Spanish succession and the crossing of bloodlines endangered Protestant England with the possibility of converting a Catholic monarch. In John Williams' *The Redeemed Captive* (1707), that possibility was the wedge used by French Jesuit negotiators who asked John Williams to embrace Catholicism as ransom for the return of his daughter from the baptized Iroquois, who had kidnaped and adopted her. Understanding that conversion to Catholicism was itself a form of oppression, why was it, class, that Native Americans became Catholics en masse while

---

[4] It remains one of the three gaps of knowledge that American education perpetuates by design, the other two being that slavery began over three centuries before the Civil War and that it was not just a sin of the South.

Protestants did not make conversion an imperative?[5] Why were Native tribes prepared to adopt white children and the English incapable of adopting Native children?

In The War of Spanish Succession, Cotton Mather saw the weakening of the Spanish Empire and the prospect of converting "American Spaniards" away from Popery.[6] His diary writings, which reiterate his obsession with spiritual forces in constant unseen struggle (as in his "The Wonders of the Invisible World"), report of his having been moved one day to a "sudden composure" when he reflected on the history of the English and Spanish as colonizers: "We have made a fair and just purchase of our Country from the Natives here; not encroaching on them after the Spanish Fashion, in any of their Properties and Possessions."[7] In that state of composure, he implies that the salvation of Protestantism from Popery would be a fair and just price for the future acquisition of lands from "American Spaniards."

Mather's plan required his learning Spanish, which according to his diary he accomplished from study in "leisurely hours." Actually, he was fudging his more likely being taught the language by a much prized "Spanish Indian" slave, described in a seemingly unrelated entry. Once he was literate in Spanish, as so he claimed, he wrote and published a translation of one of his sermons, *La Fe Del Christiano*,[8] the first Spanish-language publication in the English colonies, under the name C. Mathero.

The diary then weirdly weaves this plan into a confession of his feeling morally obligated to mentor "American Spaniards" because of his daughter's having suffered a severe burn. He blames the burn on his failure to be at home and devote more time to mentoring his daughter, and therefore vows as penance to teach "American Spaniards" the true religion. This episode, rich in psychological mystery, exemplifies Mather's rhetorical manner of attempting to redeem his errors in life by redacting his writing of the experience. It also dramatizes the Puritan weaponizing of religion against Spanish culture,

---

[5] John Eliot (1604-1690 was a Puritan missionary to the Native Americans of Massachusetts Bay Colony whose translation of the Bible in the Algonquian language was the first Bible printed in North America.

[6] This campaigning was funded by Samuel Sewall: also see his *Diary*.

[7] Cotton Mather, *The Diary of Cotton Mather* (Boston, Massachusetts Historical Society, 1911), V.I, 205. The declaration that "We have made a fair and just purchase of our Country from the Natives" is contradicted by King Phillip's War against the English, provoked by colonial expansion. Roger Williams' proselytizing that the English had no inherent right to what were Native lands was one reason for his expulsion from Plymouth Plantation.

[8] Mather, *Diary of Cotton Mather*, 296.

synonymous with Popery, foreshadowing the American relation with Hispanic culture to this day, making Mather the first spiritual apologist for territorial expansion in "Spanish America":

> [Memorandum.] following 4 d. I m. entry [recorded in March, 1702]
>
> I have been much engaged both in public and in private Supplications, that the Lord would open a way, for the Access of His glorious Gospel into the vast Regions of the Spanish America: and I know no Minister but myself who hath been so. Now, while I was this Day employing my Thoughts, upon this great Subject there was brought unto my Hands, a most wonderful Thing, which was brought hither the last Night from England; namely, a Copy of the Articles concluded between the Emperour King of England and States of Holland: whereof the sixth is, that the English and Dutch shall have Liberty to make themselves Masters, if they can, of the Countreys and Cities, under the Dominion of Spain in the Indies, and that they shall keep all that they shall conquer. Who can tell, what may be the Consequence of this astonishing Thing?[9]

THE REVOLUTION

Later, among the colonials, while pride in English descent perdured, with the emergence of an American consciousness, being "sons of England" came to compete with an emerging patriotism disconnected from England and a romanticization of Spain as the wedge to gain independence. Spain became the principal financer of the revolution. A radical sector of revolutionaries, the Columbians, looking to break with England as even their heritage proposed that the country be named Columbia, the child of the vision of Columbus and Isabella.

In 1772 the patriotic college students Philip Freneau and Hugh Henry Brackenridge collaborated on a poem that they submitted to a contest whose prize was reading it at the graduation ceremony of their school, The College of New Jersey, later Princeton University. "On The Rising Glory of America" is an epic poem in the form of a Platonic dialogue valuable in its existence in two versions that mirror the conflicted American consciousness that we inherit today.

Freneau went on to be known as the Poet of the Revolution, during which his American vision matured, and his appreciation of the emergent American consciousness profoundly changed from the ideas he once shared with Brackenridge. So much that he was compelled to rework the poem, adding and changing lines that often also gave the original, unchanged lines new nuances. The result was so diametrically different from the original that Freneau

---

[9] Mather, *Diary of Cotton Mather*, 420.

included the reworked poem in his 1789 collection *The Poems of Philip Freneau,*[10] described as "Written Chiefly during the Late War."

The first page of the new version has this footnote: "The poem is a little altered from the original (published in Philadelphia in 1772) such parts being inserted here as were written by the author of these volumes. A few more modern lines toward the conclusion are incorporated with the rest, being a supposed prophetical anticipation of the subsequent events."[11] The final product defines an American vision, distanced from the original poem, presumably the poem that today appears among Hugh Henry Brackenridge's complete writings. That poem has the same title, "On The Rising Glory of America," and sings of the impending revolution to liberate an America that Brackenridge saw as the child of superior English culture, the new nation wrought by the "sons of Britain."

Most important for our imagined text is the counter-discourse on perceptions of Spain. In the English tradition, Brackenridge detested Spain and in his poem he invokes the Black Legend of Spanish cruelty, celebrating that "The British Epithet" was inherently more "merciful," a trait presumably inherited by Americans as "sons of Britain":

> Such is the curse Eugenio where the soul
> Humane is wanting, but we boast no seats
> Of cruelty like Spain's unfeeling sons.
> The British Epithet is merciful:
> And we the sons of Britain learn like them
> To conquer and to spare; for coward souls
> Seek their revenge gut on a vanquished foe.
> Gold, fatal gold was the assuring bait
> To Spain's rapacious mind, hence rose the wars
> From Chili to the Caribbean sea...[12]

Freneau changed "like Spain's unfeeling sons" to "like Europe's murdering breed." For Freneau, Americans stood apart from the equally rapacious European conquerors motivated by the same greed, the Spanish for gold and the English for land. Not seeing the British morally superior to any other European nation, all being capable, like the Spanish, of being corrupted by gold in whatever form,

---

[10] Philip Freneau, *The Poems of Philip Freneau: Poet of the American Revolution* (Los Angeles: HardPress Publishing, 2012).

[11] Freneau, *The Poems of Philip Freneau: Poet of the American Revolution,* 42.

[12] "The Rising glory of America, 1760-1820," Internet Archive, https://archive.org/details/risinggloryofame0000unse/mode/2up, 65

Freneau's version narrows Brackenridge's "Spain's rapacious mind" to those bands led by plundering conquistadors, "Spain's rapacious tribes."

Freneau wrote not as one of the "sons of Britain" but as "American":

> Such is the curse, Acasto, where the soul
> Humane is wanting–but we boast no feats
> Of cruelty like Europe's murdering breed–
> Our milder epithet is merciful,
> And each American, true hearted, learns
> To conquer and to spare; for coward souls
> Alone seek vengeance on a vanquished foe.
> Gold, fatal gold was the assuring bait
> To Spain's rapacious tribes--hence rose the wars
> From Chili to the Caribbean sea,... (Freneau, 67)

In these two poems with identical titles and conflicting American visions, we witness the origin of today's cultural war over its potentially multicultural consciousness, the debate not involving poets "of color" but in an American literary lineage of openness to what in the future would be called "minority" as American. In this chapter of American letters, then, not just Latino writers can recover admiration of Hispanic roots in Freneau, a precursor to today's progressive, multicultural consciousness, who in numerous subsequent poems expresses his profound admiration of Native Americans. A product of his time, who must be judged against minds like Brackenridge's, Freneau's most explicit statement on American equality is this description of the slaves as quintessential Americans in his later poem "To Sir Toby": "...they, of stuff determined to be free."[13]

In addition to countering Brackenridge's invoking of Spain's Black Legend of inherent savagery, Freneau also diverged from Brackenridge's America in an 18-part epic, *Pictures of Columbus* (1774). Understandably, if anachronistically judged by today's political correctness, Freneau would be condemned for romanticizing Native Americans while lauding the Admiral who enabled their enslavement. But Freneau cannot be judged by today's standards, and there is merit in understanding his best American vision by fictionalizing Columbus to portray the American consciousness. Freneau portrayed Columbus as the first American, a European who rediscovers his natural relationship to nature and God, free of the trappings of civilization, including the tyranny of aristocracy and commerce:

> Sweet sylvan scenes of innocence and ease,
> How calm and joyous pass the seasons here!

---

[13] Fred Lewis Pattee, *Philip Freneau: Collected Poems* (Seattle: Kindle Direct, 2020), 320.

> No splendid towns or spiry turrets rise,
> No lordly palaces—no tyrant kings
> Enact hard laws to crush fair freedom here;
> No gloomy jails to shut up wretched men;
> All, all are free!—here God and nature reign;
> Their works unsullied by the hands of men–[14]

When Freneau's Columbus encounters the corpse of a native slain by one of his men who craved his gold earrings, the Admiral identified with the victim, who lived a nobler life but was cut down by crass European materialism:

> Is this the fruit of my discovery!
> If the first scene is murder, what shall follow
> But havock, slaughter, chains and devastation
> In every dress and form of cruelty!
> O injur'd Nature, whelm me in the deep,
> And let not Europe hope for my return...[15]

In "Discovery" (1772), written the year after "The Rising Glory," Freneau expanded on his not damning the Spanish, focusing on the conquistadors, who committed the evils that followed the discovery as part of "Ambitious Europe":

> Ambitious Europe! polished in thy pride,
> Thine was the art that toil to toil allied,
> Thine was the gift, to trace each heavenly sphere,
> And seize its beams, to serve ambition here:
> Hence, fierce Pizarro stock'd a world with graves,
> Hence Montezuma left a race of slaves.—[16]

In other words, in "Discovery" Freneau reiterated his challenge to the ethnocentrism of the racializing Black Legend that England had bestowed on the Spanish and as well stepped outside of the nascent "mainstream" in American culture by not condemning specifically Popery but also Protestantism:

> Religion, bolder, sends some sacred chief
> To bend the nations to her own belief.
> To their vain standard Europe's sons invite,
> Who hold no other world can think aright.[17]

---

[14] Fred Lewis Pattee, *The Poems of Philip Freneau* (Princeton: Princeton University Library, 1902).

[15] Pattee, *The Poems of Philip Freneau*, 117.

[16] Pattee, *The Poems of Philip Freneau*, 86.

[17] Pattee, *The Poems of Philip Freneau*, 87.

Americans of whatever heritages can hear Freneau speaking to them immediately as they can also hear Walt Whitman speaking to all as he wrote to tell the future that he, like them, once stood in Brooklyn and looked at Manhattan.

But American literature as vehicle of the traditional American Story has never been properly taught to instill Freneau's American vision of "men/Numerous as sands." The default has always been Brackenridge's America as the land of the "sons of Britain." In that tradition, canonical American literature also passed down Brackenridge's Anglo rivalry with Spain through conscious omission, so the Latino writer educated in the United States is inculcated the mythos of a mutual cultural irrelevance that tradition has perpetuated.

Freneau's poems on Columbus, written on the eve of the revolution, were his expression of a widely-held idea of Columbus as symbol, both of the American spirit for boldly sailing off into the unknown, and as symbol of Spain, with Columbus as seed of a new, liberating history of origin as the fruit of England's rival culture. In that American romanticization, Isabela was the spiritual mother of the American republic, a role to be resurrected among American suffragettes.

A queen presumably oppressed by an ignorant Ferdinand, Isabella gave her jewels to finance Columbus's adventure, seeing free America in Columbus's eyes, a romanticization that inspired the aforementioned faction called Columbians, like the poet and political playwright Mercy Otis Warren, who aspired to liberate the country called Columbia, the name a female symbol of America named after Columbus (also tacitly honoring Isabella). Phyllis Wheatley's patriotic poem "His Excellency General Washington" invokes Columbia:

> Celestial choir! enthron'd in realms of light,
> Columbia's scenes of glorious toils I write.
> While freedom's cause her anxious breast alarms,
> She flashes dreadful in refulgent arms.[18]

A resonance of this figurative Spanish maternity is the protagonist of Mercy Otis Warren's play *The Ladies of Castile* (1784), Maria, who symbolizes the fight for liberty of Warren's own patriots.

This wooing of Spain was not a poetic exercise: Spain largely funded the American Revolution,[19] which explains the literary Hispanophilia that extends

---

[18] Phillis Wheatley, "His Excellency General Washington," *Poets.org*, https://poets.org/poem/his-excellency-general-washington.

[19] For a detailed account of Spain's importance to the revolutionary cause, see "Spain and the American Revolution" at the *Museum of the American Revolution* website, www.amrev museum.org.

to the end of that eighteenth century. Royall Tyler's unpublished dramatic farce *The Island of Barataria* (1787)[20] was based on the second chapter of the *Quixote*. John Howard Payne wrote the play *The Spanish Husband* (1830), an adaptation from Calderón's *The Surgeon of His Honour* as well as the never published *The Last Duel in Spain*.[21] In 1800 William Dunlap presented his translation of the German Augustus von Kotzebue's five-act *Pizarro in Peru, or the Death of Rolla* and his play *The Night of the Guadalquivir*.[22]

The nation's revolutionary Hispanophilia was destined to be conflicted because the same nation was also envisioning a clash with Spanish culture when it expanded westward. Jefferson's reflections on the importance of Spain and the nation's destiny with Hispanic culture are made evident in his *Notes on the State of Virginia*, in which he instructed that the Spanish language be taught at the College of William and Mary.

Jefferson had taught himself Spanish, which was said to be excellent, and while "he was in Congress in 1775, it was generally believed that he spoke Spanish."[23] The importance that Jefferson gave the Spanish language in the nation's future is underscored in his listing Spanish as second of learning priorities sent to his nephew:

> 2. Spanish. Bestow great attention on this, and endeavor to acquire an accurate knowledge of it. Our future connections with Spain and Spanish America, will render that language a valuable acquisition. The ancient history of that part of America, too, is written in that language. I send you a dictionary.[24]

A Platonist, Jefferson disapproved of fiction, except for *Don Quixote*, which he is said to have read in the original Spanish and listed among the first books and only novel to be included in the library of the University of Virginia.[25] Cervantes' masterpiece, of course, didn't need Jefferson's publicity as it had already been the Western world's literary standard. For despite my graduate professor's lectures claiming that Defoe taught the Western world to write the

---

[20] Stanley T. Williams, *The Spanish Background to American Literature*, vol. 1 (New Haven: Yale University Press, 1951), 331.

[21] Williams, *The Spanish Background to American Literature*, vol. 1, 408.

[22] Williams, *The Spanish Background to American Literature*, vol. 1, 331.

[23] Williams, *The Spanish Background to American Literature*, vol. 1, 25.

[24] Thomas Jefferson, Letter from Thomas Jefferson to Peter Carr, August 10, 1787, *Encyclopedia Virginia*, https://encyclopediavirginia.org/entries/letter-from-thomas-jefferson-to-peter-carr-august-10-1787/

[25] Williams, *The Spanish Background to American Literature*, vol. 1, 25.

modern novel, since the start of the seventeenth century, roughly coinciding with the founding of Jamestown, *Don Quixote* had been the bible of novelists in Western literature.

One unexpected antecedent of Latino writing is J. Hector St. John de Crèvecoeur's *Letters of An American Farmer* (1782),[26] a journal that celebrates rural American life in the narrating voice of the fictional farmer James. Insightfully portraying the colonial American, this work is a staple of college textbooks. Its canonization, however, glosses over the irony of Crèvecoeur's sympathetic portrayal of James written just before the revolution as distinctively and so accurately American against the paradox of its aristocratic author's not identifying with the American democratic cause. The criticism also glosses over that Crèvecoeur is actually emblematic of an early multiculturalism. Understanding Latino as *latino*, if anybody is the first Latino writer it is Crèvecoeur.

Born Michel Guillaume Jean de Crèvecoeur in 1735 to aristocratic parents,[27] after fighting in the French and Indian War, he moved to the Province of New York and became a British citizen in 1765. He purchased a farm in Orange County and married Mehitable Tippet in either 1769 or 1770–sources disagree on the date.[28] Mehitable came from a Loyalist family, sympathetic with Crèvecoeur, a monarchist who did not believe in the call for an American nation. In the violent build-up to the Revolution, Crèvecoeur returned to France, where he stayed until 1778, when he returned to his farm in New York, where, suspected of being a spy, he was detained.

Forced to leave the country, he departed for London, where he used his English name, J. Hector St. John, under which in 1782 he published twelve essays with the title *Letters of an American Farmer: Describing Certain Provincial Situations, Manners, and Customs not Generally Known; and Conveying Some Idea of the Late and Present Interior Circumstances of the British Colonies in North America.* European interest in the United States pushed sales, and within two years that book went through several editions and was translated into five languages, making Crèvecoeur esteemed by Benjamin

---

[26] His French writings are under the name Michel-Guillaume Saint Jean Crèvecoeur.

[27] In this discussion I cite the core summary biography "J. Hector St. John de Crèvecoeur," Wikipedia, https://en.wikipedia.org/wiki/J._Hector_St._John_de_Cr%C3%A8vec%C5%93ur although my brief biography of him is also a compendium of information from introductions (without references) to the many editions of his *Letters to an American Farmer,* none really rounding out a full picture, which is consistently finessed.

[28] While the criticism accepts that Crèvecoeur was a French immigrant, the emphasis is on his perceptive portrayal of the American and on his philosophical ideas. Of late, some critics interpret his work as fictionalized documentary.

Franklin and reclaimed by his native France's intelligentsia, including France's Academy of Sciences.

Creative early sociology, Crèvecoeur's letters prefigure the conscious literary adoption of American culture by later writers, such as George Santayana and William Carlos Williams, and as in their writings, one can decipher traces of cultural interference. In the letter on "Charles Town," for example, on witnessing southern slavery, his presumably Protestant James ruminates over slavery with a French Catholic *latino* consciousness, critiquing the accumulation of wealth by lawyers and merchants "in the north," referring to the English colonies, who are compared to "what now the Church possesses in Peru and Mexico." And not in the character of the American ordinary man, James observes the Spanish connection of Carolinians in the slave trade, equating Carolinians with those who extract gold from Peru: "With gold, dug from Peruvian mountains, they order vessels to the coasts of Guinea...."

Otherwise James is the vehicle of the Anglophile Crèvecoeur, who personally sympathized with British condescension toward the Spanish, as he expressed in his unpublished, "Sketch of a Contrast between the Spanish and English Colonies." J.H. Elliott has described that "sketch" as "Crevecoeur's indictment of Spain and its American territories, ...no more than a banal encapsulation of the prejudices and assumptions of eighteenth-century Europe that still resonates today."[29]

Today Crèvecoeur's *Letters* are being interpreted as fiction by some scholars but no text I have found on Crèvecoeur broaches the suspicious circumstances of his writing in English nor raises the question of his having written in collaboration with at least a translator: Crèvecoeur's coming to live in New York at age thirty and his purporting to have acquired the flawless, native English of his character James compares to Cotton Mather's above-cited claim to his having received the providential endowment of Spanish in weeks. Crèvecoeur certainly picked up the Puritan penchant for textually redacting reality and reinventing oneself.

Indeed, it makes more sense that in the decade that he lived with his American wife, he either wrote the work in French and had it translated with her help or wrote it in his best English, which his wife later polished. That is the

---

[29] From "Contrasting empires: J.H. Elliott looks at the differences–cultural, religious, ethnic and economic–between the Spanish and British approaches to their empires in the Americas, and asks how they turned out, both for the mother countries and for the colonies and states that eventually emerged from them," *The Free Library*, https://www.thefreelibrary.com/Contrasting+empires%3A+J.H.+Elliott+looks+at+the+differences--cultural%2C...-a0149462145

obvious conclusion to draw from his production of subsequent expanded versions and new books, which came out quickly in French, raising the suspicion that they had already been written in that language. After the release of the English version of the *Letters* in 1782, he purportedly translated the work into French, adding essays originally written in French to the first twelve *Letters* and two years later, in 1784, published the new book in Paris in two volumes, *Lettres d'un cultivateur Américain*, a work that the Wikipedia contributor describes as "more literary."

Soon thereafter he returned to America, where his wife had died, his farm was in ruins, and his children were being raised by neighbors. He recovered his children and returned to Europe, where, in 1790 he published an expanded, three-volume, second edition of *Lettres d'un cultivateur Américain*. Then in 1801 he published another three-volume work on America, *Voyage dans la haute Pennsylvanie et dans l'État de New York*, 3 vol. (1801, published in translation, *Travels in Upper Pennsylvania and New York* in 1961).

In danger because he was an aristocrat as the French Revolution loomed, he hid and tried to escape to America but was denied entry by the new American ambassador to France, James Monroe. He lived in France and Germany until his death. After his wife died, notwithstanding that unpublished English works were later found in his attic, the harder evidence of his published work shows that in her absence he had only published in French. That multicultural Crèvecoeur does not exist in college texts, but his bilingual machinations to become a writer in English is a precursor of today's Latino writing.

In that same decade, in Charles Brockden Brown's *Wieland; or, The Transformation: An American Tale* (1798), the ventriloquist Carwin ridicules the notion of blind belief and the ease with which minds can be manipulated into adhering to a religion or a nationality–or an antipathy to a culture. Carwin's vocal tricks change the lives of others as well as his own when he undergoes a transformation from Englishman to Spaniard, adopting a Spanish name (never given), and even converts to Catholicism to become "indistinguishable from a native" of Spain.

Why Spain? Because the English believed, as the character Henry Pleyal states, "in the incongruousness between the religion and habits of a Spaniard, with those of a native of Britain." In other words, they believed that Hispanic and Anglo were intrinsically diametric, that conviction an American inheritance. Carwin answers: "Briton and Spaniards are votaries of the same deity, and square their faith by the same precepts; their ideas are drawn from the same fountains of literature, and they speak dialects of the same tongue; their government and laws have more resemblances than differences; and they were formerly provinces of the same civil, and till lately, of the same religious, Empire."[30]

In his subsequent novella *Memoirs of Carwin the Biloquist* (1803 - 1805), we learn that in *Wieland* Carwin was being ironic, and that his pairing of the two cultures was a way of asserting that Spain's Catholicism was as delusional as England's Protestantism, both resulting from religious ventriloquism, and the same could be said of England's projection of Spain as antithesis.

NINETEENTH CENTURY

Brown's rational explanation for Anglo bigotry was no match for the white American ethnocentric mysticism expressed in Manifest Destiny, the national belief in a providentially ordained destiny to possess Mexican lands, avenging past centuries of Spanish hegemony. The result was the trumped-up Mexican-American War (1846–1848). For Americans not enchanted by the ethnocentrism of Anglo supremacy, the annexation of half of Mexico provoked much introspection on what is American, as summarized by Whitman: "It is as if we were somehow being endow'd with a vast and more thoroughly-appointed body, then left with little or no soul."[31] Ulysses S. Grant, served in the War with Mexico and later wrote:

> I was bitterly opposed to the measure [to annex Texas], and to this day regard the war [with Mexico] which resulted as one of the most unjust ever waged by a stronger against a weaker nation. It was an instance of a republic following the bad example of European monarchies, in not considering justice in their desire to acquire additional territory.[32]

In literature that would qualify for our imagined textbook, the post-Mexican War southwest produced translated works by absorbed Mexicans now Americans, early Mexican-American testimonials on cultural encounter and clashes, and Anglo writings that contemplate the Mexican culture now part of an expanded America. In fiction, the southwest acquisition produced works of Hispanic

---

[30] Charles Brockden Brown, *Wieland and Memoirs of Carwin the Biloquist* (New York: Penguin, 1991), 83.

[31] *Democratic Vistas, and Other Papers Hardcover* (N.P.: Andesite Press, 2015), 13.

[32] *Memoirs of U.S. Grant*, The Project Gutenberg, https://www.gutenberg.org/files/4367/4367-h/4367-h.htm#:~:text=For%20myself%2C%20I%20was%20bitterly%20opposed%20to%20the%20measure%2C%20and%20to%20this%20day%20regard%20the%20war%2C%20which%20resulted%2C%20as%20one%20of%20the%20most%20unjust%20ever%20waged%20by%20a%20stronger%20against%20a%20weaker%20nation

consciousness clashing with its new American circumstance, including works by white Americans.

This writing includes Helen Hunt Jackson's novel *Ramona* (1884), which disproves the fancy of a strict border between the cultures, the story of a Scottish–Native American orphan girl in newly acquired Southern California defined by Mexican culture. Also noteworthy for the theme of cultural encounter in the west are the western stories of O. Henry (William Sydney Porter), tales of colorful, sly heroes and *bandidos*, among them an original version of El Zorro. Some of O. Henry's western stories, paradigms of Eastern fascination with the West from a writer more famous for his urbane New York stories, could be read as if a Latino wrote them.

A direct Latino antecedent of this western American chapter is *The Squatter and the Don* (1885) by María Amparo Ruíz de Burton, the first Mexican-American novel in response to the injustices that befell on suddenly-American Mexican lives. Ruiz de Burton's novel not only shows a Mexican-American literary lineage but is also precursor of later mainstream writings that incur on the Southwestern cultural intersection, as Willa Cather's Mexicanized American character in *O Pioneers!* (1913).

Of course, at this juncture our textbook would provide reference discussion on the idea of a cultural intersection as toxic to a traditional American ideal that celebrates an immutable white male protagonist and resistance to cultural or racial impurity as narrated in the traditional The American Story. In that enchantment, Leatherstocking who walked the paths of Indians didn't become a white Indian; the southern slaveholder didn't desire black women but inseminated them, nor did white Southerners learn to eat African foods and dance to African music and worship like Africans; southwestern Anglo men supposedly didn't marry Mexican women and adopt Mexican dress and the macho swagger of the Mexican vaqueros. Instead, ethnocentrically Americans applied their inherited Puritan gift of redacting reality in texts in order to perpetuate in the imagination a purely Anglo-Protestant continuity.

Before the end of the nineteenth century, American imperialism that had grabbed the northern half of Mexico, looked to expand American influence into other parts of Latin America. Among the key writers as selections of that era could be included the Cuban José Martí, a leader of the struggle against Spain for Cuban independence. Born five years after the Treaty of Guadalupe-Hidalgo (1848) ceded half of Mexico and distant from the implications of that war, Martí left in exile for New York City optimistically still harboring a belief in the U.S. as democratic role model and believing in a pan-Americanism that included Anglo America. In his eighteen-years residence in New York City, this optimism lost its credibility and he finally wrote the essay *Our America*–landmark in Latin

American letters and ironically an antecedent of Latino not only in having been composed in New York but, when first translated in 1977, in being the modern model of a unified Latin American identity.

As with Manifest Destiny, American imperialism divided Americans along the fault lines that could be traced as antecedent to today's culture war, a loss of idealism that produced a literary, post-Romantic realism, what we discover in Melville's story "Benito Cereno," based on a true account reported in newspapers. Our textbook, unlike traditional texts, would point out the allusions to both Spanish and Spanish American history interwoven into a story written on the brink of war over slavery as well as invite discussion on what today would be considered the story's multicultural Queer subtext. Another important literary response to American imperialism is William Dean Howells' "Editha," a critique of America's provoking the Spanish-American War in Cuba and the American indifference to lives lost in another culture.

Another selection for our textbook among nineteenth-century authors can be Walt Whitman's open letter "The Spanish Element in Our Nationality." In 1883, when Santa Fe, New Mexico would celebrate 333 years of settlement if one counted since a founding date of 1550 (historians today affix that original settlement in 1610), Walt Whitman was invited to write a commemorative poem. Whitman instead sent the open letter "The Spanish Element in Our Nationality," published in papers throughout the country, in which he corrected the ethnocentrism of a solely Anglo-Saxon American heritage without Hispanic contributions to American culture in the creation of the national identity.

Whitman's poems, in the tradition of Freneau, invoked Columbus as symbol of Spanish contact with the Americas and as emblem of facets of the American spirit in "Prayer to Columbus," "Passage to India" and "A Thought of Columbus."[33] In those poems Whitman also subtextually returns by way of Columbus as metaphor to the "Columbian" revolutionary spirit of American origin, not looking to England as mother, but to Spain. This harkening is expressed explicitly in his homage to the First Spanish Republic, "Spain, 1873-74": "(A glimpse of thy Mother's face Columbia,....)//Nor think we forget thee maternal;...."

Whitman's seeing Spain as maternal at the end of the century would not seem so unexpected if contextualized in a Transcendentalist resurgent Hispanophilia that William Hickling Prescott is credited with having started with the successful publication of *History of the Conquest of Mexico* (1839) and *History of the*

---

[33] One would have to assign these poems to today's students reminding them that they are to be read for what they say about Whitman's being of his time and his not considering Columbus' racial record but inventing a Columbus that embodies his inclusive ideals.

Conquest of Peru (1847). Extending that Hispanophilia, Washington Irving looked to Spain for roots that intertwined with his American culture in *The Alhambra* and *The Life and Voyages of Christopher Columbus*. His *History of New York* is written in a strange English that imitates not only Spanish but more specifically imitates Cervantes' prose. The Washington Irving that Americans were likely to know wrote about Sleepy Hollow, Ichabod Crane, and Rip Van Winkle, not the writer who was professor of Spanish at Harvard.

Irving's interest in Spanish history is presumed totally disconnected from his writing of American lore and culture. Of course, his Iberian fascination suggests parallels and branches out of the same American romanticism, which also explains the Transcendentalist Emerson's knowledge of Spanish literature, which he displayed in his reviews of translations and other Spanish-themed books. Two such reviews found in the journal *The Dial* are of books by his Harvard language-teacher colleague, Henry Wadsworth Longfellow. One was the published script of Lowell's adaptation of Cervantes's play *La Gitanilla*, titled *The Spanish Student*, essentially a Spanish play written in English, and another was a volume of Lowell's translations from Spanish poetry.

Henry Wadsworth Longfellow, a professor of both French and Spanish, was a literary multiculturalist, seeing American literature as composed of a variety of characteristics of other national literatures, "embracing French, Spanish, Irish, English, Scotch and German peculiarities."[34] Under this influence, Lowell wrote the poems "Torquemada," on the Inquisition, and "The Jewish Cemetery at Newport," on the first Jewish settlers in the colonies, who were Sephardic: "The very names recorded here are strange,/ Of foreign accent, and of different climes; /Alvares and Rivera interchange/ With Abraham and Jacob of old times."[35]

Longfellow's replacement at Harvard, James Russell Lowell, also taught Spanish and Spanish literature, which influenced his own work although less so but still an important part of his work that is not conventionally highlighted in textbooks. An updated textbook like ours might contain the poem "The Nightingale in the Study," about the playwright Calderón de la Barca, and a Lowell poem written in Spanish, "Casa de Alma," and from his prose pieces collected as *The Bigelow Papers*, a section satirizing the U.S. war with Mexico.

---

[34] Lauren Simek, "The Sounds of Narrative in Longfellows's *Evangline*," in *Reconsidering Longfellow,* Christopher Irmscher and Robert Arbour, eds. (Teaneck: Fairleigh University Press, 2014), 90.

[35] Henry Wadsworth Longfellow, *The Complete Poetical Works of Henry Wadsworth Longfellow* (Windham, NH: Windham Press, 2013), 171.

Of course, one cannot complete this discussion of nineteenth-century writings without underscoring Mark Twain as a child of Cervantes, as first argued by Olin Harris Moore in "Mark Twain and *Don Quixote*"[36] and many more scholars since then. Moore noted: "Mark Twain's admiration for Cervantes was destined to grow steadily. While he was composing *Huckleberry Finn*, he actually took occasion to put himself on record as choosing Cervantes as his standard-bearer against Walter Scott and the "romantic frauds." Moore argued that not just the life of Huck Finn but as well *Tom Sawyer* and *Innocents Abroad* descended from the *Quixote*.

TWENTIETH CENTURY

Entering the twentieth century, the incidents of Hispanic literary influences can and does fill books of criticism. Best known are Hemingway's novels set in Spain, *The Sun Also Rises* and *For Whom the Bells Tolls*, and his novella set in Cuba, *The Old Man and the Sea*. In the same vein Katherine Anne Porter's most anthologized story "Flowering Judas," is set in the Mexican Revolution, a multicultural connection that graduate students might come upon but is not foregrounded in a mainstream remembrance of Porter, who explains her obsession with Mexico in the essay "Why I Write about Mexico." Topics for discussion: What have twentieth-century American writers sought in Hispanic culture to understand their American identity? Why did those writers seek exile outside instead of—like the Beats—inside the United States?

Latino writers who were English majors were probably never be assigned to read the philosopher, poet, cultural critic, and novelist George Santayana, who since his death in 1952 has been little remembered as writer (although, judging from the number of websites currently devoted to him, he seems to be enjoying a revival). Renowned as philosopher and cultural critic, he was twice on the cover of *Time*; his only novel *The Last Puritan* (1936) was a *N.Y. Times* best-seller. Among his insights was the inevitability of today's culture war: "On the other hand, a crude but vital America has sprung up from the soil, undermining, feeding, and transforming the America of tradition."[37]

American as writer, he was legally Spanish, born in Spain, in 1863, of a Catalan mother born in Scotland. Widowed by her first husband, to whom she had promised to raise his three children in the U.S., she married a Spaniard with political ambitions in Spain. On their amicable divorce, as she had complied with her promise to her first husband, to return to America, she had to promise her

---

[36] *PMLA* vol. 37 (Jun 1, 1922): 326.

[37] George Santayana, *Character and Opinion in the United States* (New York: Scribner's 1924), 140.

second husband that his son would never surrender his Spanish citizenship. Out of loyalty to his father, whom he began to see during summers while in Harvard, never became an American citizen, although he had also realized early on that, having no roots in New England's "genteel tradition" he would always feel alienated.

Bias was an inelegant way of putting it back then, but bias was what obstructed his fellow New Englander's appreciating that, under the influence of his father, Santayana profoundly shared the Westernist underpinnings of that "genteel tradition." He did not identify with the more literally applied democratic values threatening America's traditional social order and therefore New England's genteel distinction. That cruder, threatening America included its minorities, with which Santayana wouldn't have identified, too much the Bostonian and the classist Spaniard.

Latin America at that time, from both an Anglo-American and Spanish viewpoint, was a nonentity on the world's intellectual map, and America's Southwest was not yet part of the American mindset, much less its Mexican American population. Although the future great Latin American writers of this century were starting to publish throughout his life, the English-speaking world would not discover them until the late sixties. Indeed, Santayana would be called a conservative today. But that does not make him less an antecedent Latino, being a profound paradigm of the shifting lenses–Anglo and Hispanic, American and European–through which he contemplated American culture. He is a writer too nuanced to be simplistically categorized and therefore overlooked, however transparent the "incorrect" political leanings one can extrapolate from them.

For example, while he did not identify with the impending democratic society nor would have identified with today's woke vision of an alternate America, he sublimated a private, alternate consciousness in his writings. In *The Last Pilgrim* his protagonist Oliver Alden is a metaphor of the New England culture with which another part of him didn't identify.[38] Alden had always acted out of duty but is incapable of allowing to be led by feelings. One can extrapolate from that metaphor suppressed homosexual drives as well the more common Latino critique of comparatively less emotional Anglo Americans, with whom Santayana felt no communion. In Boston, Santayana's family spoke only Spanish at home;[39] his half-sister Susana, fed up with Boston, left to live in Spain. At 48, despite the pleadings of Harvard's president, Santayana left his

---

[38] George Santayana, *The Last Pilgrim: A Memoir in the Form of a Novel* (Cambridge: M.I.T. Press, 1924).

[39] George Santayana, *People and Places: The Background of My Life* (Glasgow: Good Press, 2021).

eminent position as professor of philosophy to resettle in Europe from which he never returned.

Santayana's contemporary, the poet William Carlos Williams, offered a competing take on America, determined to claim an American identity without betraying an inherited literary and personal Hispanic "line." Williams' response to traditional America as personal challenge prefigures the post-civil rights questioning of traditional America, and foreshadows the multiculturalism that in our time is mistakenly interpreted as a recent political invention of liberalism and a post-seventies minority emergence. That Williams is not taught in standard curricula but should figure importantly in our textbook because Williams as antecedent of Latino writing is evident in several recurring themes that intersect with also Puerto Rican writing across his complete works of poetry, fiction, essays and plays.

Langston Hughes lived for a brief time with his father in Mexico, covered the Spanish Civil War as a foreign correspondent for the *Baltimore Afro-American* newspaper, wrote a series of poems on the war, and purportedly attended bullfights with Ernest Hemingway. Hughes' African American colleague, Richard Wright lived five years in Mexico before traveling to Paris, where he lived out his days as an expatriate. In 1957 Wright published *Pagan Spain*, a critical essay on Spain during the Franco dictatorship, an insightful demystification of the romancing of Spain in American letters. John Steinbeck's work offers a gallery of Hispanic characters (Kino and Juana of *The Pearl*, Lee of *East of Eden*, Danny of *Tortilla Flat*). Wallace Stevens' identified with the "soul" of a Cuba to which he never traveled but dreamed about in almost half his poems and through his exchange of letters with José Rodríguez Feo.

Better known for his *USA Trilogy* of novels, John Dos Passos, son of a Portuguese immigrant, grew up American yet also conscious of his Iberian roots, which contributed to his early left-wing political commitment. He traveled to the Soviet Union to study socialism and expressed that consciousness in his earlier writings and in his writing of the propaganda film *The Spanish Earth*, in support of Spain's Republican cause. Later, disillusioned by Communism, he wrote against it. After a season in Spain, he assumed the persona of a young Quixote in his book of essays, *Rosinante to the Road Again*.

In the second half of the twentieth century, of course, emerge the first writers identified as Latino. The three Pulitzer Prize winners, Oscar Hijuelos, Junot Díaz, and most recently Lin-Manuel Miranda most notably represent two generations that have produced a catalog of first-rate writers that I leave as summary to explore because attempting a representative list would express a preference and an omission would suggest critique. Our imagined textbook has much to include to properly cover Latino writing into the millennium and today.

The overriding point of this abbreviated, incomplete overview of American letters is to refine Stanley Williams' initial 1950's thesis based on an anachronistic monolithic "Spanish" background. In the second half of the twentieth century the Latin American emergence alerted the world to separate civilizations branching out from a shared language and literary history and against that broader *latino* background that encompassed "U.S. Hispanic" emerged a new American writing that expressed a "Latino" consciousness and indeed was also informed by the Latin American emergence but as well rooted in the breadth of American writing if not read, the modus operandi of ethnocentric criticism, to perpetuate the enchantment of The American Story.

Latino writing is indeed rooted in American literature through what Stanley Williams called its "Spanish background"; where Latino writers have no roots is in how that literature is taught in their American education, which expunges not just a Spanish background but a thematic multiculturalism as an American literary tradition. In sum, for the Latino writer, an American literary history exists of inclusive mainstream precursors with a vein of direct Hispanic cultural and literary influence, the legacy not taught in school.

PART 2:
LATINO ILLUSIONS, LATINO REALITIES

6.

A HISTORY OF FLIGHTS

I was four months old when I first boarded an airplane. The year was 1946. My mother held me in one arm as her other hand guided my almost three-year-old sister. The plane, my mother told me years later, was a bullet-pocked war veteran, the seats wooden folding chairs. We flew at the start of the postwar Puerto Rican diaspora to New York not for the better-known socioeconomic reasons. My mother was leaving my adulterous father and the life of a divorced woman in a then more Catholic Puerto Rico.

A more traditional woman might have resigned herself to the adulterous proclivity of Puerto Rican men and waited out his contrite return. It took me decades to reconstruct the details that culminated in this flight and understand why, convinced by sisters and my father's promises, we flew back to San Juan from where, shortly thereafter, we flew back again, this time to start a new life in my godmother aunt's apartment in a Bronx neighborhood still partly Jewish. Because my mother and godmother harbored the determination to someday return and kept close ties with their four other sisters who remained on the island, we were destined to take more flights.

Flights also resolved the need for my care summers after I started school.[1] At the end of every June I flew to San Juan with my godmother who scheduled her vacation to escort me. At the end of August, I flew back in the care of a flight attendant, a job in those days considered strictly a woman's, then titled a "stewardess." For the better part of my life, this shuttle between mainland and island was its centerpiece, sewing a sense of being from both mainland and island. At some point when I looked back at my life, I realized that I was born with the birth of commercial aviation, and not just me but Puerto Ricans of those times were its by-products, performers in a history determined by generations of evolving aircraft.

My most memorable flights were the first back to the island, solemn rituals imbued with the collective sadness of our mass separation, every flight foreshadowing an eventual glorious final return. Fifties dress codes contributed to the solemnity because, as in old movies, in public people more commonly dressed in what today we would describe as "up," men in suits and women in

---

[1] My sister had already been rescued from American morals, having been sent to be schooled in Puerto Rico by nuns.

dresses. Consequently, given the importance of the occasion, my mother, godmother aunt, my sister and I left for the airport dressed as if to attend church, a comparison not hyperbole because Idlewild airport –renamed in 1963 after John F. Kennedy's assassination– was practically a cathedral, the place where, souls folded in suitcases, Puerto Ricans went to be transported to their sacred ancestral land.

We always took the cheaper night flights. Family friends followed us in a second car. They helped with the suitcases and because at the airport they were going to be closer to their Caribbean temple. Absent today's terrorist threat, they accompanied us to the boarding gate, where my aunt was entrusted with a shopping bag of items requested in airmail letters. Last hugs, we passed the boarding gate, and those who stayed took the stairs to the terminal's "Observation Roof."

My aunt would only let us fly on Pan American,[2] the first and largest commercial line and one of two (the other being Eastern) that offered nonstop flights between New York and San Juan. In 1950 when I was four years old, its flagship aircraft was the four-propeller "Yankee Clipper," its commercial version of an airline that started delivering mail. In a publicity pamphlet photo of that time, the Yankee Clipper looked huge even though, from nose to tail, it wasn't that much longer than the wingspan of today's biggest jets.

Boarding those planes was more romantic than today's hike through a covered ramp. As seen in old movies, passengers paraded on the tarmac toward a movable ladder parked against the plane. One climbed up and before entering would turn around and wave toward the "Observation Roof." The flight took eight hours.

We always flew on summer night flights and the cabin lacked air conditioning, so the interior was suffocating. Cooler air awaited in the sky, but until then the only relief came from a small fan above each passenger's seat. In that cabin heat, my aunt would take me down the aisle between pairs of seats until she found ours, mine always by the window.

Having flown since my seat belt was my mother's arms, I knew how to fasten myself. My aunt, muttering to herself, first stored the shopping bag under the seat in front of my hanging feet before adjusting her seatbelt and opening her purse to take out her rosary. Murmuring, she stroked the beads with her thumb and index finger while, if we were assigned seats on the best side, I looked through the small window in the direction of the Observation Roof. I saw little more than lights and silhouettes of heads but I waved my hand in the hope that

---

[2] Founded in 1927 by an American investor with the ironic name Juan Trippe.

my mother could recognize it was me. From that Observation Roof, when my family was seeing others off, for ten cents I looked through a green, oval-shaped binocular viewfinder. Identifying a face in the small window lit a collective breast and every heart ascended in flight with them, *Adiós! Adiós!*

This time I was flying. Cabin doors shut, the propellers started whirling, the trembling cabin advanced on the tarmac for a distance that seemed endless as one of the two stewardesses demonstrated how to put on the life jacket. Knowing the lesson by heart, I didn't pay attention and neither did my aunt, who placed more trust in the Hail Marys she had been murmuring since before breaking out the rosary, since before boarding the plane, since we passed the boarding gate. As the plane started to take flight, the volume of her prayer rose with it while the other stewardesses offered small yellow or pink two-piece boxes of Chicklets. The science of chewing never failed to pop out air that clogged my ears. I trusted the Chicklets more than my aunt's prayers. Until one unforgettable flight.

It had started out especially happy because my mother and sister were flying with us. Being a night flight, after takeoff I rested my head, as I always did, on my godmother's lap, looking forward to waking up to the radiant Caribbean dawn, its crisp blue sky, where gleaming silver wings sliced across epic sculptures of bleached clouds.

But this time I woke up in a low-light, unable to lift my head because my aunt pressed it tightly against her lap. Her palm over my ear muffled cabin cries and groans louder than her appeals to Mary as the rosary bounced against my hair. Then the plane simply stopped flying, falling freely, its downward incandescent streak my visualization of the unison scream, mine among them, a fall that suddenly ceased with the leveled plane bouncing as if suspended from a cable.

Its briefly regaining altitude calmed because I thought the terror had ended, but my aunt didn't release my head from her lap nor interrupt her *Santa María, madre de Dios, llena eres de gracia...*, which she suddenly prayed at the top of her lungs as the plane fell again and I screamed into her lap for my mother (sitting with my sister in another row) and again I visualized the luminous plane descending in total dark until again it ceased with a bounce, this pause after the previous treacherous ascent offering no relief. I continued to groan in my aunt's lap during this respite, two more descents, bounces and climbs, continuous my aunt's prayer in her loudest voice, until Mary herself, I came to believe, calmed the winds and the plane, also dispelling any fear of flying.

More traumatic resulted being torn from Puerto Rico's sunlit clarity, from the warmth of extended family, to resume my growing up a latchkey kid in the solitude of a constantly cloudy apartment in New York. That solitude began with flying back alone, handed to a stewardess, who seated me in her sight among other children in her care. On those return flights the non-tourist passengers made me wonder why so many were leaving behind the island's colors and warmth.

Years later I would learn they too felt torn away and that they flew out of economic necessity, flying without imagining the drop in temperature that awaited them. U.S. citizens but cultural immigrants, they traveled without needing a passport or knowledge of the country that claimed them, of which they knew little more than that English was spoken. At that time no one knew that they were also making history: the first massive influx to the U.S. on airplanes.

The history of Puerto Rican migration opens after the First World War when, American citizens by fiat in 1917, more cosmopolitan islanders boarded ships that transported them to New York, a migration that picked up before World War II, creating a small Puerto Rican community that in the thirties and forties blended with Spanish immigrants to form New York's "Spanish" community.

Chiefly white islanders who at first experienced ethnic hostility, they later enjoyed The Good Neighbor policy's recognizing white "Latin." They also planted a collective white image that overlapped the more racially-mixed postwar WWII diaspora reflecting more accurately the island's racial composition. This overlap resulted in, even though inspired by the postwar diaspora's travails, *West Side Story*'s being written about on an ethnically-harassed, not a racially stigmatized community, virtually the latest European immigration: "I Like to Live in America."[3]

After World War II, high unemployment and the abandonment of agriculture in favor of industry in Puerto Rico resulted in the iconic post-war migration to New York, an exporting of poverty designed into the industrialization initiative. The project was bicoastal, with the collaboration of New York City planners looking to replace the loss in the garment industry of upwardly-mobile Jews.[4] Islanders began to board a repurposed wartime cargo ship, the Marine Tiger, whose name came to label any green, inept Puerto Rican in New York. For a time, the Marine Tiger also served as a symbol of the migration.

---

[3] This white image remained after the war to be represented in the Sharks in *West Side Story*, later criticized as a distortion of postwar Puerto Rican racial demographics although it was the same postwar community and vestiges of the prewar community that preserved island racial attitudes, cultivating the whiter image of migration, provoking the more realistic response of the second generation in the 1960s, the properly Newyorican.

[4] The new workers were offered to New York exploiting the early white Puerto Rican racial image of the smaller pre-war community, which enjoyed the embrace given to Latin America during the Good Neighbor Policy.

But the majority actually arrived on airplanes. The relocation went into high gear after the island government convinced Pan American Airways that it would see more profits on frequent flights with a super-cheap fare ($25.00 in 1950's currency) multiplied by entrepreneurs, tourists who would vacation in newly built hotels, plus return visits of nostalgic Puerto Ricans. Eastern Airlines soon offered the same fare, while, on the industrializing island, public service announcements conveyed the benefits that awaited anyone who flew to neighboring isle of Manhattan.

Thousands boarded planes, and the reduced island poverty along with the success of industrialization contributed to the optimism of the island's "permanent union" with the United States, ratified by a plebiscite in 1952. Officially, a *freely agreed* on permanent pact between an ostensibly autonomous Puerto Rico and the United States, the island's new status was an *Estado Libre Asociado*, literally an Associated Free State, officially translated "Commonwealth." A former UN ambassador of then-Ceylon (today Sri Lanka) once explained that "Commonwealth" misled the international body into approving a truly autonomous political status like that of the former members of the British Empire. In Puerto Rico, "Commonwealth" only camouflaged an unchanged colonial relationship.

In 1952 Pan American was already flying its new flagship plane, the Constellation. Pressurized cabins made the Chicklets obsolete and the flight was reduced to six hours. Constellation was the name of the model produced by Lockheed, so Eastern kept pace with its own Constellation, and during the Eisenhower years, its pressurized cabins relocated Puerto Ricans in New York boroughs other than Manhattan's already crowded "El Barrio," the incrementing Puerto Rican demographics already changing New York City's script to extremely unfavorable reviews.

Particular hostility was expressed toward teenagers, who were forming gangs. Emblematic of that era was Salvador Agrón, the leader of the gang The Vampires. Agrón was born in Puerto Rico and constantly shuttled by plane between dysfunctional parents. In 1959, he was sixteen and, wearing a stolen black "Dracula" cape, led his gang to a city park to rumble with another gang that didn't show. Two non-Hispanic boys in the park ended up dead, and Agrón and another gang member, Luis Hernandez, 17, were convicted of killing them. At sixteen Agrón was the youngest person in New York State condemned to die in the electric chair. Three days before his scheduled execution, his sentence was commuted by Governor Nelson Rockefeller. (Hernandez's sentence had been overturned due to a lack of evidence that he actually stabbed someone.)

Agrón had always denied killing anybody, but his teenage bombast had forever demonized him. "My mother can see me fry!," I read at 13 in *The Daily News* that my aunt or mother would daily bring home and saw the photograph of a vampire-grinning teen spreading out his Dracula cape, images that immortalized him as, how *The News* dubbed him, The Capeman. In 1977 Agrón was released from prison and died in 1986 of a heart attack. His troubled story inspired Paul Simon's musical, *The Capeman* (1998).

Around the same time that Agrón was said to have committed the murders another Puerto Rican gang was rumbling on Broadway. Playwright Arthur Laurent and composer Leonard Bernstein, who had originally planned a musical about the conflict between the Irish and Jews, saw more timely metaphors in the drama of Puerto Ricans, thus creating *West Side Story* (1957), a love story set in the confrontation of two gangs, the Jets and the Sharks, with Puerto Ricans as metaphors of those that America did not forgive for merely being–the theme that Paul Simon picked up in his musical.

The gang names in *West Side Story* are actually malapropisms. The Jets were grandchildren of immigrants who arrived on ships, while the Sharks represented a migration still arriving on planes. None, strictly speaking, had arrived by jet, not yet in commercial use, one anachronism of two, the other to which I shall return, but the musical's historical accuracy was misinterpreted as erroneous in the sixties by the diaspora's second generation that condemned the musical for stereotyping Puerto Ricans as having a proclivity toward gang violence. The musical was, in fact, accurate American history of which Puerto Ricans were a part: those were the fifties of the problematic teenager, the decade of the films *Blackboard Jungle* (1955) and *Rebel without a Cause* (1955).

In 1957, Pan Am and Eastern upgraded the New York-San Juan route to the propjet, a propeller plane aided by jet propulsion, technology from the end of WWII that took a decade to be commercially adapted. The propjet shortened the trip to and from Puerto Rico from six hours to four, a shortened flight that contributed significantly to the island's economic transformation. Speeding up the industrialization, the project stitched the island to American industry, fueling confidence in the Puerto Rican economy that, after 1959, was promoted as the "Miracle in the Caribbean" to cast shade on the Cuban Revolution. But its four-hour flight also accelerated the importation of American values, manners, and popular culture, so the economy that it was helping to build up was also nurturing contrary visions of either a viable statehood or a future independence.

A major symbol of confidence in the Puerto Rican economy was Trans Caribbean Airways. In 1945, the real estate investor O. Roy Chalk had founded Trans Caribbean in San Juan to fly mail between Puerto Rico and surrounding Caribbean islands. Seeing that for the already lucrative New York-San Juan route the only two airlines offered service in English to chiefly Spanish-speaking passengers, in 1958 Chalk leased a fleet of propjets, placed ads in the two New York Spanish-language newspapers *El Diario* and *La Prensa*[5] and made deals with Cofresí Travel, an agency focused on the Puerto Rican market.

Trans Caribbean employed the children and grandchildren of those who had arrived on the Marine Tiger and the Yankee Clipper. Flight attendants– still strictly women "stewardesses" --wore the uniform designed by Mrs. Chalk, with a hat "that was supposed to be a copy of the Spanish Cordovan hat, the blue color in aqua,"[6] representing the Caribbean's Spanish heritage. In reality their flights were more in the tradition of the rural bus with chickens and roosters and overloaded packages. Trans Caribbean became famous for its loud-mouthed jokers and pint bottle drinkers that were often denied boarding. The most colorful flights were the invariably off-schedule, officially advertised as midnight "Kikiriki" flights that arrived with the "Ki-ki-ri-ki" of Spanish-crowing roosters.

When I was a young teenager, my mother's having married and our family's economic circumstances having improved allowed me to fly in the morning. Thanks to the propjet, I flew at dawn and had lunch at the house of one of the four of my eight aunts who stayed on the island. The propjet not only cut flight time, it flew above the storms that had shaken the "Yankee Clipper" over the Atlantic. But a few good features of those earlier flights were lost. The view from the window of the propjet was now monotonously blue. Far below floated the epic cloud sculptures, now visible as a lumpy white carpet. The passengers too had changed. If on the Constellation I traveled with mainly insecure-looking islanders leaving for the first time, in the propjet many were like me, returning to visit the island or returning to homes in Manhattan, Brooklyn, or the Bronx.

The propjet was really an economical choice made by airlines over available advanced technology that had commercially debuted the same year, the Boeing 707 jet. Pan Am put it into service in 1958 and Eastern upgraded its fleets but neither immediately for service to San Juan. By the late sixties the Boeing 707 had become standard although not reigning alone for long before we flew the McDonnell-Douglas DC, Trans Caribbean's choice. The pure jet crossed the Atlantic in three hours and fifteen minutes, and it was on the pure jet that Puerto Rican passengers began the practice of applauding when the wheels of the plane touched the island.

---

[5] This was the moment when he decided to invest even more in the expanding mainland Puerto Rican community, seeing the advantage of buying the two papers and eliminating competition between them by merging them into one, *El Diario* (1963).

[6] "Trans Caribbean Airways," Wikipedia, https://en.wikipedia.org/wiki/Trans_Caribbean _Airways

Landing on the island had always provoked a public expression of jubilance, but something about the jet's arrival drew an ovation. Tourists looked around appearing to think: maybe these people, unfamiliar with technology, were even simpler than we thought. Feelings of returning home may explain the urge to applaud, but applause also burgeoned from another chamber of the Puerto Rican psyche. The jet's consistent choreography, invoking the energy to make tons weightless, its silky cruising speed, and finally its ballet-precise descent provoke the secular reaction of a people with a legacy of flight as also a spiritual event.

Those feelings explain why, if at first the applause celebrated only the return to Puerto Rico, over time the custom spread to arrivals in New York, appreciating the same aesthetics in acknowledging that now also New York was home. Of course, those who applauded and still applaud are of a certain, folkier social class, not the islander who flies to Atlanta or Boston, whose not applauding becomes an identifier.

In 1970 Pan American added the Boeing Jumbo 747, with its distinctive bulb top and its first-class lounge. I never got to see it, but for a brief time the jumbo offered a tail-section lounge with a bar and meeting space. A lounge with a bar may have sounded like good business in the abstract, but in addition to not paying for itself, as explained to me by a stewardess, the bar proved problematic with unruly passengers, resulting in that space's being filled with seats.

In 1971, American Airlines acquired Trans Caribbean, marking this New York-San Juan flight, originally promoted as a scheme by the Puerto Rican government, as a major market. By the end of the century, Pan American and Eastern had gone bankrupt, but one could fly to Puerto Rico on several more airlines and from many more cities, notably from Atlanta through Delta and TWA until the latter went bankrupt in 2001. TWA's route to Puerto Rico was picked up by Spirit, an economy airline about to shake up the industry by eliminating meals and entertainment, charging for suitcases and seat selection.

Through the second half of the twentieth century, island financial crises prompted more migration from Puerto Rico, this time from the social class that would not be confused with the Sharks and not bound for New York because an island class-conscious travel culture had already been established. At Luis Muñoz Marín Airport, the upper- and middle-class white passenger was probably not flying to New York or even the Northeast, more likely Atlanta, or Orlando, where Puerto Ricans were becoming that city's largest Latino demographic. Behind this pattern operated other cultural tensions aggravated by the advantages of the jet.

For the islander, the jet assuaged the trauma of leaving, symbolizing the possibility of a quick return. For mainland Ricans the jet liberated the homing consciousness to migrate out of New York to Hartford, Allentown, Chicago, Boston. In three hours and fifteen minutes Puerto Ricans scattered over the Northeast could converge on the island for a wedding or a wake. In other words, the jet redrew the mental map, putting the island so much closer, providing the illusion that little would change, that things continued as they always were, while the same jet daily delivered evidence that diaspora and island Puerto Ricans were changing in opposite directions.

Those who left the island as the poorest now landed economically middle class without a middle-class Hispanic culture. That lack degraded them and islanders mocked their poor or no Spanish. In defense, the Newyoricans resorted to the contradiction of flaunting the same English that on the mainland was spoken proudly seasoned with words in Spanish. Contradicting the pride thrown back at white America, they defensively invoked its supremacist anthropology, defending their New York blunt manner as culturally superior to subtler, devious Hispanic formality. They counter-criticized islanders who flaunted a Hispanic identity that was just a translation of American culture, islanders' daring to mock the Newyoricans' having become English speakers when they themselves have become bilingual to the point that even many educated islanders could no longer complete a thought purely in Spanish.

Islanders dismissed those retorts that they heard coming from a lack of knowledge of authentic Puerto Rican complexity, being the despair of a minority mentality intellectually limited by its American circumstance to truly understand today's Puerto Rico. Mainland Ricans based their Puerto Rican identity on giving importance to a diaspora history that the island already disowns, already prefers to forget. The Newyorican does not appreciate how, despite being politically trapped in a colonial fake autonomy, today's islanders have creatively subverted their political connection with the United States and evolved culturally and intellectually sovereign, part of the collage that is modern Latin America.

The mainland Puerto Rican community was indeed seeing the island through a different lens, having developed a personality of its own informed not by living an islander's situationally-applied American consciousness but by having to live actual American lives. Second generation youth, having seen their parents act with good island manners socially interpreted by white America as a recognition of deserving the humiliation they received, lost island subtlety, island obliqueness, learning from New York to respond brazenly, "in your face." Hostility turned mere living into a political act, and anger became the American identity from whose point of view Newyoricans tried to understand their Puerto Ricanness. A constant vigilance against contempt makes clinging to being Puerto Rican a recovery of a lost history, recovering the *abuelita* who once embraced every family member.

Unfortunately, that *abuelita* was becoming extinct even on the island more Americanized and materialized even as it speaks of itself as rooted in a tradition disconnected from mainland concerns. In that denial, Puerto Rico therefore did not respond sympathetically to the problems of a racial and social class that, compartmentalized in Puerto Rico, by accident of fate in New York now misrepresented an entire people. To the islanders whose mythic Puerto Rico had historically been a Spanish *patria chica*, the common denominator of-color-conscious Newyorican is an unrecognizable concatenation of the poorest white *jíbaro* mythos and the traditionally compartmentalized black *cocolo* marginality, and whose first language is English.

Newyoricans also grated because their return made the islander's remote U.S. citizenship disturbingly real, bursting an autonomous psychological bubble that otherwise spares of a self-doubting, angry minority consciousness. Not personally experiencing American intolerance and resenting the pathetic image that the diaspora image imposed on all Puerto Ricans facilitated rationalizing that those mainland working-class people, virtually no longer Puerto Rican, were the cause of their own problems and that, for the more educated, white middle-class Puerto Ricans, American equality was possible.

That illusion was devastated by Hurricane María, in whose aftermath Trump did not treat islanders more respectfully. Gone with that wind was the sustained denial of the uncomfortable Puerto Rican reality imposed by Newyoricans, who had only inspired a killing of the messenger until Trump imposed the same harsh reality. María made landfall in 2017, and its devastation produced as collateral damage the denouement of an identity drama that began twenty-five years before, with the start of the postwar diaspora, and whose rising action had picked up speed after the first jet landed in San Juan in 1970.

However problematic, the mainland-island relationship does not impede that during a political crisis or a natural disaster both sides of the Atlantic make a truce. The island's government and humanitarian organizations appeal to the mainland Puerto Rican community's political influence in Washington. They essentially request that the community on the other side of the ocean forget how difficult the island can be, invoking the vestige of sentiment that Puerto Ricans are one. Thus motivated, many from the mainland flew to Vieques in support of the protest against the practice of Navy bombing and, more recently, ambassadors of that same solidarity boarded a jet to aid the island after María. Ironically too, owing to the resulting economic crisis after decades of island government's dysfunction, jets were now also instrumental in Puerto Rico's bleeding of professionals who resettled on the mainland, leaving behind the shattered economy in exchange for a more stable life in Orlando, Atlanta or this time even in New York.

This more recent migration converges with the Latin American immigration that began arriving in New York in the eighties. Nationally, of course, the greatest number of Latin American immigrants crossed the Mexican border, but except for Central Americans who cross Mexico to reach the border, hundreds of thousands arrived throughout the country on airplanes. Different from Puerto Ricans, they immigrate to begin a process of procuring their American citizenship.

Nevertheless, these *latino* immigrants repeat the same ceremony – even though the same can be said of those who cross the border with Mexico – in landing far from the traditional American immigrant mythos with its romance of ships arriving in New York Harbor in the sight of Lady Liberty. Whether landing from San Juan or Buenos Aires, the proverbial "coming to America" is not the same as it was for the Italians and Irish. Whether in the east or west, *latinos* don't see Lady Liberty and for every Latin American, including Puerto Ricans, the "Old Country" is America itself, an ever-concurrent present that never becomes the past one can shed. Moreover, their heritage is not immigrant but native as Hispanic is a major tributary of the nation's cultural history.

In the broadest view of hemispheric history, the causes of Latin Americans' emigrating can be traced to the Conquest but can also be narrowed down to more recent history: the economic or political dysfunction of countries, of course, prompted an exodus. But the American history of this immigration is incomplete without the historical context that prompted it, the native U.S. Hispanic history to which those immigrants were, in effect, also migrating.

Latin Americans emigrated in the Digital Age that, back home, had daily provided news about a United States that now respected civil rights and provided material benefits to its Hispanic minorities. Those opportunities, of course, had been won by the struggle of "U.S. Hispanics," eastern Puerto Ricans and western Mexican Americans, who in alliance with African Americans and Native Americans, had transformed the historically intolerant country, guaranteeing a better life for all *latinos*, including those yet to come. One hopes that history will not be rewritten as today that seems to be a political objective in the country's eastern half.

I underscore the more mottled eastern half because the Mexican American southwest, rooted in its geography and therefore its particular history, always keeps present its narrative. Constituting almost a third of the United States, those states are their own monument to their Mexican-American history. In contrast, as the opening chapter in the history of transoceanic Latin Americans in the United States, Puerto Ricans will only have as monument their history of flights that collective memory should preserve and curate. For that reason, monumental is the first Latina Supreme Court Justice Sonia Sotomayor, born in the Bronx of the postwar diaspora, the first transoceanic influx from Latin America, and who embodies the American legacy to be inherited by *latinos* recently arrived on airplanes.

My flight to Puerto Rico after Hurricane María took me to an unrecognizable island, not physically but psychologically. Trump had expressed the same antipathy he instilled at the border with Mexico, showing no respect for the difference that islanders had felt confident would separate them from Newyoricans and border crossers. Those beliefs that had comforted in seeming incontrovertible suddenly ceased to be valid, the wound aggravated by the deteriorating economy and the lack of federal interest in rescuing it, mainly from Puerto Rican governmental dysfunction.

This was not the industrialized island that a postwar generation had known. A sense of cloud hung over however bright the tropical day. With so many forced to leave, with so many now depending on political assistance of those Puerto Ricans who had been so easy to dismiss as Puerto Ricans, one sensed an identity crisis, a struggle to preserve island difference after having POTUS throw rolls of paper towels in their collective face.

Meanwhile, round-trip flights to and from the island continue crossing latitudes and longitudes of what is now a virtual large country, the island a hub to which flights depart from New York, Chicago, Boston, Atlanta and Orlando. Departing also from Puerto Rico's American ambiguity–a flight to Puerto Rico can be taken either from a domestic or international airport–today those flights are destined to land not just in San Juan but as well in Ponce, Mayagüez and Aguadilla. No one confuses the state of Oregon with another country but in the case of Puerto Rico it is popularly confused. Puerto Ricans self-define as undefined, also both between domestic and international: Puerto Rico has its own Olympic team.

Puerto Ricans also live the contradiction that at the same time that more efficient aircraft reduced the time to cross the Atlantic, the fissure within the culture grew to the size of an ocean. And still, no matter from which diaspora in our history of flights, no matter from what region of the virtual larger Puerto Rico, something said in the media or some conversation unexpectedly incites to recognize that on the island originates a key component of one's sense of self. At that moment, the soul that seemed settled and acclimatized feels a nostalgia whose first symptom is to become aware of a chill it had been ignoring, resisting, denying.

Suddenly the music most danced to – although much of it is now created in New York – and the food one most likes to eat reminds of a forgotten Caribbean warmth. We pay closer attention to a constant call less audible every day. One feels the urge to board a jet, go home even if one never came from there and even though one will not be entirely welcomed by a Puerto Rico that at least still preserves good manners. The flight, in fact, will be to an island that may have never existed, perhaps even prompting the vow never to return because Puerto Rican can be experienced more authentically on the mainland.

In New York's JFK, descendants of those passengers who dressed up and packed their souls in suitcases fly to the island maybe to keep in touch with blood, whose thickness every day grows thinner, or convinced just to enjoy the beaches, the music, the food. More consciously homing will fly passengers from more recent diasporas. In our more profane times, they all wear jeans or shorts and sneakers, dragging wheeled carry-ons filled only with material items. They arrive by medallion taxi or in a gypsy cab or in an Uber or on a public bus or in an Air Train or in the car of a friend or significant other. Friends who once accompanied in a second car to witness the takeoff from the "Observation Roof" today send text messages or call, virtual *abrazos* to those about to take a flight still existential but that long ago stopped being spiritual, departing from an airport now just an airport remodeled many times since the start of this history, when JFK was a cathedral called Idlewild.

7.

THE MAKING OF MIGUEL PIÑERO AND "THE WORLD OF THE NUYORICAN"

I suspect in praising me
You were not concerned so much with my desert
As with your power
That you praised me too arbitrarily
And took credit to yourself
In demonstrating that you could thrust
anything upon the world.

–Robert Frost

PIÑERO

In 1974 Joseph Papp produced the play *Short Eyes*[1] on Broadway to critical raves, showering overnight fame on playwright Miguel Piñero, who wrote this play as a member of a writer's workshop at the Sing Sing federal penitentiary in Ossining, New York. *Short Eyes* was nominated for six Tony awards, won that year's New York Critics Circle Award for "Best Play," and was later made into a movie. Over the next fourteen years, four more of Piñero's plays were staged, all Off-Off Broadway, each earning a *Village Voice* "Obie." He also acted in several films that included *Fort Apache: The Bronx,* and in numerous television series, notably as a drug lord in *Miami Vice.* He also wrote scripts for several hit television series, including *Miami Vice, Kojak,* and *Baretta.* In his scripts he always wrote a part for himself, a fictive version of his true-life person, a thief and drug addict, a lifestyle unchanged by success and fame until he died in 1988, at forty-two of cirrhosis of the liver.

His impure life is cleansed by the legend of the Lower East Side street genius given street cred for co-founding The Nuyorican Poets Café and giving a voice to what the other co-founder, poet Miguel Algarín, commercialized as "the World of the Nuyorican." Piñero's fame rubbed off on the Café and other poets who read there, drawing national media attention that imparted the confidence to

---

[1] The title comes from the Spanish-accented pronunciation of "short heist," prison jargon for child molestation.

purvey their New York Lower East Side as emblem of all mainland Puerto Ricans, replacing the mythos of El Barrio in East Harlem, and for a time making Piñero the most famous "Nuyorican" or mainland Puerto Rican writer.

That general assumption was also the basis of Leon Ichaso's 2001 biopic *Piñero,* in which the community to which Piñero supposedly gave a voice is represented by audible but invisible Café audiences that cheer readings of his poetry. Like a Greek chorus, the crowd tells the movie viewer how to respond and through them Piñero should become his admirers. Being their voice, this film is also implicitly about them, so judging him harshly becomes a judgment against those who identify with Nuyorican. And so, I write risking that accusation. Nevertheless, I proceed to put into sharper focus those years in which I witnessed the making of Piñero and the "World of the Nuyorican," which while politically correct as subjects to rally around are more culturally and intellectually problematic than pop summaries camouflage.

When *Short Eyes* premiered in 1974, "Nuyorican" as epithet lacked the credence that came with the growing media attention that Piñero brought to The Nuyorican Poets Café, which was promoting "Nuyorican" as a cultural identity. Calling the mainland Puerto Rican community "Nuyorican" sounded cool, a defiant re-Anglicization of the islander's defamatory *newyorican.* And even though Piñero's unfortunate life of drug addiction and crime should have made him unrepresentative of a more civil and vastly nuanced community that had challenged its depiction in *West Side Story,* for younger Ricans the glow of fame somehow justified making of Piñero that community's poster boy.

More plainly, "Nuyorican" promoted as epithet of a cultural identity was actually public relations that marketed both Piñero and "The World of the Nuyorican" as something that neither of them actually were, representative of the greater mainland Puerto Rican community. From conversations I have had with its chief promoter Miguel Algarín, the promotion was premised on scant knowledge or interest in mainland Puerto Ricans outside of New York's Lower East Side, a general disconnect among younger city Newyoricans exploited to promote also the Café. Pit that conclusion beside the fact that Piñero as a voice of the mainland Puerto Rican consciousness was belied by his writings that expressed his loathing of Puerto Ricans and that, despite his using the word "nigger" to describe them and himself, in his writings he created white alter egos. But to dissect those contradictions we must start at the beginning.

Piñero was not yet a member of the group calling itself The Nuyorican Poets when Miguel Algarín, unable to continue hosting events in his living room, rented an Irish pub, eventually asking the producer Joseph Papp for Public Theater space. Joe provided the space, and those poets were soon joined by a theater workshop called The Family, started by inmates at New York's Sing Sing penitentiary. The poets and playwrights read their works in that donated space until Joe, who had already picked up *Short Eyes*, helped find the present locale of The Nuyorican Poets Café, to which he continued to lend support, later picking up a play by Reinaldo Povod.

Joe Papp helped The Nuyorican Poets project as an act of solidarity with New York's poorest communities, a chunk of which resided near the Public Theater, populating the area called Alphabet City (Avenues A, B, and C) in the Lower East Side. Considering himself a gentleman of the Left, he acted on his social consciousness: having grown up Jewish in a more antisemitic time, he knew first-hand the experience of belonging to a stigmatized group. If, as Leon Ichaso suggests in *Piñero*, one can read Papp as someone who ripped off "the street," he must also be remembered as someone who midwived the streets' creative possibilities out of a genuine belief in unburnished potential, which is to say in others like himself, who rose from working-class origins, was not a college graduate, and was self-taught in theater.

Joe also appreciated The Nuyorican Poets Café as an off-off-Broadway venue and lent support as a gesture of commitment to New York theater, in whose survival he envisioned a role for the city's future Hispanic middle class that would emerge from the rapidly increasing Latin American population. At that time the predominant Hispanic population was still the Puerto Rican community, from which he had already discovered the actor Raúl Juliá.

Papp's futuristic vision prompted him to acquire and make part of The New York Shakespeare Festival a summer showcase of Latin American theater, *Festival Latino*, started in El Barrio by an Argentine actor and his Salvadoran wife, who stayed on as its directors. At their request, in the summer of 1986 Joe hired me as press representative of *Festival Latino* at the Public Theater, whose centerpiece that summer was the already-running Broadway production of *Cuba and His Teddy Bear*, written by his other Nuyorican Café discovery, Reinaldo Povod (1960 – 1994), who was "the son of Puerto Rican mother and a Cuban father of Russian descent."[2]

My first *Festival* task that summer was to set up a press conference before Latin American journalists and serve as two-way translator, both for them and the English-monolingual Povod, who wore his signature black and white captain's cap–ironically felicitous because before the press he was at sea. Desperate, he covered up his inability to answer any question by laughing it off. If he understood any question, he was unable to articulate answers in either language, forcing me to "translate" substance from gestures or a response no more detailed than a shrug or, a "Yeah, that's right." The contributor to Wikipedia describes Povod as Piñero's "protégé," and watching him I realized

---

2 "Reinaldo Povod," *Wikipedia*, https://en.wikipedia.org/wiki/Reinaldo_Povod

that he was playing Piñero's defensive trick: if one trips, play the naive artist, perform a clown act.

The year before Piñero died, to illustrate, thirteen years after the production of *Short Eyes*, *The Village Voice* interviewed him on a Lower East Side sidewalk. He was still getting high and hanging out on the same street. Shirtless and wearing a porkpie hat, he posed for a now iconic photo that ran captioned with his exaggerated love of heroin. He had played that routine before, in other interviews, rationalizing his drug-taking as an aid to creativity ("half inspiration, half inhalation" was an oft-quoted quip). This junkie-artist image-making was his clown act, implying aesthetic choices that Piñero made unconsciously and deflecting questions with self-consciously-played naive-genius responses.

To his credit Piñero acknowledged to himself that he was the sum total of his drugs and crime and, authentic to himself in a constant sense of guilt and sin expressed in his plays and poetry, he found it difficult to perform the seriously touted playwright. His uninterrupted lifestyle– street denizen, mugger, heroin addict, thief– seems to have been crying out that he had found it hard to fit into the body of the talented creature whom Joe Papp had stitched together out of needled body parts. Threatened by having to live as and identify with that Piñero, whom the world expected to articulate things he could not, he took refuge in his Lower East Side persona.

This inner conflict makes both the true and embellished accounts of his wildness interchangeable as expressions of self-recognition: his either mugging a woman for her mink coat or his jumping a subway turnstile, either way getting arrested on either the Lincoln Center opening of *Short Eyes* or the night of his Tony nomination was surely meant to poison Papp's monster and his feeling of being authored by Papp's world outside his streets.

Piñero's problem of self-recognition is actually a theme in *Short Eyes*, and the play's success amplified his problem, scripting him in a publicity-rich, true-life drama of the outlaw who became a literate, narrating protagonist. This character had come into vogue since the English-language publication, in 1963, of *Saint Jean: Actor and Martyr*, in which Jean-Paul Sartre contemplated the unrepentant criminal-turned-novelist-and-playwright Jean Genet as model existential man, unable to see distinction between good and evil. Genet was Piñero's expressed role model.

There were also American role models, in whom marginalization also encompassed race. This American drama with a Hollywood ending was narrated in Claude Brown's *Manchild in the Promised Land* (1965), which told of his surviving Harlem, prison and drugs, and in *Down These Mean Streets* (1967), the Afro-Puerto Rican Piri Thomas's memoir of racial rejection from his own in Spanish Harlem and his also overcoming drugs and incarceration. In

1968, Eldridge Cleaver published that decade's most influential book of the race-prison genre, *Soul on Ice*. In all three, the narratives document existential and institutional injustice. In Piñero and *Short Eyes*, Papp found vehicles that tapped into that trending curiosity, which extended into the eighties.[3]

In *Short Eyes*, Piñero's protagonist, the convict Juan, becomes the confessor of the child molester Clark, who had committed the crime that made him the most hated species in the prison and whose only explanation for opening up to Juan was a mysteriously felt affinity. In pairing with Clark, Juan departs from his prison Hispanic group–which makes his name a pun, his being different or Juan/One. Most of the characters of *Short Eyes* are Hispanic and trapped in Piñero's personal prison, being Puerto Rican and therefore as social misfits. Otherwise, culturally being Puerto Rican has nothing to do with this play really about the only cultures that Miguel Piñero knew, street and prison.

Clark's being in prison and feeling an "affinity" with Juan makes Clark virtually Puerto Rican in Piñero's universe. This metaphorical cross-pollination is repeated in *The Sun Only Shines for the Cool* (1984), in which Willie Bodega is a non-Puerto Rican who hangs out at a dive of pimps and prostitutes, Piñero's synonym for Puerto Ricans, and whom the younger character Cat Eyes describes as "a gringo who raps like a nigger," nigger being another Piñero characterization of Puerto Rican. In sum, by any measure *Short Eyes* is not an ethnic play and has nothing to do with being "Nuyorican." Appropriately, the glossary that accompanies the published script of *Short Eyes* is of prison jargon.

In two one-act plays Piñero created the alter ego Mike Poor. In *Tap Dancing and Bruce Lee Kicks,*[4] Mike is described as a "self-educated poet-writer coming to grips with his drug use," who pitches to his L.A. agent the idea of writing "a story about the building where I live," which we learn is populated with drug addicts to whom he is dealing. Mike also appears in another one-act, *Cold Beer* (1979), also set in Los Angeles and in which Mike Poor is described as an emulator of Charles Bukowski, the alcoholic cult poet, the subject of the movie *Barfly*. Bukowski's books surround Mike as he "chain smokes and chain drinks his beer," both being "part of his poetic image...." *Cold Beer* satirizes the madness of a culture that is paying him money to write about anything in his

---

[3] This vogue capped out after Norman Mailer sponsored the release of convicted murderer John Henry Abbott, author of *In the Belly of the Beast: Letters from Prison,* published in 1981. Soon after being released Abbott killed another man and returned to prison. In 2002, he committed suicide in his cell.

[4] Date uncertain. Although this play appears in *Outrageous: One Act Plays* by Miguel Piñero, it is not included in *Outlaw: The Collected Works of Miguel Piñero*.

supposedly exotic life when in fact he perceives himself as an American poet, a personal liberation from his public image.

Midnight Moon at the Greasy Spoon (1981) is about two aging Jewish owners of an urban diner, its world a stage for an assortment of characters disappointed in life, that theme punctuated by the death of one of the owners. The dialogue between the two old men, reminiscent of Neil Simon, is a departure from the playwriting persona expected of Piñero. But the play did not benefit from the Public's dramaturg refinements, that polished *Short Eyes*, and The *Times* review was generous in underscoring the play's vitality despite its "disarray" in the staging, the highest praise acknowledging an improvement an improvement in his work, this play being "a departure for Mr. Piñero, and a sign of his expansion as a playwright."

Piñero had arrived at that "expansion," in other words writing outside what was assumed to be his ethnic world, after writing the one-act prison play *The Guntower* (1976), which had hinted at that ambition. The African American prison guard Simmons expects the only other Hispanic character in the play, the prison guard German Rosado, to back up his rebelling Puerto Rican incarcerated brothers, whose "country is controlled by this country." Simmons receives the surprising response consistent with Piñero's personal figuration of himself: "...This is my country...I am an American citizen and proud of it. *This country has never made me as blue that I would want to be red*...[Italics mine] so don't call me a Puerto Rican. I am an American." Underscoring that this country has never made him blue evokes the leitmotiv throughout his work that Puerto Rico and being Puerto Rican always had.

Piñero's plays are not about Puerto Ricans but about his damaged idea of them. His full-length *The Sun Only Shines for the Cool* exemplifies the pattern, Puerto Rican characters mainly setting for the protagonist who is not Puerto Rican or doesn't want to be Puerto Rican. In *Short Eyes*, Juan is Puerto Rican but different from the others who are just setting. Whether as Mike Poor, Juan or Willie Bodega, the character stands apart from Puerto Ricans consistently stereotyped by Piñero as drug takers and criminals. Just images of drugs and crime and prostitution become ethnic stand-ins.

In *Tap Dancing and Bruce Lee Kicks*, for example, the dialogue has no ostensible evidence of any ethnic environment, but the suggestion is that Mike Poor would be writing about his junkie world that is also presumably ethnic and evocative of Puerto Rican. The same device is used in *Eulogy for a Small-Time Thief* (1984), in which the closest thing to an ethnic marker is the phonetically ambiguously-named David's taking drugs and being by trade a mugger. The point of view in Piñero's plays is, even though expressed by an underclass character, a judgmental white mainstream voice, a consistency that leaves little to interpret.

This judgmental white mainstream consciousness continues in his poetry, all invariably evocative of the Lower East Side, scripts of his walking around and thinking out loud, at times revealing a sense of guilt about his lifestyle, at times ranting stock grievances about capitalism and whites. His was not a Puerto Rican Lower East Side, not Loisaida, but a romanticized place of "Jews and Gentiles, Bums and Men/of style...., where "streets are hot," and where "fancy cars & pimps' bars & junk saloons/&greasy spoons make my spirits fly...." That sinful world, "the only place that I can see," was actually an adolescent memory of the Lower East Side that by 1980–when he wrote "Another Lower East Side Poem"–was already gentrifying. His poems were memories as a minority formula fiction.

Harsh realism in *Piñero* is depicted in the scene when, in Puerto Rico, Piñero reads before an audience, significantly older, that doesn't cheer as the young crowds did at the Café. The actor who plays him, Benjamin Bratt, is given the lines that have Piñero defend his being as Puerto Rican as his two parents. Whether or not Piñero actually made that claim, his writing doesn't sustain that he believed that he was or would want to be as Puerto Rican as his parents, who in the film are characterized as the lowlife causes of his unhappy life.

Interviewed by Lynn Geller for *Bomb Magazine*,[5] director Ichaso compared his film to *Barfly*. In that film we never get a sense of Bukowski's admirers or of his being their mouthpiece; Bukowski is an exotic literary figure, a life martyred presumably in the name of art, a metaphor. Not being a minority personage, Bukowski did not have to epitomize the populist ideals that prevailed in the seventies. Piñero, on the other hand, was being measured by the politics of finding comparable native genius across the democratic spectrum. His minority voice was implicitly interpreted as a sociopolitical response to racism and economic oppression experienced by an entire community.

The publicity copy for Leon Ichaso's *Piñero* compared Piñero to Genet, whose hatred of bourgeois French life, the target of his criminal life, was presumably the counterpart of Piñero's anger at middle-class America as a "Nuyorican." Such politically correct presumptions are based on the superficial similarities of their both being ex-cons and writers when the two are separated by one profound difference. Genet hated bourgeois French life and Piñero did not hate middle-class America. Although back in the seventies Piñero was comparably assumed to address his anger at middle-class America, that was a false assumption. Contrary to that hype, he fantasized being middle-class America (Clark, Mike Poor), which shared his indictment of Puerto Ricans. Piñero's

---

5 "Leon Ichaso by Lynn Geller," *Bomb*, January 1, 2002, https://bombmagazine.org/articles/leon-ichaso/

writing reveals that he conflated his perception of Puerto Rican ethnicity and antisocial behavior so he could speak of one as the cause of the other, of Puerto Ricans characterized not by their ethnicity but by their inherent sinfulness.

In other words, his being Puerto Rican made him sin. But the sins that socially marginalized him also artistically redeemed him because writing as a thief, junkie and convict universalized him out of the narrow confines of just pathetic Puerto Rican ethnicity, allowing him to make comparisons with Genet. Consequently, seeing in the legendary "street" Piñero a voice of the mainland Puerto Rican community only makes sense if one also sees that community as exclusively its culture of poverty, the operative stereotype since Puerto Ricans first arrived in large numbers after World War II.

Piñero's overnight prominence gave the media license to hyperbolize with the best of intentions, bestowing on him both title of laureate of the Lower East Side and implicitly the laureate of an otherwise ostensibly mute Puerto Rican/ Nuyorican community. Popular legend took hold and grew to proportions that exaggerated Piñero's importance as writer and cultural icon.[6] Only someone who believed the legend told by those who felt empowered by telling it could have made hagiography of Piñero. Such a convert was the Cuban-American Ichaso.

Almost three decades after the production of *Short Eyes*, Ichaso's *Piñero* hyped its protagonist as a literary genius, with the movie's promotion making additional claims about its subject's contribution to rap music, American literature, and mainland Puerto Rican culture. In that interview for *Bomb*, Ichaso told of the day that he first met Piñero, who looked homeless, scratching himself and covered with what seemed like bug bites. That sight of Piñero contrasted sharply with the image he had of him as the famous author of *Short Eyes*.

After that meeting, Ichaso kept hearing many stories about Piñero but still was not motivated to make a movie about him. Then at some point after Piñero's death he realized that Piñero was being forgotten, "falling into the cracks," and Ichaso decided that a film would rescue him from oblivion. Ichaso lamented that Piñero's writings were out of print and his plays rarely produced: "Jesus, what a shame—somebody that was so influential in the seventies, one of the people responsible for spoken word as we know it today, who used to do his poetry with music. Plus it was a fascinating life. He became as much a New

---

[6] When I first wrote this sentence, I remembered a Woody Allen prose piece of that time, in *The New Yorker*, that satirically referred to, from recollection, "a Puerto Rican playwright who one day woke up and discovered that he was famous." In researching through Allen's published books of prose, that reference was apparently later edited out.

Yorker as anybody else and yet his is also the story of uprooted men who started a life here without forgetting where they came from."

Ichaso knows how to promote his movie, but didn't know much about poetry and, frankly, about Piñero. Along with poets of other minority groups, a generation of aspiring Puerto Rican poets who came of age in the sixties were influenced by African American and Beat jazz readings. Writing in that same style or variations thereof, they converged on The Nuyorican Poets Café.

Along with Pedro Pietri, after the success of *Short Eyes,* Piñero became the best known Nuyorican among them. But he was neither an originator nor a role model for today's "spoken word" poetry, which has a much longer history. Moreover, as discussed above, nothing he wrote gave any inkling of his remembering "where he came from," Puerto Rico simply being where he was born before coming to New York. In fact, everywhere Piñero traveled, he tagged it with his vandalism as if to deny to himself that he had left The Lower East Side.

Ichaso translated into film the *hype* about Piñero, even poeticizing his physical appearance: we never do see the bug-bitten figure he described nor do we see the strung-out drug addict. The real Piñero was closer to Rasto Rizzo and instead we saw Joe Buck as cast for the role was the much better and healthier-looking Benjamin Bratt, who near the end talks of dying without looking worse for the wear of his life. An even more serious error is the film's assumption of Piñero's importance as community icon, contradicted by the reality that becomes starkly evident in the black-and-white footage of his "funeral." Little more than the Café's regulars listen to presumably many eulogies, from which we see and hear only Amiri Baraka read part of Piñero's "Lower East Side" before the thin procession walks ceremonially down the street in the trail of their dead poet's ashes being cast into the Lower East air by Miguel Algarín.

"THE WORLD OF THE NUYORICAN"

After Joseph Papp, the second key figure in the making of Miguel Piñero was the poet Miguel Algarín, the elder Father in a trinity in which Piñero was the "junkie-Christ," who came to embody the Nuyorican spirit that resided in the temple that was The Nuyorican Poets Café. From that pulpit Algarín preached on "The World of the Nuyorican," as he posted it on the Web. Piñero as the most celebrated poet of that world was a walking advertisement for the Café. Algarín, as administrator and head poet, managed both the Café and the hype surrounding Piñero after whose death he became the legend's executor.

Their close relationship is portrayed in Ichaso's film, on which the real Algarín also served as consultant. But the fictionalized Algarín is a sanitized portrayal, a stabler academic mentor trying to guide the incorrigible genius. He is not a poet himself nor the entrepreneurial administrator of the Café, characterizing keys to understanding that close friendship. In fact, in Algarín's case the mentoring worked as well in the other direction because, seeking recognition as an equally flamboyant poet, Algarín inhaled second hand the wild behavior of his ex-con and street-bad friends.

A professor of English at Rutgers University, Algarín was never academic in the traditional sense, producing no critical publications, and nothing on Piñero's writings, being instead magisterial in publicity and the politics of race. The procurement of The Nuyorican Poets Café's present site from the city, the having of Joseph Papp's ear, and the media attention garnered by the Café were fruits of that political savvy on seventies racial politics. To his credit, he turned the Café into an iconic, internationally-known performance space that continued to thrive decades after Piñero and the original Nuyorican Poets were dead and the city had gentrified the Lower East Side.

But in marketing Nuyorican, Algarín must also be credited with distorting the collective image of the Puerto Rican community for his own personal gain. For in the course of making the Café internationally famous, Algarín also successfully promoted "Nuyorican" as a hip mythology of the entire New York Rican and, by implication, mainland community, replacing the gang stereotype that had lingered since *West Side Story* with the life and lifestyle of the Lower East Side's bad boys, The Nuyorican Poets, and particularly Miguel Piñero.

Outside of becoming a synonym for mainstream Puerto Rican and evocative of the spoken word poetry scene, Nuyorican doesn't culturally say much more, so the epithet frequently defers to Puerto Rican, as demonstrated in the title of Algarín's first anthology *Nuyorican Poetry: An Anthology of Puerto Rican Words and Feelings.* "Nuyorican" was also an Eastern precursor and segue to racialized Latino, replacing the ethnic foreignness of "Hispanic" or "Spanish," emphasizing a racialized American identity. Before Latino, Nuyorican had replaced the island's white Hispanic history with a populist presentism of racialized Puerto Rican, and Algarín promoted "The World of the Nuyorican" with an anti-intellectual shield of authentic populism, replacing as focal point the diaspora's point of origin, the uptown island-centric, *jíbaro*-nostalgic El Barrio, with the tacitly racialized "Puerto Rican" Lower East, Loisaida.

Algarín proselytized on the "World of the Nuyorican" disconnected from the history of Puerto Rican culture or its literature. From my conversations with Algarín, it became apparent that he had studied Elizabethan England in greater detail and knew more about that English history than about Puerto Rico and the culture that El Barrio's first generation sought to preserve, however racially problematic. In this disconnect, "Nuyorican" as response promoted a cultural distortion.

The diaspora's second generation, influenced by the Civil Rights Movement, broke with El Barrio's preservation of the island's white *jíbaro* mythos, and had turned "Puerto Rican" into a race ("White, Black, or Puerto Rican"). That generation's migrating to the Lower East Side redefined Puerto Rican by neighborhood, El Barrio or Loisaida, where Nuyorican came to be romanticized as synonymous with the entire mainland community, which in fact as a demographic had spread from New York to Rutherford, Allentown, Chicago, Los Angeles, and as far as Hawaii and, along the East coast, from Boston to Orlando.

Certainly, Nuyorican evoked a stereotype of urban New York Puerto Rican youth perhaps more accurately than the fading metaphors of *West Side* Story. But the community's changing demographics and expanding geography made for a reality that required more nuance, which the pop culture hegemony of "Nuyorican" overshadowed and distorted, enduring despite the Café's being engulfed by Manhattan gentrification. Popularly and in the media "Nuyorican" was still spoken of as a cultural epithet while it had evolved to become the nonethnic brand for spoken-word poetry, of which the Café had become an institution.

Exactly what was being romanticized by the adoption of Nuyorican as ethnic epithet in the first place was never really clear, especially with its Piñero paradigm, associating Nuyorican with drug use and crime. And nobody seemed to notice that also being romanticized was *staying* in that world, another evocation that makes Nuyorican a complete fabrication that simplistically camouflaged the mainland Puerto Rican reality. For unlike Piñero, who could live no other life, and unlike the original Nuyorican Poets, who died young as consequence of their Loisaida lifestyles, the New York Rican was going somewhere else, maturing to produce Raúl Juliá, Marc Anthony, Sonia Sotomayor, Jennifer Lopez, Rosie Perez, among a list of nationally familiar New York Ricans we don't immediately associate with "the world of the Nuyorican" promoted by Algarín.

One can say that the mainland Puerto Rican community was growing up while the Nuyorican Poets, especially Piñero, were its Lost Boys in a Lower East Side Never Never Land. This metaphor I extrapolate from Piñero's portrayal in Ichaso's film, whose Peter Pan male story line about Piñero makes him a paradigm of the Nuyorican problem of growing up and never becoming a psychological adult in the New York Rican experience. Algarín confused that characterizing dysfunction with a cultural trait: "The World of the Nuyorican" is a mythos about growing up in New York but not about having grown.

Piñero saw two male models from which to choose and recreated them in his plays: either the world of his deadbeat, abusive Puerto Rican father no different than the pimps and hustlers. In contrast were those white men who had been his teachers or whom he had watched on television, the white men he emulated vicariously in his plays but which he could not become in real life. Seeing before him the threshold to manhood and beyond that an unknown world in which he saw no place for his adult self, not able to duplicate his white models and not wanting to be Puerto Rican, he recycled his Lost Boy experiences—drugs, thievery.

Director Ichaso did not have to intend to organize *Piñero* around this Peter Pan motif; whatever the camera recorded in the Lower East Side became Piñero's Never Never Land, a fictive home. His reading in Puerto Rico takes place in a brightly illuminated room before a visible, stodgy, more gray-haired and indifferent audience while his readings in the Café take place before a darkened audience we never actually see but must imagine from their effusive cheer. The island setting and that audience's response was real, we see their faces, while the darkened Loisaida audience and its hype is to be imagined, "the only place that I can see."

In *Piñero* the timekeeper of reality is the movie's Wendy, Piñero's girlfriend Sugar. Throughout the film, Sugar reminds Miguel that in an adult world people get married, have children, have responsibilities. But when she asks Piñero to marry her, in other words begs him to grow up, we know he can't and we think we know why. One can extrapolate that he probably knew she would end up a young widow, but a stronger impression is that, over the adulthood she is proposing, he simply preferred living in a van, taking drugs, hanging out around the block and later reading poetry in the Café forever.

Consistent with this Peter Pan chronology, from the first frame to the last, few cosmetic changes are made in *Piñero*. Until his last breath, Piñero remains young and Benjamin Bratt looks exactly the same at the start and the final scene, when after countless inhalations or injections of heroin we never see him take and more than a decade had passed since *Short Eyes*. Piñero was in his forties. Did Ichaso himself realize too late that his story had overlooked the passing of time, that "Nuyorican" seemed to transcend time? Was his awareness of having overlooked the passage of time the reason why, in the final editing, he shuffled the chronology of the scenes, turning this narrative flaw into artistic plotting?

IN MEMORIAM

Piñero ends with the now iconic photo– shirtless, wearing that porkpie hat– first published in *The Village Voice* for that street interview in which he expressed his love for his drug addiction. Reading that interview was one of three indelibly pathetic memories I have of Piñero. The other two were of the times he came around the Public to ask Joe for money. I never actually saw him walk into the theater; I was just told he was present. Each time he produced a silence in the entire house, a sense of the Public's being disgraced, the second time shortly before his death.

In *Piñero* he only returns to the Public when Joe produced Ray Povod's *Cuba and His Teddy Bear,* and jealous of his protégé's success, in front of the Public he hawked his complimentary tickets. That scene, however, didn't do justice to Piñero's jealousy and his certain feeling of being abandoned by Papp. Ten years before, Pinero's *Short Eyes* had opened the Public's door for Povod. In the intervening decade Piñero had advanced no farther than stagings at the Nuyorican Poets Café and, in one fashion or other, peddling for television and movies his unchanged self, an accomplished thief and junkie.

Povod's play, which eventually moved to Broadway starring Robert DeNiro, must have painfully reminded Piñero that, as playwright the Public's doors were now closed to him who, given every opportunity, never redeemed himself. But he needed to prove that those doors were still opened, that they owed him something. Returning to see Joe must also have been a way of not just reliving past glory but of claiming damages because he held Joe responsible for having given him the opportunity and thus exposing him to the truth that he was incapable of growing up.

Also absent from the film was the bigger picture of Piñero's slipping from importance as Joe Papp gravitated away from the Nuyorican playwrights, his vision having broadened of future contributions to New York theater by immigrating *latinos.* The following summer Povod's play was no longer running and the Nuyorican playwrights were notably absent from the formal program of *Festival Latino.* Pressured by Algarín that the *Festival* should present more local talent, Joe appended some short performances and readings.

Both Piñero and Povod died before the last *Festival Latino* in 1990, ending that chapter of the Public's history. The following year, Joe, who had been battling cancer, died. The Public's personnel, with whom the *Festival Latino*'s founders-administrators had grated since they arrived, unburdened the theater of a program that had always been treated as a summer chore imposed on them by its founder's overzealous liberalism.

Today *Short Eyes* and Piñero's other plays are anthologized and may be assigned in multicultural studies courses. Occasionally, in a multiculturally-sensitive season, one of his plays is performed by some group, and Latino literary anthologies might include poetry by Piñero. In 1970, director Robert Young adapted *Short Eyes* as a feature film, but it has yet to reappear in a major theatrical revival. The week of *Piñero*'s release, the *Times* Art section ran a piece on mainland Puerto Rican poets, on that broader application of "Nuyorican," and none of the interviewed poets actually mentioned Piñero.[7]

Piñero achieved as much owing to his raw talent as to those decades that judged them as timely, an insight into his underworld, and that time had passed. Looking back since, while not denying his raw talent, in the end Piñero resulted a shining object, a miracle that Joe Papp wanted to pull off but that never cooperated. *Pinero* was not uniquely revealing nor insightfully documentary, more a hyping of a talent not really a genius, and the mainland Puerto Rican community really had no reason to resurrect his memory other than to remind itself of the "Nuyorican" stereotype that Piñero sowed and which others have had to outgrow. Not the entire community sees Piñero that way, of course. In a Lower East Side café, a candle shines before a photograph in memory of the most publicized embodiment of "The World of the Nuyorican."

The Café proceeded without Piñero, became a New York focal point of spoken word poetry. Young poets from Long Island and New York City packed it to read at notorious poetry slams. Today, except for the bouncer and bartender, few if any others are Nuyoricans or any Rican. One day I arrived at my Long Island college to teach and saw a poster announcing a reading of three "Nuyorican Poets" scheduled for that week on campus. The young poets in the photos were, white, African American, Asian. They were now the Nuyorican Poets, and whatever Nuyorican supposedly meant about the mainland experience was bartered to keep the Café relevant. Today, while still called The Nuyorican Poets Café, it thrives as a nondescript, more inclusive New York performing space.

---

[7] Mireya Navarro, "The Poetry of the Nuyorican Experience; Writers Following in the Literary Tradition of Miguel Piñero Thrive in a Poets' Cafe," *The New York Times*, January 2, 2002

8.

WILLIAM CARLOS WILLIAMS, LIN-MANUEL MIRANDA, AND THE ENIGMA OF IDENTITY

In 2016, one year after the premiere of the musical *Hamilton* at the Public Theater, Lin-Manuel Miranda was awarded the Pulitzer Prize. *Hamilton* was playing on Broadway in 2017, the centennial year of the publication of *Al Que Quiere* (1917), the first important book of poetry by William Carlos Williams, who was posthumously awarded the Pulitzer Prize in 1963 for his last collection of poems, *Pictures from Breughel and Other Poems* (1961). Besides being the first author of Puerto Rican descent to receive this award, also little known, Williams was Miranda's precursor as playwright and not just owing to their ethnic backgrounds.

Miranda's musical is based on the Alexander Hamilton portrayed in Ron Chernow's biography *Alexander Hamilton* (2004), which interprets Hamilton as a culturally marginalized man not justly recognized as a writer and thinker. Eight decades earlier, Williams had written the never-staged libretto for a grand opera in three acts titled *The First President* (published in 1936), portraying a humanized, robust and loving George Washington. Williams' motive for dramatizing a historical figure foreshadowed the reason Miranda gave *The New York Times* why he wrote *Hamilton*: "to galvanize us into an understanding of who we are today."

In 1950 Williams also wrote *Tituba's Children*, a dramatization of a theatrical metaphor that intersperses the communist-hunting hearings of Senator Joseph McCarthy with the colonial-era Salem witch trials. Tituba, a slave from the West Indies (in literary history she evolves from Caribbean Indian to African), was accused of teaching witchcraft to young white youth in her charge. Not a musical but with verse dialogue, in this drama written nine years after Williams' first visit to Puerto Rico in 1941, the pivotal year on whose influence I will elaborate later, Williams celebrated Tituba as another national heritage from his mother's Caribbean.

Tituba was accused of having highjacked the souls of colonial youth in her charge with her African witchcraft. In other words, Tituba sowed the impure spirit that Williams understood as quintessentially American, sowing as well the impure nation made up of *Tituba's Children.* This recognition of his Caribbean lineage makes Williams a precursor of Miranda if we understand that he wrote *Hamilton* identifying with the bastard son from the Caribbean island of Nevis whose social impurity made him another emblem of the cultural marginalization that as Puerto Rican Miranda shares with other minorities.

Williams is also a precursor as a writer who foreshadowed multiculturalism. Today's multiculturalism recognizes that the country may have been envisioned monoracial but prospered because it exploited its heterogeneity. The final de facto product is a multicultural and multiracial country, this problematic history patriotically corrected with the redacted history of the traditional The American Story, a narrative of the country as immutable and white. In challenging that tradition, Williams foreshadowed Miranda. Inspired by today's multiculturalism, Miranda wrote about the American Revolution reimagined as a multiracial event.

Finally, Miranda also invokes Williams in subtextually announcing that the real struggle is to reclaim the national narrative, the metaphorical wider warning of Hamilton's character in the closing song about himself, "Who Lives, Who Dies, Who Tells Your Story." Williams had questioned the traditional American Story that starts with the Puritans[1] by giving the nation's history a truer American reading in the essays of *In the American Grain* (1925).

Understandably Miranda would not have thought of Williams as precursor, either as Puerto Rican or as playwright. Williams did not resonate strongly enough as either Puerto Rican or playwright for Miranda to have made the connection. When Miranda was a college student in the late 1990s, despite the release in 1994 of my *The Spanish American Roots of William Carlos Williams,* Williams was still better known as the major mainstream poet, notwithstanding the acknowledgment of his mother's being from Puerto Rico. For years after my book's publication, American and island intellectuals resisted giving credence to my ascribing any Puerto Rican literary and cultural significance related to Williams' work, a connection at best toned down to an autobiographical curiosity. After all, as Wallace Steven's called him, Williams was "the America of poets."

And even if Williams had been recognized as Puerto Rican, Miranda would doubtfully have recognized Williams as a writing precursor because even though Miranda personally identifies as Puerto Rican, he does not create as a Puerto Rican playwright, writing as a generic Latino American reminiscent of Borges' duplicity in "Borges and I." Williams performed a similar split in creating in two voices, Bill's in direct language and Carlos' in baroque encoding.

---

[1] Whose exclusivity, according to Williams, "had nothing to do"—from his bilingual "no tienían nada que ver"—with the true inclusive idea of America.

But, if one were to compare Williams and Miranda head to head, on this question of their personal and writer's cultural identity the two sharply diverge.

Miranda personally identifies as Puerto Rican while writing as a Latino that, being American, has nothing to do with his island-centric Puerto Ricanness. Williams never publicly identified as Puerto Rican while his work that contemplates his mother actually invoked Puerto Rican precursors and aligned with contemporaneous island writings. Compared, Williams and Miranda offer contrasting paradigms of that subjectivity that we call an identity, a thesis that behooves first distinguishing the profoundly different role of Puerto Rican consciousness in the life and work of Williams and Miranda.

Williams' mother Elena Hoheb was born in Mayagüez. She and her brother Carlos were orphaned at a young age and later Carlos, a doctor who practiced in Santo Domingo, Dominican Republic, financed Elena's art studies in France until a Dominican political crisis ruined him. Elena had to leave her studies, that interruption the central tragedy of her life, and she returned to Santo Domingo where she felt compelled to marry Carlos' English friend, William George Williams. They moved to New York, married, and ended up living in Rutherford, New Jersey, where William Carlos was born in 1883. Elena lived unhappily for the rest of her life, not having married for love and surrounded by the condescension of people unable to appreciate her Hispanic and French refinement.

Williams' father, William George was indeed born in England, as traditional critics enthusiastically underscore, but at the age of five, fleeing the consequences of a scandal that Grandma Welcome never disclosed, she took William George to the island of St. Thomas, where she had hoped to marry an English resident of that island. A changed destiny led to William George's growing up in the Dominican Republic, where he became bilingual and a Hispanophile.

William Carlos did not specify, but his father's being more literary and more the Hispanophile than the Frenchified Elena, he was probably the parent who read him the classic Spanish poets of the baroque Golden Age, affixing Góngora and Quevedo alongside Shakespeare on Williams' mental bookshelf. Both parents chose to reject U.S. citizenship, a decision that pained Williams deeply although, owing to the devotion he had for Elena, he did not follow the pattern of sons of European immigrants, who Americanized, shed their parents' past.

Instead, he tried to sustain a stasis between his Bill persona and his Carlos persona, preserving his son's devotion yet determined to be recognized as an American poet. Ezra Pound's quip that he was a "foreigner" because he grew up in a Spanish-speaking home was emblematic of the challenge to be recognized as an American poet. With that motive he reread American history, questioning the presumably truer American lineage of Pound, who condescended to him, and in that inquiry, discovered a new importance to his Hispanic roots. Williams was not a Catholic, but he recognized that it was Spanish Catholicism that sowed the truer American hemispheric disposition to inclusion, using the then popular euphemism that implied race, its "mingling spirit."

Williams reminded that Spanish priests came to "lay hands," baptize, and fulfill their duty to incorporate the native soul into the Church. If the "squeamish" Puritan came expressly not to touch the native, the Spanish "married America," sexual relations that the English condemned as bestiality. For these reasons, according to Williams, contrary to the patriotic mythology of The American Story, the Puritans "had nothing to do" with America and it was the Spaniards who had earlier sown the essentially American "mingling spirit" that he inherited precisely because his mother was Puerto Rican.[2]

Armed with that confidence, Williams launched a personal war against the traditional American culture that threatened to marginalize him as it had marginalized Elena, when they were the ones who embodied the truest American spirit. Traditional America had perpetuated itself under the illusion of being an outer European province, the America of a falsely American tradition, which should wane with modernity. Of course, both his argument on the origin of the true American spirit and his effort to establish his own American authenticity were consequences of his always keeping in mind the Hispanic roots that nourished him by way of his Spanish readings, his mother and her memories of Puerto Rico.

But his was a rocky romanticization of those Puerto Rican roots as it also depended on Elena's unreliable narration. Like Blanche Dubois living in her aristocratic Southern past in A Streetcar Named Desire, Elena escaped from her sad Rutherford life to memories of an idealized Puerto Rico, presumably more cultured and implicitly also far from her son, who was more crudely American. In reality, Puerto Rico was the island to which she would never bring herself to return. If Elena felt anything of the patriotism that flared up on the island in the nineteenth century, she did not express it. Williams surely heard that patriotism expressed by the family friend, Dr. Julio José Henna, an associate of the nineteenth-century independence advocate Ramón Emeterio Betances, whose true influence must be conjured from Williams' devoting a chapter to him in The Autobiography.

---

[2] A romanticization of the Conquest indeed but, as Frank Tennenbaum, would demonstrate two decades later in Slave and Citizen: The Negro in the Americas (1945), making no reference to Williams, profound was the contrast between slavery practiced under Catholicism and Protestantism.

Williams was fifteen years old when U.S. troops occupied the island in 1898. Williams wrote that his mother decided to forget her island as if it had been desecrated. He mentions Puerto Rico in passing in *The Autobiography* (1951) in the context of identifying or locating other relatives, notably excluding his two visits to the island. He did not elaborate on them to biographer Paul Mariani,[3] explaining that he accepted the first invitation, in 1941, to the University of Puerto Rico's Río Piedras campus, because he was curious about his roots. The second trip, in 1956, to read at the University's campus at Elena's Mayaguez, was taken out of an interest in gathering more material for *Yes, Mrs. Williams.* One has to deduce as well that the second visit was really a consequence of his 1941 trip, which, from all evidence, changed the Puerto Rico that he had only known from Elena's memories, the visit during which Puerto Rico became a literary reality.

In 1941 Williams was invited to speak at a conference of America's writers held at the Rio Piedras campus of the University of Puerto Rico and accepted the invitation because, according to his explanation to Mariani, he was curious about his roots. His talk, dressed in a strictly literary discourse, titled "An Informal Discussion on Poetic Form," was really intended to argue that the U.S. was less like England and more like Spain in being a fusion of cultures and peoples.[4] One key moment of this trip, absent from Mariani's biography but reported in San Juan newspapers, was his being introduced to Puerto Rico's most renown poet, Luis Palés Matos and receiving his book *Tuntún de pasa y grifería* (*Tomtom of Kinkhead and Black Things*, 1937).

The Spanish Civil War had begun in 1936, impacting also Latin America. In Puerto Rico, the war reinforced the already active *hispanismo* consciousness that had been counteracting Anglo-Americanization. The exile to Puerto Rico of notable Spanish artists and intellectuals further reinforced that consciousness, making Puerto Rico a showcase of Hispanic culture, that trend peaking in 1956 when world-acclaimed cellist Pablo Casals was invited to found the international Festival Casals de Puerto Rico and in the same year the ailing poet Juan Ramón Jiménez, now a resident of his wife's birthplace, was awarded the Nobel Prize, which the president of the University of Puerto Rico received in his name.

Tellingly, Williams makes no mention of Jiménez, a lyrical purist the antithesis of Luis Palés Matos, who was born in 1898 and grew up not in patrician San Juan but in the heavily African coastal town of Guayama. Blond and blue-eyed, growing up in the care of black women, surrounded by Afro-Puerto Rican music and ceremonies, early on he began writing poems with

---

[3] Paul Mariani, *William Carlos Williams: A New World Naked* (New York: W.W. Norton, 1990).

[4] Mariani, *William Carlos Williams: A New World Naked*, 446.

African imagery at first influenced by Vachel Lindsay's white-man's perception of Africa, inspiring Palés' experimentation with exotic African and local negritude imagery at times tinged with poeticized *criollo* racist irony.

In those playful and naively racist beginnings, Palés discovered the Afro-Caribbean identity that his people had historically denied and were then denying during that era of nostalgia for its Spanish past to counter Anglo-Saxon colonization. Right-wing critics dismissed his racial adulteration of the traditional white *criollo* vision and left-wing critics condemned him as racist because of his exaggeratedly sexual representations of blackness, actually a Romantic celebration of Afro-Caribbean vitality against Western decline.

Palés was indeed guilty of romanticizing the black man as a noble savage, but, at the same time he was challenging the *criollo* culture that still clung to its Spanish past stifling Puerto Rico's true, Afro-Hispanic identity, what Palés called Afro-Antillean. Black sensuality redeemed the island *criollo's* hollowed out spirit, a people dying "of nothing." His expression of love for black woman's beauty was not solely an erotic impulse but a recognition of the African spirits inherited through her womb in the Caribbean, making the mulatta symbol of island Afro-Hispanic mixture.

Williams patently digested *Tuntún de Pasa y Grifería,* in which he recognized a kinship that he himself had expressed long before they met. Nine years before Williams read Palés' celebration of black woman's beauty, he had written "The Colored Girls of Passenack—Old and New" (1932): "I have had my breath taken away by women of color that no white woman equals for me."[5] Moreover, Palés was a baroque poet as was Carlos in code, both descendants of the poet Williams called "the Man," Góngora. And to seal matters, Palés wrote formal poems but in spoken language, "en Boricua,"–the colloquial way of saying "in Puerto Rican speech"– the equivalent of Bill's giving prestige to the American Idiom.

In sum, Williams discovered a brother, an addition to what he ambiguously called, always in quotation marks, his "line," which began with Góngora, included Quevedo, Lorca and Neruda, and now Palés Matos, whom he adopted as one more of "Elena's sons." That metaphor was grounded in reality: Elena was the daughter of his maternal grandmother, a racially-mixed woman from Martinique who married his Dutch maternal grandfather, thus embodying the Afro-Antillean heritage that Palés celebrated.

---

[5] *The Farmer's Daughters* (New York: New Directions, 1961), 55.

Williams' reaction to *Tuntún* also behooves a rereading of poems that he wrote as a young man about his mother Elena's idiosyncrasies, his criticism of her psyche coinciding with Luis Palés Matos and other Puerto Rican writers' cultural criticism of the island's *criollo* consciousness. Notable is his quarrel with Elena's propensity to escape, dodge crude reality:

Ah, Madam, what good are your thoughts

romantic but true
beside this gaiety of the sun
and that huge appetite?

–"Brilliant Sad Sun"[6]

Palés satirized that propensity: "only sometimes Don Quijote/ being daft and scatterbrained,/of your Maritornes whoring/constructs a Dulcinea."[7] Essayist Antonio S. Pedreira had summarized that *criollo* defect in the first sentence of the preface to his classic essay on island psychology, *Insularismo* (1934): "These words will lack that admiring tone that our complacency has created to measure our reality."[8] Without knowing it, Williams criticism of Elena's proclivity to live in *sueños* echoed Palés Matos' Afro-Antillean mission to rattle *criollo* escapism that denied the island's defining Afro-Hispanic heritage.

Shortly after returning to New Jersey, Williams published his translation of Palés' "Preludio en Boricua" with a praising introduction, and subsequently wrote poems and stanzas imitative of Palés' poetry, an imitation I demonstrate in detail in *The Spanish American Roots*. But the literary impact of *Tuntún de pasa y grifería* does not stop at a few poems and a translation. In that collection in which Palés celebrates the African spirits that swarm the geography that informed him, the idea of geography shaping the consciousness served Williams in advancing the writing of his poem about "a man as a city." To what extent he had already worked on *Paterson* is unknown, but interviewed by critic Edith Heal, Williams claimed that he was looking for a "scheme" to begin the poem "Paterson," and came upon it "in 1941."[9] In the first pages of *Paterson* one comes across verses on African women on the cover of *National Geographic*,

---

[6] William Carlos Williams, *The Collected Poems, Vol.1 1909-1939*, ed. A. Walton Litz and Christopher MacGowen, (New York: New Directions, 1986), 270.

[7] Julio Marzán, *Selected Poems: Poesía Selecta By Luis Palés Matos* (Houston: Arte Público Press, 2000), 26.

[8] Translation mine.

[9] Mariani, *William Carlos Williams: A New World Naked*, 445.

imagery that patently inspired him to imitate the rhythm of two of Palés' most iconic lines

Culipandeando, la reina avanza
y de su inmensa grupa resbalan...[10]

Behind her, packed tight up,
in a descending scale of freshness...[11]

Tuntún also made Puerto Rico a more substantive heritage than the island presented by Elena's sentimental reminiscences. No longer just an emblem of his Spanish roots, Puerto Rico acquired a Caribbean specificity. For that reason, it can also be deduced that as a consequence of his reading *Tuntún* he also came up with the necessary "scheme" to finally produce the promised book about his mother, *Yes, Mrs. Williams*. Put off for decades, originally intended as a biography, it ended up being a celebration of Elena as the embodiment of the Caribbean, an adaptation of the Palesian metaphor of the turbulent mulatta.

In other words, by way of Palés Matos, Williams discovered that his Spanish-language literary roots included a specifically Puerto Rican legacy. But several reasons can explain why, if he boasted of the influence of Góngora and Quevedo, he did not divulge the literary influence of his Puerto Rican roots. One reason what that it was his pattern to conceal sources: "Let them write what they may and/perfect it as they can they will never/come to the secret of that form."[12] The other would not have been because "Puerto Rican" was not prestigious, a bias that would not have applied to "Spanish" Puerto Rico back then. The most plausible reason was that this association was not of remote, vague roots but of his immediate identity, which would have blurred his established American identity as poet.

Consequently, the 1941 experience changed him privately, leaving him, one must deduce, conflicted. He had been invited to that 1941 conference in recognition of his achievement as American poet, of course, and because the island governor's then-wife, the poet Muna Lee recognized his being "a Puerto Rican poet" but as well because of his publicly expressed Hispanic consciousness in *In the American Grain*, coinciding with the prevailing island Hispanism, which on the mainland was far from threatening. Hispanic prestige had been defended by the Transcendentalists against the populist bigotry underpinning

---

[10] Luis Palés Matos, *Poesía Completa y Prosa Selecta, ed. Margot Arce de Vázquez* (Caracas: Biblioteca Ayachucho, 1978), 156.

[11] William Carlos Williams, *Paterson* (New York: New Directions, 1963), 13.

[12] "The Cure," in *The Collected Poems of William Carlos Williams, Vols. II* (New York: New Directions, 1986).

the war with Mexico. More recently it had been boosted by F.D. R.'s Good Neighbor Policy (1933) in then "Spanish" America. Popular ethnic xenophobia always existed, as the Williams family and notably Elena were constantly reminded, but among the learned there prevailed a modicum of Hispanic prestige, what empowered Williams, honoring Elena, to keep the Carlos in his name as a poet and title a book *Al Que Quiere.*

That Hispanic prestige also benefitted a small island migration that began arriving in New York after Puerto Rico was extended U.S. citizenship in 1917, a community of predominantly white *criollos* that became part of the then-monolithically understood Spanish community expanded by the Spanish immigration that had begun in 1880 and would further grow owing to conflicts that culminated in the Spanish Civil War (1936-39). Williams openly identified with that community, supporting the Republic and publishing translations of Spanish poets. He also kept in touch with the writers and intellectuals of that composite "Spanish" community who were actually Puerto Rican.

One conduit to that community was the family friend Dr. Julio José Henna, a sure recommendation to his medical studies, and founder of the French Hospital that later hired him. His membership in that community was what led him to Dragon Press, run by the translator and Hispanist literary critic Angel Flores, who published Williams' first book of short stories, *The Knife of the Times and Other Stories* (1932). In other words, prior to 1941 Williams' idea of his Puerto Rican heritage happened to coincide with the prewar migration's Hispanist *criollo* consciousness, not the Puerto Rican consciousness he would have after returning in 1941 and discovering Luis Palés Matos.

But if his great admiration for the classical Spanish poets did not compel him to identify as Hispanic, Palés Matos' being his soulmate did not compel him to identify as Puerto Rican. He was too American and familiar with American xenophobia to risk expressing difference publicly and, to assure his American credentials, he still sensed the need to express his Carlos side in baroque code. After the war, whether as Bill or as a Hispanic-purist Carlos, Williams found it even more difficult to acknowledge any connection to the problematic, more racially mixed diaspora.

Williams never refers to the postwar migration even though he more than anyone else was aware that it was made up of what he called the "pure products of America." He maintained this silence despite being a daily, meticulous reader of newspapers and magazines, and an assiduous follower of culture.[13] No mention of the widely-reported creation of the cosmetic Commonwealth to feign the dismantling of colonialism, nor of the subsequent shooting up of

---

[13] Mariani, *William Carlos Williams: A New World Naked,* 9.

Congress by Puerto Rican nationalists. He could not have avoided the "Bridge between Two Cultures" publicity campaigns, with photographic spreads in *Life* and *Look* magazines. Even though he kept abreast of New York's artistic life, he never commented on the 1957 success of *West Side Story*. And yet, surely because he sensed not having many more years left, in 1959, two years into the play's Broadway success, he published *Yes, Mrs. Williams*, which associated Elena and him with what was considered the infestation of an inferior breed of "Spanish."

To summarize, Williams' Carlos consciousness claimed Hispanic literary roots through his Puerto Rican mother Elena, never identifying as Hispanic or Puerto Rican. And yet in poems on Elena he echoes Puerto Rican themes that he later discovered in the poems of Palés Matos. Should we in retrospect, knowing what we now know, repeat with Muna Lee and insist that Williams is also a Puerto Rican poet? More ironic still, based on today's social definitions, Williams doesn't even qualify as Latino, the epithet intuitively attached to Lin-Manuel Miranda.

Lin-Manuel Miranda publicly identifies as Puerto Rican but neither do his plays nor his musical compositions contain any elements from which one could extrapolate a Puerto Rican theme or consciousness. Nevertheless, in writing *Hamilton*, a musical that celebrates America as a multicultural and multiracial country without any influence of Hispanic culture, Lin-Manuel Miranda becomes the more authentic Latino writer.

Miranda's first major play was *In the Heights* (2005), a musical adaptation of the classic drama he surely read or saw in his high school (because it was taught in all of them), *Our Town* (1938) by Thorton Wilder, about the lives of the inhabitants of a fictional small American town. Miranda's play portrays the lives of members of the community that formed during his youth in Washington Heights, predominantly Dominican, as if it were a village. Reminiscent of *Our Town* in being about individual competitions and the lure of a larger world, residents of the "Heights" (Upper West Side Manhattan) are portrayed as immigrants who, according to the Dominican narrator Usnavi, are looking for "a better life."

Miranda wrote an earlier, one-act version of *In the Heights* in his sophomore year at Wesleyan University, where it was staged, drawing the attention of influential Wesleyan graduates in the theater world, who invested in Miranda's fleshing it out in preparation for a Broadway play. That assignment would require the collaboration of Puerto Rican writer Quiara Alegría Hudes. After an off-Broadway premiere, the collaboration turned out to be a smash Broadway hit that has been performed internationally. A film version had to wait for its premiere until June 2021, delayed by a year due to the Covid pandemic.

The play triumphs because of Miranda's genius as a composer despite the slackness of the libretto, according to Charles McNulty of *The Los Angeles Times,* who described it as "overstuffed and oversimplified."[14] Clive Barnes of *The New York Post* criticized it as "sentimental and untruthful."[15] My own critique is that the musical is set in a neighborhood as fictional as *Our Town* but not as metaphorically evocative. The actual Heights does not have the history of African-American Harlem or El Barrio to imagine it as a metaphorical village while imposing a suspension of historical reality.

The Dominican immigration represented the start of the non-contiguous Latin American immigration, *latinos* fleeing poverty and/or political oppression, attracted not just by the promise traditionally afforded to European immigrants but to the post-civil rights benefits gained by minorities in the Civil Rights Movement. In *In the Heights,* the characters from a predominantly black country enjoy a harmony with their American life only limited by finances in a script that dodges the social experience of living in a country torn by race. Can one write of Latinos, especially Dominicans, as if making no social statement if, being predominantly black, they are inherently metaphors making a social statement?

Starting out with that implausibility, gives a license for more. The most paradigmatic is the situation of Nina, the Puerto Rican student who was attending Stanford University in California and returned to the Heights after having lost her scholarship because her two jobs did not allow her to keep good grades. Her father runs a taxi cab service in The Heights. If a New York Puerto Rican went all the way to Stanford, it had to be because she had all her expenses paid and if not, she could get a student loan to supplement her studies. Hard to believe is that she and her parents hadn't worked out the finances before she left for California. It didn't make sense for the father to sell his business, which would appear to be his having already attained a "better life." They lived in the gentrifying Heights in Manhattan.

In 1979 The Puerto Rican Traveling Theater promoted Edward Gallardo's *Simpson Street* as the first English-language play by a second-generation writer from the Puerto Rican diaspora. When I saw the production, having grown up during my early childhood near Simpson Street in the Bronx, the play seemed to lack credibility, the characters' embodiments of social formula. A young man from a family in conflict over obviously working-class but presumably Puerto Rican grievances ends up hoping to solve his problems by escaping to

---

[14] "In the Heights," *Wikipedia,* https://en.wikipedia.org/wiki/In_the_Heights.

[15] "In the Heights," *Wikipedia,* https://en.wikipedia.org/wiki/In_the_Heights.

California, the state where many Americans were finding the golden promised land and in this case a symbol of redemptive assimilation.

Decades after that production, Gallardo revealed in the *Miami Herald* that he was Cuban. One deduces that he had fooled the actress Miriam Colón, the founder of the Puerto Rican Traveling Theater. In retrospect, Gallardo simply borrowed the types and images and thus assembled a "Latino" drama before the epithet existed. Similarly, *In the Heights* relies on abstracted Dominican and Puerto Rican characters with no dimensions other than cliched American socioeconomic circumstance.

White Miranda played the role of the Dominican Usnavi– a name suggestive of the influence of Pedro Juan Soto's protagonist in his novel *Usmaíl* (from "U.S. Mail")– and like Miranda as a Dominican the cast of characters is Dominican or Puerto Rican in name more than in having any specific manner of behavior or expression or memories, nor were the actors cast to do so being variants of generic Latino. Given that they are all Latinos, there is a nuance of wanting to escape the suggested ghetto that otherwise the play romanticizes.

In that ambiguity we experience the joys and frustrations of longing for "a better life" from budding Americans, a dream apparently achieved outside the Heights and presumably away from *latinos*. Nina returns to California promising Benny that she is coming back (to return from Stanford to her high school graduate boyfriend, really?), Kevin and his wife leave the neighborhood after selling his taxi business, Vanessa the hairdresser has always longed to live in Greenwich Village but belatedly discovers a love for Usnavi who had always talked of returning to Santo Domingo and now seems to be the only one inclined to stay in the Heights. A taste of Latino to exactly what point is not clear except to enjoy good music.

In 2005, when *In the Heights* was first performed, Latino consciousness was beginning to be the epithet of American identity for all Latinos/ *latinos*. In *In the Heights* Miranda created metaphors of emerging multiculturalism, the subtextual theme that would inspire *Hamilton*. More explicitly American in theme and, for obvious reasons, without Latino characters despite the Latino actors, *Hamilton* fulfills Latino expectations in invoking solidarity with racial minorities and the multicultural consciousness that aspires to redefine America. Exuberant solidarity at the cost of much not well thought out.

Miranda was rudely awakened to this criticism when he transported the original cast to perform *Hamilton* in Puerto Rico. He wrote *Hamilton* as an American either reflecting on or just adopting a Latino identity, and presented the musical before islanders wary of the difference between Latino and *latino*. The island's nationalists protested his romanticizing a figure in the history of Puerto Rico's colonizers. Miranda, who identifies personally as Puerto

Rican, had evidently compartmentalized not only his own Puerto Ricanness but the existence of a consciousness of Puerto Rico as something more than an object of poeticized pride. And island nationalists were not the only ones who accused him of writing with a one-eyed view of history.

The African-American novelist and playwright Ishmael Reed reacted by writing the play *The Haunting of Lin-Manuel Miranda* (2019), in which he criticized *Hamilton* as the result of an excessively felicitous reading of the nation's history, of a blindness to its sadder reality. Miranda as Reed's character is awakened in the night by some of the historical figures he omitted from his musical, including the slave owned by Hamilton's sister. Like a tourist being forced back to places he had failed to see on his first visit, Reed's Miranda learns of a history that his musical overlooked and apologizes for his ingenuousness.

Miranda is arguably a victim of a Latino/ *latino* ambiguity. In Spanish neither *puertorriqueño* nor *latino* are racial epithets, what Latino and Puerto Rican evoke in English. So as Spanish *puertorriqueño* or *latino* Miranda would not intuitively respond with the racial consciousness that Reed presumes would be intuitive for a Latino Puerto Rican. On the other hand, his Puerto Rican consciousness is evidently of an island tradition of fervent cultural patriotism that does not translate into addressing Puerto Rican culture intellectually. And neither is Miranda, strictly speaking a Newyorican, as his personal story does not descend from the postwar diaspora. His parents, both professionals fleeing an economic crisis in Puerto Rico, arrived in New York City much later, a product of the island's industrialization and the already achieved civil rights opportunities and socioeconomic and educational benefits gained by disgraced Newyoricans. He is a graduate of Hunter College High School.

In other words, Miranda grew up in New York but far from the marginalization that "Newyorican" evokes, which might explain why none of his theater descends from *West Side Story*. I am not referring to the dramatization of gang stereotypes but to the backstory of poorer and darker islanders induced to uproot themselves for the benefit of the rise of those who better fit in the new, whiter industrialized island. Miranda does not express an awareness of ties to that history in the two works that have established him as a playwright and composer. To create the musical *The Capeman*, Paul Simon wrote as if he were a postwar diaspora Puerto Rican inevitably invoking *West Side Story* as a theatrical precursor.

Miranda identifies with Puerto Rico after a childhood in which he traveled annually to Puerto Rico to spend a month with his grandfather in the town of Vega Alta. He has donated money to restore the island after Hurricane María and used his personal influence to petition Congress for measures to alleviate Puerto Rico's crushing debt. His passion for Puerto Rico was also expressed in his organizing that original-cast production of *Hamilton* on the island. The island is definitely *latino*, so given his island-centric identity, in *In the Heights* as composer and playwright, Miranda's Latino voice was an artistic creation.

Very Latino too was his updating American history with minority actors. Postmodernist Latino does not understand literature as a vehicle of ideation, using metaphors as modes of revealing, an "elitist" expectation. It is foremost experiential, documentary; hence the facility of adopting presentism, history being the preservation of accumulated metaphors. And from Latino literalism and presentism follows replacing a presumably white supremacist Hispanic history with a racially-liberated Latino consciousness. The metaphors we know as the Founding Fathers inscribed ideals that do not have ideational power if coming from a congress of white men, so Latino requires that African American and Latino actors perform the revolution so that Latinos can believe the revolution was also about them.

Ironically, in having conceived the multicultural *Hamilton*, Miranda was vindicating Williams' thesis that the truest, American "mingling spirit" was sown by the Spanish, who seeded the multiracial consciousness that Miranda inherited as Puerto Rican long before Latino presumed to invent it. Nevertheless, because of that naive coincidence, Miranda is celebrated as a Latino writer. In contrast Williams does not enter into the Latino discourse because, to begin with, his writing is traditionally literary, using ambiguity and metaphor.

Williams also traced his Puerto Rican heritage to Hispanic roots aware of Hispanic as a default whiteness but not racializing it, what a woke Latino generation was to do. Furthermore, not lending itself to the contemplation of nuance, Latino also ignores that in *Yes, Mrs. Williams* Williams introduced his mother Elena as having inherited African roots through her mixed mother from Martinique, the self-recognition of race that he learned to embrace from Luis Palés Matos. Seen from another angle, in both *Yes, Mrs. Williams* and his poems on Elena, Williams engages, if unconsciously, in the Puerto Rican literary discourse notwithstanding that island intelligentsia refuses to recognize his participation.

In the windy tunnel of identity, perspectives blow from all directions. Williams, who never publicly identified as Puerto Rican, leaves us with poems and prose that translate into English a Puerto Rican literary discourse of whose existence Miranda gives no evidence of knowing. On the other hand, while his parents' hometown embraces him as native son, and Miranda publicly announces his Puerto Rican identity and his concern for Puerto Rico's material needs, that identity does not inspire him to writing anything to do with Puerto Rico's historical, cultural and racial struggle to define itself nor about the mainland Puerto Rican's struggle with identity. Williams, who presaged multiculturalism, is not recognized by the Latino consciousness while Miranda enjoys the status of Latino superstar for advancing multiculturalism. Finally, there are islanders who believe that neither is truly Puerto Rican, denying that Puerto Rico long ago ceased to be an island and is now the hub of what novelist Eduardo Lalo calls "Greater Puerto Rico."

In 1997 the Nagasake-born novelist Kasuo Ishiguro won the Nobel Prize as a Briton. There are British and Japanese who debate his identity. The same could be debated about the novelist William Henry Hudson (1841-1922), author of *Green Mansions*, of British parents whom, even though he wrote in English, Google describes as an "Argentine author." The "American philosopher" George Santayana was born in Spain and never became an American citizen. At the age of 49, he left Harvard and the country for Europe to never return, leaving a canonical bibliography of insight on American culture, which he claimed to have "borrowed." The Frenchified Julio Cortázar left Argentina to never return but wrote as an Argentine writer, his hallmark novel *Rayuela* set in a Buenos Aires short on setting details, its author a speaker of French-accented Spanish. As I write Jhumper Lahiri launched her latest novel that she wrote in Italian, her new language of choice, which she subsequently translated into English.

Williams maintained a strictly intellectual relationship with his Puerto Rican identity and Miranda maintains a strictly personal and non-intellectual relationship with his. Identity is defined by the story one chooses to tell. In the end, as Miranda discovered the Hamilton inside him through the telling of Ron Chernow, we are all left singing the song Miranda wrote for Hamilton, "Who Lives, Who Dies, Who Tells Your Story."

9.

A SADASS PARABLE ABOUT IRIS CHACON

Late-night comics Jay Leno and David Letterman were a study of cultural contrast. Jay Leno was Mediterranean warmth, every member of the band his buddy. He opened his show giving his audience handshakes. His skits stopped people on the street. Sometimes he knocked on people's doors. In contrast, Letterman kept his distance behind cameras. Humor was the office where he worked. Occasionally he walked among the audience, part of his job. One sensed no personal rapport between him and the audience, between him and band members. A tribute to Letterman's comic skills is that, even though he personally seemed humorless, one enjoyed his humor. He was also considered the hipper late-night host, delivering cutting edge, and perhaps for that reason in 1984 the Puerto Rican singer, dancer and continentally legendary bombshell Iris Chacón chose Letterman's show to start bowling over the U.S. male audience.

She didn't get far.

Introduced to the U.S. mainland audience as– to cite Letterman's recital of her publicist's copy– "the Dolly Parton of Puerto Rico," she appealed to a birdbrain's appreciation of Parton, the comparison really a disservice to a serious and talented songwriter. Parton knew how to game the media with her huge breasts, gained entry then played country smart and not dumb blond. Chacón played a one-dimensional hyper-sexy Latina that, given her limited performing talents, took her farther than one would have imagined.

Her career took off in the seventies. She was a not especially gifted, flowing-haired brunette singer whose dancing was just really an excuse to showcase her bountiful booty, the kind that arrests the eyes of Caribbean men. Her hyperbole became iconic. In his novel *La Guaracha del Macho Camacho* (*Macho Camacho's Beat*), published in 1974, novelist Luis Rafael Sánchez fictionalized her with the stage-name "La Langosta" ("The Lobster"), adding the tagline, loosely translated, "with the meat in the tail." On her first Letterman appearance, accompanied by two male dancers, she stepped out on stage in a performing swimsuit that revealed in yesterday's standard definition TV her high-definition thighs and butt.

Statuesque, when she walked over to the guest's chair, the comparatively reduced Letterman seemed unable to contain in his sight her sizeable presence. She sat in the chair but Letterman was unable to manage her determination to call attention to herself. Talking to herself over his first question, she removed her shoes, complaining that she just couldn't sit normally, then stood on the sofa chair and sat on its arm, her knees facing Letterman, giving the camera a wide angle view of her thighs, to which she called attention by smoothing her hand over them.

Breasts, knees, thick thighs and crotch aimed straight at the speechless Letterman, he tried to look around her broad shoulders, find a space without her, remarking that it felt like "talking to a barn." Taking issue, she ginned up her intention to prove that Americans were in dire need of her sexual defibrillation. The scene, whether rehearsed or spontaneous, called for Letterman to play her American foil, what used to be called the "straight man" (the unfunny one in a comic duo) to her gag, which he did without requiring his putting on an act. His fingertips tapped her knee in the goofy, sexless way of Oliver Hardy as he asked her to behave, sit down.

This not being Puerto Rico nor a Univisión studio, Letterman's giggles notwithstanding, his occasional glances into the camera or toward his audience solicited sympathy for putting up with what he knew that they understood as the funny sleaze before him. At some point, in a kind of jest that could have also been sincere, he said "Come on, that's enough." Fortunately, at that moment it came time for a commercial break, fortuitous given the confusion as to what the audience was actually watching, either a rehearsed gag or chaos.

The following week I discussed Chacón's appearance with a woman friend, a professor of Latin American literature at one of the C.U.N.Y. colleges. Born in New Jersey of Puerto Rican parents, she said that she had watched mortified. I asked why if daily on Spanish-language television one saw the same high-tension sexuality, the heavily made-up plump dancing girls, the busty and big-butt-popping bombshells. Precisely, said the professor, a feminist. Spanish-language television daily insulted women although she did admit to watching some shows. Just to spend some time entertained in her cultural world she had to tolerate elements that she couldn't excuse as "*latino* difference." Unfortunately, Spanish-language TV still appealed to the least common denominator, she lamented. But she watched knowing that those sexual elements that we tolerate at home are embarrassing when taken on the American road. Before our own audience, she might have interpreted Chacón's self-parody on Letterman as just stupidly humorous, but seeing her perform that way before an American audience embarrassed her.

Chacón landed on mainland network TV after starring in a 1983 island television ad that, before the Internet, went media viral. An island agency with an account to sell Amalie motor coolant created an ad that pivoted on exploiting Chacón's most marketable asset. A car, hood up, has overheated on the road. Chacón pulls up to the befuddled-looking owner who says that he doesn't understand because he had poured in coolant. Chacón emerges from her car in a gold lamé body glove with leopard spots and says that she has something that would definitely help. She turns her backside to the camera, and while bent over to reach into her car trunk, says *"Tengo un TREMENDO coolant"* ("I have an AWESOME coolant"), then turns around again holding up a gold-colored plastic container of Amalie.

Hearing in her accented pronunciation of "coolant" the Spanish word for derriere "culo" timed exactly as she bent over to remove the container from trunk, the driver stares at hers, bug-eyed. (Actually, the ad's true cleverness more subtly hinges on the ambiguity of the hyperbolically pronounced *tremennnnn-do*, at once physically big and great as product.) Buzz over that ad made it to the front page of the *Walt Street Journal*. Next thing we know la Chacón is boarding a plane to hit the American market and appeared on a number of primetime and daytime shows from 1984 through the early 1990s.

She arrived at, excuse the expression, the tail end of an era for her kind of bombshell vedette in English. Feminism had been on the rise since the seventies and it wasn't a Latina feminism but the Anglo Puritan standard. In the eighties, when I was writing for the *Voice*, the Argentine writer Luisa Valenzuela invited me to join her and a group of our friends who were attending a woman's writer's conference in Mexico City, where shared feminism did not result in cultural sisterhood on the subject of women and sexuality.

Latin American and liberated Arabic women writers chose to dress in attractive garb and wear makeup, finding themselves crossing words with American feminists who apparently expected that all the liberated women present should have burned their bras and worn only denim shirts and jeans. For those Anglo-American feminists, of course, Chacón was the incarnation of the kind of oppression they were determined to overcome. In other words, Chacón arrived just in time to be judged by that lens that made her look so retrograde. And to complicate matters further, there was another cultural impasse that contributed to Chacon's miscommunication in her mainland invasion. She was marketing the wrong erogenous zone.

Breasts in American sexuality are, excuse the expression, titillating but not considered intrinsically sleazy. Had Chacón arrived, like Pamela Anderson or Dolly Parton, foregrounding only her breasts, all she would have had to do was sit and exhibit. In other words, Chacón's lobster tail had already crossed a cultural red line, an American obsession with minimalism back there, and her sitting on the chair arm to flaunt her tremendous "coolant," came off as downright dirty.

That was still the state of American sexuality in the 80s. But if at once retrograde, she was also ahead of her time, as Andrew S. Vargas noted on the website *Remezcla* in "Way Before Kim Kardashian's Butt Broke the Internet, There Was Iris Chacon."[1] The traditional squeamishness about big behinds was in the process of being reversed among prominent female sex symbols, from Jennifer Lopez to Beyoncé to Kim Kardashian. Lopez is the grand dame of that movement, yet, while her career was still on the rise, her handlers knew how to navigate through mainstream tastes. Her appearance on Letterman's show was a revealing contrast to Chacón's when she was there for public forgiveness owing to an incident that had occurred a week earlier.

News reports had put her in an ugly rap-scene shooting on a date with Sean P. Diddy, and Letterman seemed to express a genuine liking for the real Jennifer behind the hip-hop publicity stunt that she had been performing by dating a rapper. Letterman sounded as if speaking from the heart when he commented that the image of her in a setting with a gun did not fit the feelings that the country had for her. Shortly thereafter, perhaps because he had reiterated before a national audience what so many others had already urged, Jaylo ended her relationship with the rap star and that scene. For this purification, Jaylo wisely wore a black skirt and a white blouse, distracting from her prodigious body by looking like a private school student.

Like Parton successful in other talents, Jaylo did not need to emphasize just her physical attributes, but Chacón didn't have another talent and had to play her only cards at once as she was on the downside of her prime. Moreover, as noted earlier, history worked against her because she had rocketed at time when her kind of entertainment was still popular in Latin America but made it to mainland television when it had become passé. She begs comparison with a contemporaneous predecessor, one who created the television role in which Chacón was being cast, whose career began a decade before Chacón's and continued for several decades beyond, but who charted her American visibility more successfully, the Spaniard Charo.

Charo didn't clash with American sexual requisites because at the time that she emerged men still ogled at women, starlets cashed in on their ogling, and because she fit the American bill perfectly. To begin with, she was blond. She had started out on television introduced by the popular bandleader Xavier Cougat, and like Dolly Parton, used a sexual window to gain visibility but then, through the medium of that fame, exhibited a serious side: she was a flamenco

---

[1] Andrew S. Vargas, "Way Before Kim Kardashian's Butt Broke the Internet, There Was Iris Chacón," *Remezcla*, November 20, 2014, https://remezcla.com/film/tbt-way-kim-kardashians-butt-broke-internet-iris-chacon/

guitarist who had studied under Andrés Segovia. In addition to her blond looks and cute smile, also very mainstream American was the selling point of large breasts.

Mainly Charo pandered to stereotypes of "Spanish," performing as a ditz who made people chuckle with silly-comments in her thick Castillean accent. One hallmark was her referring to sex as "coochi-coochi," which she repeated as she pumped her small hips. Charo was not a serious invitation to sin and did not pretend to arouse, only to make funny sexual references; she was a big-breasted little Spanish sexual clown, not hot smoldering but sexily cute, who when she started to play a flamenco guitar made her body disappear and ultimately succeeded in leaving a hint of being much smarter than she performed as ditz. The audience laughed with her. But where Charo fully knew how to perform on American TV, Chacón appeared to have no real appreciation of the culture into which she had crossed, and so she broadcast herself as too sleazy for American television and too naive to know better.

On the other hand, Charo had the advantage of being Spanish, which even though this may sound contradictory, is a culture that had been so heavily Catholic that its sexual mores fit right in with American TV compared to bombsells who were her Latin American counterparts. For, not to diminish feminism's objections to this commericial pandering, in Latin America sensuality is perceived natural to personal aesthetics. On Univisión it was not unusual for a bombshell, after performing, to then be interviewed and talk of her life, her devotion to her husband, their children, and even her faith. That transition does not shock us, for whom sensuality and sexuality are optional major components of personal vanity but is unlikely to be seen on English-language TV. Actually, if Chacón had one saving grace, her act was a subtle parodying of the Latin vedette.

On Spanish-language TV, where bombshells are staple entertainment, then, Chacón would not have felt compelled to educate the audience on how high-voltage sensuality worked. She would have performed her song and dance, and Letterman could have actually conducted an interview. But her setting out to perform not in a familiar *latino* milieu, with no space for her to be the woman, what she would have been among *latinos*, bespeaks of how culturally distant she felt from that American audience to think it better to solely be her act.

Sexual mores are really just specialized expressions of cultural Weltanschuungs, and the chasm between the two cultures in question is what Hispanic/Latino American biculturals reconcile throughout their lives. In the matter of sexuality, I have had to reconcile competing male models. And I was also the brother of an older sister with whom I had discussed many times her Latina sexuality in the context of Anglo culture, her feeling that no matter what she did, she was being viewed as too sensual. I also couldn't help putting my sister in Chacón's place.

While teaching as a visiting professor of Spanish at a New Jersey university, I was assigned at an office that happened to be across the hall from the chairman of the English department, a woman with a Jewish surname. She was middle aged, and because of her surname, I was surprised to discover that she was indeed Jewish but also Brazilian. Being two *latino* professors of English (what I normally was in my tenured other life), we regularly chatted.

In the course of one conversation, she closed her office door and confessed to feeling oppressed by the feminist standards that predominated in the English department. Every morning she feared for her career when considering how much make-up to wear or whether she should add something of her favorite jewelry. Her just being a *latina* with such impulses to look attractive as a *latina* patently made her feel retrograde before her presumably more politically advanced women colleagues whose dress was more consciously sexually neutral.

I confessed that I too felt the pressure to tone down my Latin masculinity that, no matter how much dialed down, was always made to feel excessive. We *latinos* are constantly being shamed into buying into the ultrasonic preaching that the Anglo sexual standard is the ultimate correction when theirs is the mores of a culture uncertain about what to do with sensuality, descending from a Puritan tradition of treating the senses as sinful and of never having made an art of it.

I thought back to contrasting expressions of sexuality my sister and I experienced throughout our lives and Chacón's having to discover it on the job, unintentionally making her the butt of Anglo-American laughter. After fulfilling her first string of bookings, although she would sporadically appear on TV for another decade, it became evident that her debut was unsuccessful. Her final appearances of that tour, on David Letterman and Merv Griffin, were more subdued, in which she admitted to learning much, and the talk was more like a post-mortem review of a job interview that she had failed miserably.

On the internet Latinos today assess Chacón's incursion onto the mainland more generously, as Vargas represents, crediting her appearances for paving the way for later Latinas. Another possible interpretation perhaps not Latino-wide enough for discussion and in violation of Latino's solidarity feature: that her experience epitomized the gap between mainland and island Puerto Ricans, the latter's assumption of being prepared to confront American culture without the help of mainland Puerto Ricans, thank you. Had they consulted beforehand, they would have been warned that before showing up Chacón's sensuality was already being held against her, about to be put on display for spoofing and that

Letterman would be there to keep things American, protecting the audience from the sinfulness of sleaze by making it funny– what Jaylo's people knew when cleaning up her mess with the rap scene.

Puerto Rican literature portrays islanders as prone to denying unpleasant reality, and Chacón encountered unpleasant reality her first night on that Letterman debut. But as Letterman resisted her, this was not yet a learning experience. She persisted, defending her sexiness to the point of humiliation, determined to be seen as wildly sexual before *americanos* who had welcomed Charo before her but needed to experience the real deal. She repeated this effort until the reality of that mainland experience sank in and the learning began. A decade later, Chacón ended her career.

10.

DOES YOUR CHILD SPEAK
ANOTHER LANGUAGE AT HOME?

This question appeared on a questionnaire that I had to fill out to begin my daughter's education in a New York City public school. Why was I being asked? Would speaking another language at home obstruct my child's education in an English-speaking classroom? Knowing what I knew from having grown up since the age of four months in polyglot New York City, even though at home my daughter did speak Spanish (because it was her Ecuadorean mother's first language, because Spanish was another intellectual enrichment I had to offer and because as a household rule my wife and I didn't celebrate ignorance, not even ignorance that passed for cultural superiority) I answered No.

What benefit would there have been to answering Yes? The truth would have measured my daughter on a bilingual child's American scale and from that point on any common English mistake that might routinely be said by any kid, out of my daughter's mouth would give the teacher license to wax anthropological, attributing my daughter's error to her problem of speaking another language at home. I thought back to my high-school English teacher who demoted my final grade from B to C, discounting accumulated higher scores of which I kept a record, lowering my grade to what he thought, his exact words, "you deserved." When my stepfather asked him to explain my low grade, he justified his judgment of my merit by underscoring the problem he had often encountered with students "who spoke another language at home."

As I registered my daughter, I looked around the lunchroom. A few other parents sat at the rectangular lunchroom table: a couple of Jewish parents but the majority *latina* mothers. Farther removed, separated from ours by two empty tables, Koreans were crowded together, laughing and chatting. In this Queens elementary school, one of the city's best, the dominant cultural power had shifted in the past decade from Jewish to Korean. Korean clout was such that the parents not only ran their own exclusive PTA and, after bringing a civil rights suit against the city, managed to postpone testing for a year so that their children, who spoke only Korean at home, could improve their English and have a fair opportunity to enter the gifted-children's program.

Highly protective of their children's Korean identity, the parents never allowed its adulteration by answering invitations to birthday parties. Of course, they never invited non-Korean children to their parties. They hired Korean school buses to transport the children home or to Korean after-school programs. Koreans evidently held an ethnocentric view of the inadequacy of American culture beyond its providing material comfort. This conviction prompted the need to preserve a Korean identity by remaining exclusively united not only in school but in their business and real estate practices throughout Queens. I was told a pattern was not to purchase a single house but to organize and transform entire blocks.

Although far more modest but comparatively just as Herculean, my mother tried to insulate my sister and me from the worst influences of our having been brought to New York by keeping us connected to island family. Especially ironic was that effort's having been carried out because of motives comparatively identical to the Koreans': my extended family's attitude toward American culture, our Hispanic values being presumably superior. My matriarch aunt financed the salvation of my sister, who was returned to Puerto Rico to attend an island Catholic elementary academy to prevent her from acquiring the looser morals of American girls.

Puerto Ricans of those days, reiterating José Enrique Rodo's cultural comparison in his essay *Ariel,* admitted to the great material achievements of American culture while holding on to a claim of superior Hispanic personal values. Today, American Dream-bound Latin Americans, distanced from that once monolithic Hispanic heritage and more steeped in America for popular consumption, arrive prepared to surrender their children to this culture whose first lesson is to foreswear learning a foreign language.

This capitulating to English was the pattern among the handful of *latinas* in this virtually suburban, small-town-like neighborhood at the city's eastern end beside Nassau County, in which except for my wife, all were married to middle-class non-Latinos– high-school teachers, middle-level managers and salesmen. They had all saved their children from the social limitations of Spanish-speaking, this de-Latinization so paradoxically "Latino." De rigueur their lightened hair, bland, un-Latin woman's dressing in jogging clothes and sneakers, their sharply articulating their child's polysyllabic, mainstreaming Anglo-Saxon given names: Jeremy, Christopher, Jonathan, Priscilla. Sitting a few feet from me, we were miles apart.

From their perspective, I was the only father at the table, and as I would subsequently learn, stood out as the only husband who had just bought into the co-op who was Puerto Rican, whatever that mythos evoked among Latin Americans learning to adopt American ways. From my perspective, our differences came down to three. They spoke English with an accent and I had two first languages, having acquired English since infancy, plus owing to my being brought up my American stepdad, I actually grew up in the middle-class

American culture in which they were raising their own children. And, unlike me, they could answer truthfully that their children spoke no other language at home.

Does your child speak another language at home? How inspiring it would have been if the question were intended to profile the new first-grader in order to help the school provide additional lessons in literacy in that other language, a recognition of that child's being linguistically gifted. But that intention would not have reflected the more pedestrian, call it patriotic, American linguistic attitude. Instead, behind the doubtless high-toned reasons for asking– to better understand the child and provide the necessary resources– the question was actually part of an agenda to teach American children to want to understand only English.

The historical argument for monolingualism is not altogether without merit: a country composed of many European cultures with a history of internecine warfare had to discourage other languages from hastening the nation's dissolution or sowing clashes of regional ethnocentricities. According to this Platonic argument, ever hovering above us is a national unity Idea closer to being attained at the moment that the country exclusively speaks English. Also implicitly argued is the notion that diverse communities would become homogenized in English-speaking and evolve into ethnically nondescript American.

Of course, this ideal cultural democracy does not exist. The nation coalesces competing ethnocentric subcultures that preserve their identity even after adopting English. Among those subcultures, the mythically defined hegemonic Anglo-Saxon "mainstream" supersedes ethnicities while proselytizing ideal democratic America. The great symbol of that democratic unity is English. Patriotism to that ideal behooves overlooking English's historical, undemocratic proclivity to demote non-Europeans, prompting ethnic groups to preserve, in cultural self-defense, their original identity and heritage, creating fragmentation. In other words, patriotism means seeing nothing disharmonious in seeing America as a performance starring its select cultural citizens supported by a cast of purely civil citizens whose exotic cultural lives they are free to exercise on a plane that neither changes nor informs the only recognized blend called American culture.

In recent times, the monolingual ideal has been more fiercely advocated in popular cultural dynamics because, as conservatives complain, an elitist liberalism has capitulated to the unpatriotic truth of a de facto multiculturalism. It offends conservatives that the government offers a full range of services in other languages, especially acknowledging the demographic importance of Spanish and that these policies are actually the historical consequence of the Founding Fathers' never having designated a national official language. My purpose is not to advocate against that possibility nor to attack English as the hegemonic language, nor am I advocating a bilingual country. I am juxtaposing American linguistic reality beside Anglophone myth.

Jefferson did no less in addressing the issue with his contemporaries and in ordaining that Spanish be taught at the University of Virginia because, looking westward, he foresaw a destiny with Spanish. That future was one motivation for his teaching himself Spanish and advising his nephew to do the same, especially because, "the ancient history of America is written in that language."[1] Another reason was his love of the novel *Don Quixote*, the only novel he ordained be offered at the university library. Unfortunately, Jefferson's linguistic openness was not passed down to his descendants, who barreled westward to force the speaking of English, so consequently Americans inherit the fear of an identity crisis should they actually speak a foreign language. This powerful monolingual tradition subverts modern educational curricula that struggle to teach foreign languages.

Foreign language teaching is an effort to ennoble something that popular American culture discredits every minute. Americans have become accustomed to associating foreign languages with powerlessness that immigrates to attain the status of English. This is very much a working- and middle-class attitude. My very cultured first ex-wife had forgotten her birth control pills when coming from Puerto Rico and would have to wait for a prescription after a doctor's visit. She had an old prescription and took it with her very continental-sounding accent to the local Queens pharmacist who, of course, unleashed his American cultural power. In my senior high-school year I worked for a Madison Avenue pharmacy that received very refined Europeans daily, very often bending the rules for them. I took my wife to that pharmacy, where she walked in alone, and given her good looks, accented charm, she walked out with the pills.

Given the fashion value attached to continental languages in upscale New York, one might imagine that if students are being made to study a language, French and Italian might be favorites. But if continental European iconography lines New York's major avenues and dominates the couture labels, French (which in parts of New York has been resuscitated by Haitian students) and Italian have been disappearing as available subjects in school curricula among working-class and middle-class kids who really just want to be American. For that reason, unfortunately, loss of French and Italian teaching has to be blamed

---

[1] Thomas Jefferson, Letter from Thomas Jefferson to Peter Carr (August 10, 1787), https://encyclopediavirginia.org/entries/letter-from-thomas-jefferson-to-peter-carr-august-10-1787/

on Spanish, the big ticket that enjoys neither pedigree nor prestige in the ears of English speakers.

Cutting out the other languages, Spanish resoundingly succeeds in schools for three reasons: two are its phonetic consistency, which has earned it the reputation of being the easiest language to study, and owing to Hispanics' being the largest minority, the rationalization that Spanish is reputed to be eminently "useful." But most American is the third reason: as any foreign language goes against the grain of a culture that doesn't encourage such speaking, students forced to learn a foreign language they will never use, least of all to communicate with local Hispanics, have understood the language requirement to be largely ceremonial, and *Spanish, like algebra, is the easiest to merely study and regurgitate for a grade with no intentions of actually learning or using it.* Quite sensibly, therefore, students choose the language that will not wreak havoc on their cumulative grade.

Teachers, schools, and the entire culture all collaborate to deliver that encoded wisdom surreptitiously by celebrating the ethnocentrism that sustains the myth that Spanish is a foreign language. I can hear it now— *We know, we know, don't repeat the history because it won't make a difference*—but I repeat the litany: Spanish predates the arrival of English on North America by a century, and it is now spoken across the entire nation as its unofficial second language. Still, it is taught as the language of some other place.

Spanish and that other place are kept mentally distant from the stereotypes spoken in popular anthropology about local Hispanics, whose neighborhoods those students of Spanish would no more think of visiting to practice their lessons than their teachers would dare make that suggestion, provoking an outbreak of parental hysteria. One arguably understandable reason for this mental cordoning off is that most "Spanish" neighborhoods are working-class, if not paradigmatic ghettos. Remember *The Bonfire of the Vanities.* In all events, be they neighborhoods peaceful or violent, a complete immunity from such "minority neighborhoods" defines a white middle-class identity.

While in more educated and upper-class minds, actual foreign Spanish does preserve a measure of cachet, local Spanish is redolent with socioeconomic disparity, invoking in English speakers a Calvinist streak that subtly damns those usually poorer Hispanic Others to their own impoverished predestinations. Hence the whiff of predestination that allows for routinely associating Spanish-speakers with "the help." Newly arrived, hipper middle-class Latin American immigrants, especially those whiter, rapidly know to avoid being confused with stigmatized "minority," often Caribbean if not Mexican American. Consider: If this culture can convince native Spanish speakers to drop Spanish altogether, how should we expect non-Spanish speakers to be disposed to learning it?

And the greatest irony is that behind Anglo peacocking before Hispanic culture and the bluster against bilingual education, the mainstream posture toward Spanish is a self-defensive canard. For however imbalanced the images evoked by the juxtaposed cultures, the fact remains that the United States' first and oldest Cold War has been over language and its Anglophone self-preservation being geographically planted in a predominantly Spanish-speaking hemisphere.

And then there's the threat of Spanish-speakers, whether as natives or immigrants, who do not perform according to the traditional immigrant American scripts they are expected to follow as other immigrants have done, putting their particular ethnic ways, especially their language, behind them. The assumption is that Hispanics are immigrants, which many are, but come to a country where their Hispanic heritage is not, and Spanish is an American language not just of their past but their hemispheric present. The presumed immigrant Latino's Old Country is hemispheric America itself, and what past native Hispanics remember is the history of Texas, California, Florida, Louisiana, Arizona, ...no need to go on.

Today Latin America may still be "emerging," having evolved measurably. Tellingly, in the face of a composite of Latinos and *latinos* as both the largest minority and the newest politically influential ethnic bloc, a conservative counterforce shrilly warns of a cultural invasion and cries out for the formalization of English as the national language. The suggestion is that Spanish speakers cannot or refuse to speak English, which is not the case; the vast majority of Latinos speak English; it is the American mainstream that gets sick over their not doing so exclusively. And if the criers for English Only actually do achieve making English the national language, formalizing an exclusiveness that does not change the status quo except to provide a new motive for harassment, exactly what does that accomplish in a country that safeguards freedom of speech.

Does your child speak another language at home? I confess to having become functionally bilingual only after boyhood years of working to be monolingual in English, determined to lose my childhood Spanish: very little American me. Raised for most of my early childhood in a Spanish-speaking household, I still spoke Spanish before starting school. But even before school, the new gadget television had changed my linguistic preference. Between the lines of television dialogue, I heard the lesson to forget my Spanish, a shedding that continued despite my growing up still hearing it at home, that lesson interrupted and contradicted when, at the end of the school year, I was sent to spend summer in Puerto Rico.

The contrast between my two lives created conflicted attitudes toward Spanish-speaking. No matter how humble my associations with Spanish while

I lived in New York and despite the allure of the world that I saw on television, my island summers were a miracle of natural beauty and constant activity, in glorious technicolor, with more dimensions than my New York life. While on the island, the shedding of Spanish made no sense and embarrassed me.

On returning I found it harder to warm up to a comparatively faded-color dullness not just in what I saw but the evocations of *americano* English, which I couldn't help contrasting to the sensuousness of Caribbean Spanish. My inner conflict would continue for months until, my Paradise fading, stockpiled years of resentment of our working class after an instilled lesson of Spanish's inferiority worked on me again to define my American life. This indecision continued consciously while a change simmered unconsciously, until erupting in my sophomore college year.

Having begun to write and take my English more seriously, I realized how comparatively illiterate I was in Spanish. The idea of being literate in one language and sounding haltingly stupid in the other suddenly seemed unacceptable. Moreover, King's having recently marched on Selma also having ignited a political consciousness, my rationalizing the difficulty and impossibility of possessing both languages, seemed like collaborating with colonialism. I took an advanced Spanish course to not just cruise toward a grade but to learn the grammar.

I finally learned the grammar as if I had stepped out of a stupor. But I still had much to read, so much more vocabulary to acquire, and after that acquire a natural personality and not sound like a digitized translation. After graduating, I concentrated on my writing in English, but through my writing activities met other Latinos like me, writing in English as they completed their graduate studies in Spanish and one thing led to another that after my M.F.A. I was convinced to switch my graduate studies to study the Latin American literature that I was discovering with the rest of the world: Jorge Luis Borges, César Vallejo, Pablo Neruda, Luis Palés Matos, Nicolás Guillén, Gabriel García Márquez, Juan Rulfo, Mario Vargas Llosa, Carlos Fuentes, Julio Cortázar, etc.

In retrospect, the arc of that transformation originates well before my entering college, with my Hispanophile dad, who as a lover of Puerto Rican culture had mastered Spanish and even how to dance like a Latin to Latin music. Afyter his marriage to my mother, in fact, we moved to Puerto Rico, where for half a year we lived and I attended a *colegio* his business deal fell through. We returned, this time to the North Bronx. Thanks to Hemingway and his generation's vogue with "Spanish," my dad's appreciation of my Hispanic heritage was better than mine.

Because Dad worked in El Barrio as a furniture salesman, he was also our conduit to the latest Puerto Rican community news, rumors, and musical releases. He would come home with the latest LP's by Tito Rodriguez, el Trío Los Panchos, Armando Manzanero or rerecordings of classics, such as Gardel's tangos and Mexican songs interpreted in Spanish by Nat King Cole, whom I would later learn was another Hispanophile, beloved in the Spanish-speaking world. My dad's love of Hispanic culture catalyzed my renewed appreciation of the importance of Spanish to me.

More specifically, I am also crediting my dad's unwavering American spirit as my model for feeling comfortable about possessing both Spanish and English unselfconsciously. Dad, no intellectual, but one of the most insightful people I have ever known, was a multiculturalist decades before the term existed and instilled the confidence that my speaking Spanish did not preclude my being "as American as any." He had parted with old friends that he considered false Americans, who believed that other patriotism: that true Americans are loath to be "foreigners" and speak a foreign language.

Finally, I was also fortunate to come from an extended family that, from humbler origins, had climbed to middle class and above in the new island industrialization. The Puerto Rican post-World War II diaspora consisted mainly of hill people and urban poor strongly encouraged to leave the island as part of an industrialization plan set in motion to benefit other social and racial classes. Many of my mainland generation, in other words, did not return to an origin Paradise.

For many, going back meant leaving grimy New York streets only to a pathetic hilltop where one felt cut off from the meaningful planet among hicks, to be made fun of because they spoke a tortured Spanish. When other minorities were rediscovering pride in "roots," many of my generation found themselves between a genuine "roots" pride, which made assimilation a secular sin, and a love-hate relationship with being Puerto Rican, an inner conflict to which few readily admitted, more often expressed in not making the effort to recover or preserve their Spanish. It was easier to blame Spanish for marginalizing us in our smaller world excluded from the broader global conversation on race being carried on in English.

In the seventies, I was working for a bilingual education program at a New York City public school, and asked a Puerto Rican boy his name. He answered "Efrem." I added, "Do you mean Efraín?" His answer took me back to when I was his age: "Don't speak to me in that horrible language!" Clearly, Efrem was angry, and he had yet to discover that when he grew up, his island extended family might just simply drop him from their roster, taunting a gold plumage of one-upmanship because they were not changed by the mainstream baptism of self-doubt and still possessed the insular confidence that they could address *americanos* eye-to-eye because they still spoke Spanish.

Does your child speak another language at home? Lacking material wealth to pass on, I wanted to leave my daughter the best I had gleaned from my two cultures, the essence transmitted through my two languages. That was my original personal mission. But looking back, I realized that I had concatenated my personal and professional language standards. Of course, I had wanted her to have the ability to articulate her bicultural complexity unhumbled in either culture, but I was also influenced by the standard that after college I had set for myself even higher the consequence of a translation workshop first offered the year that I entered Columbia U.'s Graduate Writing Program.

That course had a coordinator, the departmental chair, Frank MacShane, but was taught by a gallery of renowned translators from several languages, one notably before whom the class shivered not just because of his stern demeanor but because of his awesome linguistic authority. I refer to the late Willard Trask, who translated from French, Spanish, and Italian. His refinements of our crude translations were a revelation on semantic precision, on the mechanics of how to best communicate on the same intellectual plane.

In one of my poetry-writing courses, Mark Strand quipped that translation was "writing without the responsibilities," which might feel true to someone translating from a language not native to the translator. I say this because from literary translation I began to hear more clearly how much my spontaneous speech translated from the Spanish. For all I knew, that process could be taking place with everything I said in English. Writing, on the other hand, more distinctly flagged linguistic interference, and I came to see that for me writing was a form of translation but with full responsibilities, involving the same editing to smooth out linguistic-interference bumps, to hone in English what Trask demanded of our translations. I didn't feel particularly victimized for long, soon realizing the truth of the dictum, true even for monolinguals, that writing is only rewriting. Hemingway on being a good writer: "...one must have a built-in, shock-proof shit detector."[2]

In Jorge Luis Borges's story about the fictive titular planet "Tlon" ("Tlon, Uqbar, Orbis Tertius") the inhabitants practice the art of reproducing things, a duplicate that they call a *rhon.* The most highly prized reproduction has no original, being a reproduction "of inspiration, of hope." My poems were like those reproductions of pure inspiration, not just because I was bilingual but because all art is *rhon.* From Borges's metaphor, I spun off my own as the title of my first poetry book, *Translations without Originals,* which contained no translations or poems having to do with being bilingual, the only linguistic

---

[2] Ernest Hemingway, see https://www.goodreads.com/quotes/468339-the-most-essential-gift-for-a-good-writer-is-a

connection my given name, which suggested that as a child I spoke another language at home.

I was never comfortable with intentionally bilingual writing, Spanglish, any more than, owing to that stigma in Puerto Rico, inserting English words in my Spanish, Spanglish not a display of knowing of two languages but a glorification of half-knowing both languages. I did, however, come to appreciate that intuitive referencing of both languages was also a wellspring of originality as William Carlos Williams discovered.

While reading his complete works for *The Spanish American Roots of William Carlos Williams* (1994), I stumbled on the most explicit demonstration of my personal reason for writing that book, his being my precursor poet as the son of a Puerto Rican mother: a less-known poem titled "Translation." I also came upon a second, unrelated poem, "Hymn to Love Ended," (a Quevedo-style pun–Hymn/Him), subtitled "Imaginary Translation from the Spanish."

"Translation," does not announce from what language as the title is a gloss that informs the poem foreshadowed decades earlier what Borges would describe in "Tlon," a reproduction of an inspiration. The other poem revealed that the other "Translation" could be an "imaginary translation from the Spanish," the language that Williams spoke at home as a child. Williams' "Translation," in other words, also foreshadowed my and other bilinguals' writing from another language that informed them but doing so not as a sociological event, not dwelling on the bilingualism at work any more than poets or novelists need to verbalize that what they are writing is concomitantly a lesson on how to write a novel or a poem.

On the other hand, in those two poems Williams informs us that his bilingualism cannot be excluded from the reading of his entire work, which does not preclude that as poet in English one is also steeped in Anglo literary history, and through those superimposed lenses one compares what rings true and what rings false of what one culture has to say of the other. Hence Williams' important revision of American history.

In other words, Williams should be read as the great Modernist and defender of the American Idiom but as fruits of and not coincidental to his having also been a child who spoke another language at home. Unfortunately, in traditional America patriotic truth trumps literary truth, so the criticism cherry-picked from his biography to canonize a monolingual patriotic model, William Carlos Williams, great American poet.

That intertwined personal and professional baggage weighed on my decision to answer no and protect my daughter from the inevitable miseducation she would receive from teachers with no idea themselves of its origin. How many teachers are personally affected by the American mythos of domestic Spanish speakers as unauthoritative narrators? How many have been instructed on Spanish's being not just any other language, but the language with the longest history of rivalry with English. It was the language that has threatened English since the Reformation and the Conquest, the language that subsequent generations of Spanish speakers have refused to shed in deference to English throughout American history, threatening a desired Anglophone nationhood, and so the language that needed to be discredited. American English harbors that history. If not consciously acknowledged as multiculturalism corrects, that ancient disdain tacitly subverts democracy and always poses the possibility of insinuating itself in an unfortunate teacher's unconscious perceptions of my daughter if I revealed that she spoke another language at home.

Does your child speak another language at home? After New York's World Trade Center was toppled by terrorist airplane hijackers, overnight, at least temporarily, much changed in American thinking. Older conflicts were demoted in importance. After the attack, Fidel Castro offered to help however Cuba could. Within weeks the formerly outcast Pakistani president was persuaded to cooperate against former Islamic fundamentalist allies. West-looking white Russia, fighting its own war with radical Islam in Chechnya, discovered how much it had in common with the United States. In America, a citizenry that had paid scant attention to international news now eagerly waited to hear from fraternal terrorist hunters in Germany, Spain, England, France, Italy. In other words, Americans for whom the world seemed limited to the dimensions of a television screen were now exposed to the real wider Earth as directly connected to their daily lives.

Attorney General Ashcroft announced a nationwide headhunt for citizens who spoke Arabic and Farsi. His appeal prompted public conversations on the importance of human over technologically-gathered intelligence. To be protected from human failing, Americans suddenly required the services of foreign languages. Ashcroft's appeal to find such fluent Americans implied a change that promised to manifest itself in school curricula that had been steadily eliminating foreign language classes.

Suddenly too the traditional xenophobia was replaced by another, anti-Muslim xenophobia. At the border with Mexico, agents kept an eye out for a different kind of interloper. What threat does a Mexican, rooted also in Western Culture through Spanish, pose in crossing the border? Surely the *coyote* smuggler's trade continued unabated across hot dangerous terrain that no cell phone-carrying terrorist would choose to cross. But Mexicans risk their lives to sell flowers or work in restaurants or dig ditches, not to harm Americans. Next to demonized Middle Eastern languages, Spanish began to sound downright like home. The mood seemed rife with possibilities not just for Spanish but an auguring of a new American regard for languages.

Nevertheless, because history is an older and wiser teacher, I still intuited that under the public expression persisted a nostalgia for America before it was violently changed like New York's skyline. For too many Americans, protection only meant even more insulation, erecting even higher walls,[3] perfecting the isolationism that was part of pre-September 11 peace. For diehard traditional America, tantamount to security being threatened by bombs was being robbed of their traditional identity by having to acquire a respect of other languages. For now, I will record that for a brief span Americans demonstrated a capacity of seeing kinship where they once saw foreignness and of seeing a gift and not a challenge in those who answer "Yes" to the question of whether a child speaks another language at home.

---

[3] I was writing before Donald Trump campaigned promising to build a wall.

11.

PABLO NERUDA'S DILEMMA

In April 1972, a spring marred by continued war and Nixon's bombing of North Vietnam, New York City played host to the poet Pablo Neruda, head of Chile's Communist Party and an internationally famous critic of the war who would doubtless have been barred from visiting this country if at that moment he had also not been the reigning Nobel Laureate in literature and a bona fide diplomat, Socialist Chile's recently appointed cultural ambassador to France. His week-long visit ended with an appearance at a large meeting hall in Columbia University's Butler library, where a woman friend Yanis and I showed up extra early, hoping to secure a seat closest to our favorite poet.

Unfortunately, as so many of his other fans planned the same, half the rows were already occupied, and we ended up sitting—an important detail—almost in the center of the huge hall. I was twenty-six and the previous year had become an alumnus of Columbia's Graduate Writing Program, which co-sponsored this event. For the longest time Neruda had been my poet-revolutionary role model, and my aspiration to emulate him would have been motivation enough for me to show up wherever he was appearing.

But on this occasion, there was another, ingenuous reason. Five years before I had attended his reading at the 92nd Street Y's Poetry Center, and four years later, 1971, the year that he won the Nobel prize, I received one of the Poetry Center's four Discovery Awards and read with the three other winners on the Y's stage with its history of readings by distinguished poets, including Neruda. As I read, I remembered the night that, from the penultimate balcony row, I wondered if I could write in a voice that rose from the core of the hemisphere.

And so I went to Butler Hall also to fantasize about our crossing destinies, expecting the immediate reward of being reaffirmed in my awe and then later savoring the experience in conversation over dinner with Yanis at one of the newly proliferating Cuban-Chinese restaurants. What I never imagined was that within the hour a very private Neruda and I would be eye-eye as he whispered words that would leave an imprint as lasting as his poetry.

Neruda entered in the middle of a file of four men in suits– the Dean of the co-hosting School of International Affairs, the then-director of the co-hosting Graduate Writing Program Frank MacShane, the others doubtless Chilean security– who, except for the writer MacShane, were of a demeanor alien to any artistic or literary galaxy. The Dean carried a rolled-up sheet of paper, and everyone else walked in empty-handed, including Neruda.

He sat in the central seat of a long table facing the packed library, before a microphone and flanked by MacShane and the Dean of International Affairs, who as host introduced himself, welcomed us, and unrolled the sheet in his hand. Reading from his sheet, he introduced Neruda, welcomed as the Nobel Laureate poet, who was present as a Chilean diplomat and was there to respond to questions the audience might have.

Neruda, a short man with thinned-out dark strands combed straight back, wore a gray tweed sports jacket and a tie. His caret shaped, mischievous eyebrows aptly framed a corneal gleam that by then, the pinnacle of his career, seven continents understood to be playful: in life, this much-loved poet had already become his admirers. He would die the following year. After a statement of gratitude for the invitation and after that statement was translated, the floor was opened to questions.

Someone asked for Neruda's reaction to the Cuban embargo. A second question inquired about socialist Chile's ties to the Soviet Union. Another touched upon the bombing of Vietnam. Every question received, diplomatically phrased, Socialist Chile's official position. I seemed to have misread the invitation, realizing just then that this event was not to be a poetry reading but a Q&A on power not of the poetic sort. In the middle of Neruda's answer to the fourth or fifth question, Yanis whispered in my ear that I should ask him "to say something about Puerto Rico."

Yanis was an N. Y. U. doctoral candidate from Puerto Rico and an advocate of independence. She later explained why, in addition to her being a shy nationalist, she thought that I should be the one to pose the question: because as a recent alumnus I was the one invited by MacShane and, coming from me, the request would be interpreted in the objective, journalistic vein of its predecessors. I reflexively declined, sensing that the subject of Puerto Rico's political status was out of bounds because—in retrospect this sounds howlingly stupid— it threatened to politicize the event.

Then I recalled reading a news report that cited an anonymous State Department source who described Washington's UN strategy on Puerto Rico as a persistent downplaying of protocol, discrediting its relevance in discussions of foreign policy. Coming to think of it, where did I get the idea that, after all the explosive questions lobbed at Neruda, requesting a statement on Puerto Rico was forbidden? Was I afraid that by broaching the subject I would be identifying myself and thus intellectually ghettoizing myself? But if I didn't ask, I was bowing cowardly to a subtle censorship. More concerned now with my censoring myself and feeling obliged to resist such mind control, I raised my hand.

Neruda acknowledged me and, on my feet, I asked him in Spanish to say "a few words about Puerto Rico because Americans don't know about its true political situation." The men around him huddled frantically, fanning an atmosphere of disturbance. Shouts from the audience demanded that I translate what I had said, and I complied. My question, to my surprise was an inadvertent Molotov cocktail, igniting flash fires of murmurs around me.

In the middle of the turbulence Neruda calmly answered in Spanish that he would gladly read "those poems" but didn't have them–which his translator immediately communicated. I urged him in Spanish to say just a few words on the issue's complexity although, satisfied that I had spoken out, I was ready to retreat, sit down and melt back into the audience. I remained on my feet, waiting —as Neruda repeated the same answer through the translator—to thank him at least for having made his statement in those poems. But on the heels of the translator's final words, ". . . but as I said, I don't have those poems," from the standing crowd in the back of the hall a voice shouted: "I do!" Suddenly, standing in the middle of the hall, I was waist-high in swiveling heads and immersed in the electric silence that amplified every step of the Hispanic, apparently graduate student as he walked along the length of the side wall down to the table to hand Neruda a thin paperback.

Canción de Gesta (*Song of Protest*) is a book that Neruda began to write in the late fifties to protest Puerto Rico's becoming a "Commonwealth" in permanent union with the U.S., a veiled colony. It is said that he had written two poems for that book when Fidel Castro rode into Havana with his *barbudos* and the exhilarating, contrasting liberation inspired a gush of poems on the Cuban Revolution, poems among which he included the anti-colonialist Puerto Rico poems, in the now refocused *Canción de Gesta*. Although among his least noteworthy as poetry, its liberated-Cuba/colonial Puerto Rico symbolism made it popular among the Latin American left. Neruda flipped pages then commenced reading "Muñoz Marín," a lambasting of the author of the present "Commonwealth" status, Puerto Rico's late, first elected governor.

Luis Muñoz Marin was the son of the provincial patriot Luis Muñoz Rivera who in the nineteenth century had won concessions of autonomy from Spain, including the island's printing of its own currency, an autonomy of which Puerto Rico barely got a taste when the U.S. occupied the island and, out of closely held secret motive, unexpectedly claimed it as a booty of war. Muñoz Rivera's son, Luis, was a U.S.-educated former Greenwich Village poet who inherited his father's esteemed political reputation and was married to the American poet Muna Lee, whose family link gave him access to Franklin

Delano Roosevelt. Confidence in the young leader prompted FDR to approve the elections that made Muñoz the island's first elected governor.

In two decades as governor he industrialized a once stagnant agricultural economy and, giving up on his youthful efforts to make Puerto Rico independent, collaborated with the U.S's working around a U.N. mandate to end colonialism by drafting the island's compromised present political status, supposedly an autonomous territory in "permanent union" with the United States, officially titled *Estado Libre Asociado*. Literally translated, it is an oxymoron, a "free associated state," but more patriotic journalists and politicians are wont to fix it as a "freely associated state."

Its official translation in English, however, is "Commonwealth," adopted from the fully autonomous English "Commonwealth of Nations." Coincidence in that title influenced the U.N.'s declaring it an acceptable formula for decolonizing the island.[1] Its actual autonomy has been fought for unsuccessfully in court and, in the most recent financial crisis, denied by Congress that it actually ever existed.

Depending on your politics, Muñoz was either a Cold War pragmatist who vis-a-vis Cuba turned the much smaller Puerto Rico into a showcase of capitalism or he was a vile symbol of Latin American capitulation to Anglo-American culture and the dollar— a contradiction that has inspired fiction, drama and poetry. Today a bust of him, dapper with mustache and bow tie, lusters the five-cent U.S. postage stamp. Neruda's poem portrays him as a lackey who betrayed not only Puerto Rico but all Latin America.

As the final line of his critical poem left Neruda's lips, flanking suits shot to their feet, their response obviously surprising Neruda, who looked around perplexed before catching on. I don't recall that the actual Q&A session had lasted much more than thirty minutes. No "last call" prefaced my being called on. By every indication my request for a statement had provoked the powers to curtail the program.

On his feet, Neruda was receiving a final, long ovation when, for no other reason that I can give in retrospect except feeling responsible for having subverted his program, I went over to wait by the door through which he would exit, the direction in which Neruda had started to take steps, pausing to smile and wave farewell to the applauding audience. When he finally approached that door, from behind a row of heads but a few feet away I loudly thanked him

---

[1] A confusion explained to me by a former U.N. ambassador from the country formerly Ceylon today Sri Lanka.

in Spanish for the reading of his poem, expecting no more than a hand sign and a smile.

But on hearing my voice, he stopped and looked in its direction. I gestured and in the silence between us, became aware of the gaze of administrators and security men accompanying him. In Spanish I apologized for the disruption that I had apparently caused. To my surprise, he stepped forward in my direction, waving off his entourage and cutting into the crowd. He was in front of me but continued even closer, startling me, his face in my face.

Lightly clutching my left sport jacket lapel, his vibrant black eyes in mine, he whispered intensely in Spanish, "No, don't you apologize. I would have read the other, stronger poem,[2] but, you understand, I couldn't, I just couldn't. But don't you apologize. You did the right thing. You did the right thing." *"Hiciste bien. Hiciste bien,"* he said, punctuating each of those two phrases of approval with a tug on my lapel. With that, he turned and returned to his place in literary history.

I recounted to Yanis what had just transpired, although as I repeated his exact words, they had become secondary to my overall excitement over his having spoken to me in a special way that, for some reason, I interpreted as his having intuited that I too was a poet. That fancy sedated for another time the gravity of what had just occurred: my having been perceived as a threat to the social order for merely asking a question about Puerto Rico. Nevertheless, dinner afterwards became a celebration, and for the next couple of days I basked in my private triumph of having won a grand prize, those private seconds, which I would always treasure.

That Sunday, however, the *New York Times* Oct, 22, 1971 report on Neruda's week in New York, "An Impassioned and Popular Writer," abruptly plummeted me to a different reality. According to the reporter Henry Raymont, owing to Neruda's position as both "cultural envoy" and "diplomat," he had demonstrated a "reluctance to be drawn into an ideological discussion." His being the iconic "Communist poet," suggested the possibility of disturbance, which on his week-long tour at other campuses in other states did not materialize. The one exception "came at a symposium at Columbia University on Thursday night after a group of Puerto Rican nationalists insisted that he read one of his poems in which Puerto Rico is portrayed as suffering under the 'colonial oppression' of the United States. When he sought to avoid the request, saying he had not brought the poem along, one of the youths produced a copy and Mr. Neruda felt compelled to read it, drawing a long ovation."

---

[2] "Puerto Rico, Puerto Pobre" ("Rich Port, Poor Port").

Raymont's seeing a "group of Puerto Rican nationalists" who carried out a plan seemed to have resulted from his own agenda, evident from the opening of his piece, to subtly deflate the importance given to this Neruda by exposing the kinds of causes he supported, consistent with this presumed group of nationalists who practically mugged him into speaking up. Thus Raymont reminded me of the casual mines buried along my path to a writer's career, the likelihood that my work would be spray-painted with vandalizing preconceptions of my "minority" words as predictable and dismissible. That realization drained me of all heart for writing, even a letter to the *Times*. Why, I asked myself, should I bother to invest years to master this craft only to have the stock of my words routinely devalued in this insider-controlled culture.

Looking back, I can't measure how many days I walked around in a funk over that thought, until I began to reflect in tranquility what had transpired at Columbia. Of course, many times since that day I had uncased the jewel of my moment with Neruda and admired it—but I found myself returning to the context of the Q&A incident that preceded it, to his invoking his poems when I had only requested a statement. Until then I had been caught up in my exuberance over how Neruda had addressed me.

Against Raymont's morphing me into a journalist's stereotype, Neruda had respected me as real. By letting me know that he felt that *he* had let *me* down because, now a diplomat, he couldn't just say what he pleased, he underscored the dignity of my question as the respectable expression of one among many debatable world issues that orbit the United States.

Once I realized this, the therapeutic effect of his few whispered words kicked in, and to this day against that seasonal spiritual trough, the potency of his words as antidote has yet to expire. With that I believed that I had fully understood the meaning of our encounter, hearing Neruda's words beyond the context of that afternoon, encrypting his solidarity against the ceremony of power that surrounded us both, later performed in that *Times* report.

But increasingly I also kept thinking about Neruda's apologizing for not being able to read "the stronger poem." I hadn't appreciated the connection that he was apologizing for his not standing by his own words as he was about to urge of me. Maybe because while I was reluctant to contemplate a tarnished image of my idol (who although he did rescue me, did so admitting to having failed me), I had also been suppressing a glimpse that he had communicated his human frailty. Over time I did address that lingering, imperfect image of Neruda, but only after I realized that the private moment between us, which in my mind I had isolated from the entire episode, actually continued a discourse that began with his unexpectedly referring me to absent poems.

I had at first accepted his response of "not having the poems" as an elegant circumvention. But he hadn't mentioned poetry in any of his previous responses, and I had not requested that he read a poem. And when he subsequently spoke his hushed words to me by the door, his concern was not with the politics involved so much as the poetry. Not with the tone of a publicly-compromising politician who behind the scenes spits on restraining protocols and thereby reassures of his true position; instead, he revealed the pain of having failed me by not reading the stronger poem. From that pain, I construed that, as the Graduate Writing Program was co-hosting the event, he assumed I too was a poet, because he had addressed me as one who understood the difficulty of his having to censor his own poem.

This interpretation helped me to finally decipher why, when he approached me, and even though we were already standing at a distance from his entourage so no one could hear his low voice, he stepped up even closer and grabbed my lapel: in his apologizing and holding me, in whom he apparently saw something of himself, he was also confessing to a need to touch, and therefore be in touch with again, the younger Neruda, the poet who would have never refrained from reading the stronger poem, the poet for whom he had grown nostalgic after that long week of diplomacy before returning to New York.

12.

EPILOGUE: "HISPANIC":
A SEMANTIC CIRCUS

In a "A Conversation With Grace Flores-Hughes," published in the *The Washington Post*, July 26, 2009, we learned that during "her long career in government, Grace Flores-Hughes spent some time working as an assistant in what was then called the Department of Health, Education and Welfare." In that position in the early 1970s, she successfully advocated for "Hispanic" as the epithet to appear in the Census. She claims to have "coined" the consensus epithet Hispanic, and "is proud of my work," circumventing—one extrapolates from the interview—the future trending of Latino. But exactly why she believed that she "coined" the term even for the Census is unclear. Into the seventies the alliance of Mexican-Americans and Puerto Ricans was referred to as "U.S. Hispanic," and in conversational English every Latino subgroup was still called Hispanic.

Flores-Hughes' claim of coining the official census epithet competes with the line of thought that Nixon actually requested that the Census Bureau include Hispanic as a racialized census category to create an available minority voting bloc that might counteract African Americans in the pocket of the Democrats. Karen Fields and Barbara J. Fields[1] cite as the source of this Nixon thesis Richard Rodriguez's April 14, 2003 Bradley Lecture before The American Enterprise Institute, "The Invention of Hispanics and the Reinvention of America."

The problem with that theory is that the census hasn't actually racialized Hispanic and provided for a white and non-white Hispanic, perhaps Flores-Hughes' doing. A 2003 Census Bureau Report on race and Hispanic origin explains that, starting in 2000, skipping 2002, and again in 2003, provided this "guidance··· on how to handle the interpretation of race and Hispanic origin data":

- People who are Hispanic may be of any race.

- People in each race group may be either Hispanic or Not Hispanic.

---

[1] Karen Fields and Barbara J. Fields. *Racecraft: The Soul of Inequality in American Life* (New York: VerSo 2012).

- Each person has two attributes, their race (or races) and whether or not they are Hispanic.[2]

The *Post* interview of Flores-Hughes and Rodriguez's lecture were post-millennial, by which time, reflecting from the vantage of the emergence of Latino, one could look back and ask Flores-Hughes why not Latino or why Hispanic? The interviewer posed the question this way: "why still Hispanic?" Invoking Latino as *latino*, she answered that because Latino "encompassed speakers of Portuguese and Italian and French."

Flores-Hughes' answer notwithstanding, one has to suspect that she used the Latino/*latino* homonym effectively to circumvent the unpleasantness of answering that *latino* could be confused with racialized Latino, with which many white Hispanics did not identify.

Another incident that demonstrates how Latino's slippery semantics provide the opportunity for unreliable national discourse was the killing of Trayvon Martin by George Zimmerman. Not to diminish the gravity of Zimmerman's reckless judgment and bias expressed in the killing, but the "racial" aspect was a melodrama of racially obsessed white American journalism. Zimmerman's German paternal surname afforded the media the opportunity to narrate a white-on-black drama when it was plain to anyone with at least one eye that Zimmerman was impurely of German descent.

His mother was Peruvian and his family was, to all appearances, decidedly more Peruvian than German. Didn't that fact make him Latino? Cannot white Hispanics also be racists? So if the Census Bureau can handle white and non-white Hispanic, the media apparently can't and wrote of the tawny Zimmerman as if he were Teutonic.

Lastly, consider the title of Jonathan Zimmer's op-ed piece in the June 12, 2009 *L.A. Times*: "Judge Sotomayor, a Mythic 'Hispanic.'" Zimmer opens with the following italicized thesis summary: "The supposedly racial term was pushed by Nixon to lump distinct Spanish-speaking groups into one voting bloc. There's no such thing, and the judge should be appointed on her merits." Zimmer proceeds to explain that he put the titular "Hispanic" in quotation marks because– repeating but not citing Richard Rodriguez's argument–the epithet was "invented" by Nixon and before then "Sotomayor was growing up with her Puerto Rican family in New York City."

---

[2] "U.S. Census Bureau Guidance on the Presentation and Comparison of Race and Hispanic Origin Data," United States Census Bureau, https://www.census.gov/topics/population/hispanic-origin/about/comparing-race-and-hispanic-origin.html#par_textimage_0

Spanish is obviously not Zimmer's strong suit. Sotomayor was born in 1954 to parents of a generation made acutely conscious of being *hispanos* by the ongoing effort to Americanize Puerto Rico. Her parents were among those who went to school one morning and had English thrust on them because their teacher was suddenly forbidden to speak Spanish and had been instructed to have the children sing "*pollito*, chicken; *gallina*, hen."

Her parents came to a fifties Hispanic New York that consisted of earlier immigrants from Spain, more skilled and whiter Puerto Ricans, and sprinklings of *cubano*, who in English all called themselves "Spanish." Growing up, Sotomayor understood that being Puerto Rican she was *hispana*, which in Spanish usage alternates with *latina*. There is nothing mythic about being Hispanic even if Nixon racialized or exploited that traditional unifier of diverse subcultures.

But Zimmer apparently read Rodriguez's unreliable rhetoric, that hyperbole about Nixon's "inventing" Hispanics, and evidently felt enlightened. Rodriguez, to confront inelegant race but not really, more poetically accused Nixon of "inventing" Hispanics until he eventually got around to explicitly getting at what he was obliquely meaning, that Nixon's racializing Hispanics as a voting bloc distorted him: "Richard Rodriguez the Hispanic is not brown; Richard Rodriguez the American is brown."

With Rodriguez as authority, Zimmer apparently felt expert on "Hispanic" to spread that it was an identity that mainstream America had invented. He evidently wanted to come out ahead of the curve to bestow on Sotomayor the laurels deserved for her having been appointed to the Supreme Court as acknowledgment of her achievement and not as a token racialized Hispanic.

For any Hispanic/Latino/*latino*, of course, his coming to her rescue is laughable. Let's bet a dollar that, if asked if in her whole life for one second she stopped being Hispanic, Sotomayor would also laugh.

REFERENCES

Abbott, John Henry. *In the Belly of the Beast: Letters from Prison.* New York: Vintage, 1991.

Adams, Henry. *The Education of Henry Adams.* New York: Modern Library, 1999.

Algarín, Miguel and Bob Holman. *Aloud: Voices from the Nuyorican Poets Café.* New York: Holt, 1994.

Algarín, Miguel and Miguel Piñero. *Nuyorican Poetry: An Anthology of Puerto Rican Words and Feelings.* New York: Morrow, 1975.

Anon. *Lazarillo de Tormes.* Biblioteca Virtual Miguel de Cervantes. https://www.cervantesvirtual.com/obra-visor/la-vida-de-lazarillo-de-tormes-y-de-sus-fortunas-y-adversidades--0/html/

Beltrán, Cristina. *The Trouble with Unity: Latino Politics and the Creation of Identity.* New York: Oxford University Press, 2010.

Beresford, Bruce. *Black Robe.* The Samuel Goldwyn Company, 1991. 1 hr 41 min.

Borges, Jorge Luis. "Tlön, Uqbar, Orbis Tertius." *The Garden of the Forking Paths.* New York: Penguin, 2018.

Brackenridge, Hugh Henry. "A Poem, On the Rising Glory of America." Poetry, https://www.poetry.com/poem/19314/a-poem,-on-the-rising-glory-of-america

Brown, Charles Brockden. *Wieland and Memoirs of Carwin the Biloquist.* New York: Penguin, 1991.

Brown, Claude. *Manchild in the Promised Land.* New York: Scribner, 1965.

Calderón de la Barca, Pedro. *El Médico de Su Honra.* DocPlayer. https://docplayer.es/58046-El-medico-de-su-honra.html

Cather, Willa. *Oh, Pioneers!* Boston and New York: Houghton Mifflin, 1913.

——. *O Pioneers!* Radford, Virginia: Wilder Publications, 2008.

Cleaver, Eldridge. *Soul on Ice.* New York: Delta, 1999.

Chernow, Ron. *Alexander Hamilton.* New York: Penguin Books, 2005

Chu, John. *In the Heights.* 20th Century Fox, 2021.

Contreras Lowery, Raoul. *A Hispanic View: American Politics and the Politics of Immigration.* New York: Writers Club Press, 2002.

"A Conversation With Grace Flores-Hughes." *The Washington Post,* July 26, 2009.

Crèvecoeur, J. Hector St. John. *Letters from an American Farmer.* The Avalon Project. https://avalon.law.yale.edu/subject_menus/letters.asp

——. "Sketch of a Contrast between the Spanish and English Colonies," unpublished.

——. *Voyage dans la Haute Pennsylvanie et dans l'État de New York,* 3 vol. Paris: N.P, 1801.

Crow, John A. *An Anthology of Spanish Poetry: From the Beginnings to the Present Day, Including Both Spain and Spanish America.* Baton Rouge: LSU Press, 1980.

"Cuban and Other Hispanic, and Minorities - Confederate Soldiers." *Geni.* https://www.geni.com/projects/Cuban-and-Other-Hispanic-and-Minorities-Confederate-Soldiers/24842

Dávila Arlene. *Latinos, Inc.: The Marketing and Making of a People.* Berkeley and Los Angeles: University of Carlifornia Press, 2001.

——. *Latinx Art: Artists, Markets, Politics.* Durham: Duke University Press, 2020.

De las Casas, Bartolomé. *A Short Account of the Destruction of the Indies.* New York: Penguin, 1999.

Derysh, Igor. 2020. "Pence Aide Katie Miller Admits She Was Unaffected by Seeing Family Separations: 'It didn't work.'" *Salon,* July 7, 2020. https://www.salon.com/2020/07/07/pence-aide-katie-miller-admits-she-was-unaffected-by-seeing-family-separations-it-didn't-work/

Díaz, Junot. *The Brief Wondrous Life of Oscar Wao.* New York: Riverhead Books, 2008.

Dos Passos, John. *Rosinante to the Road Again.* N.P.: Franklin Classics, 2018.

Dufour de Pradt, Dominique. *Mémoires historiques sur la révolution d'Espagne.* Paris: Rosa, Perronneau, 1816.

Dunlap, William. *Pizarro in Peru, or the Death of Rolla,* translation from German by August von Kotzebue. New York: G. F. Hopkins, 1800.

Farias, Cristian. "Ted Cruz Tried To Show Off His Español To Marco Rubio, But He Fell Flat." *Huffington Post.* February 14, 2016. https://www.huffpost.com/entry/ted-cruz-spanish_n_56c0f58ae4b08ffac125b341

Fernández Retamar, Roberto. *Calibán: Apuntes Sobre la Cultura de Nuestra América.* Havana: Editorial Diagenes, 1974, 2nd edition.

Fields, Karen and Barbara J. Fields. *Racecraft: The Soul of Inequality in American Life.* New York: VerSo, 2012.

Flores, Angel. *Spanish Stories Cuentos Españoles.* New York: Bantam Books, 1960.

Flores-Hughes, Grace. "A Conversation With Grace Flores-Hughes." *The Washington Post,* July 26, 2009.

Freneau, Philip. *The Poems of Philip Freneau: Poet of the American Revolution.* Los Angeles: HardPress Publishing, 2012.

Gallardo, Edward. *Simpson Street and Other Plays.* Houston: Arte Público Press, 1989.

García Márquez, Gabriel. *One Hundred Years of Solitude.* New York: Harper & Row, 1970.

Guevara, Ernesto Che. *The Motorcycle Diaries.* New York: Seven Stories Press, 2021.

Guillén, Nicolás. *Sóngoro Cosongo.* Madrid: Libresa, 1997.

Hemingway, Ernest. *For Whom the Bells Toll.* New York: Macmillan, 2016.

——. *The Sun Also Rises.* New York: Vintage, 2022.

——. *The Old Man and the Sea.* New York: Scribner, 2003.

Hijuelos, Oscar. *The Mambo Kings Play Songs of Love: A Novel.* New York: Ferrar, Straus, Giroux, 2015.

Howells, William Dean. "Editha." The William Dean Howells Society. https://public.wsu.edu/~campbelld/howells/editha.htm

Hudson, William Henry. *Green Mansions.* N. P.: Compass Circle, 2022.

Huntington, Samuel P. "The Hispanic Challenge." *Foreign Policy.* 2004.

——. *Who Are We? Challenges to America's National Identity.* New York: Simon and Schuster, 2004.

Ichaso, León. *Piñero.* Miramax, 2001.

Irving, Washington. *The Complete Works of Washington Irving.* N. P.: Musiacum, 2017.

Jackson, Helen Hunt. *Ramona.* New York: Signet, 2002.

Jefferson, Thomas. *Notes on the State of Virginia:* electronic edition. Documenting the American South (website). https://docsouth.unc.edu/southlit/jefferson/jefferson.html

Kazan, Elia. *Viva Zapata!* 20th Century Fox, 1952.

Lankes, Ana. "In Argentina, One of the World's First Bans on Gender Neutral Language." *The New York Times.* July 20, 2022.

Laurent, Arthur. *West Side Story.* New York: Random House, 1958.

Lazo, Rodrigo and Jesse Alemán, eds. New York: New York University Press, 2016.

Lowell, James Russell. *The Complete Poetical Works of James Russell Lowell.* Los Angeles: HardPress Publications, 2013.

Longfellow, Henry Wadsworth. *Prose Works of Henry Wadsworth Longfellow.* 2 vols. Boston: Tickner and Fields, 1847.

——. *The Complete Poetical Works of Henry Wadsworth.* Windham, NH: Windham Press, 2013.

Mailer, Norman. "The White Negro." *Mind of an Outlaw.* New York: Random House, 2014.

Mariani, Pail. *William Carlos Williams: A New World Naked.* New York: W.W. Norton, 1990.

Marqués, René. *En una Ciudad Llamada San Juan.* Río Piedras: Editorial Cultural, 1970.

Martí, José. *Nuestra América.* Havana: Casa de las Américas, 1974.

Marzán, Julio. "Richard Rodriguez Talks to Himself," *The Village Voice,* February, 1982.

——. *The Spanish American Roots of William Carlos Williams.* (Austin: U. of Texas Press, 1994).

Mather, Cotton. *Diary of Cotton Mather.* Boston, Massachusetts Historical Society, V.1, 1911.

——. *The Wonders of the Invisible World.* London: N.P., 2020.

Mckee Irwin, Robert. "Almost-Latino Literature: Approaching Truncated Latinidades." In *The Latino Nineteenth Century: Archival Encounters in American Literary History.* Ed. Rodrigo Lazo, and Jesse Alemán. New York: New York University Press, 2016.

Melville, Herman. "Benito Cereno." In *Great Short Works by Herman Melville.* New York: Perennial, 2004.

Milian, Claudia. *Latining America: Black-Brown Passages and the Coloring of Latino/a Studies.* Atlanta: University of Georgia Press, 2013.

——. *Latinx*. Minneapolis: University of Minnesota Press, 2019.

Miranda, Lin-Manuel. *Hamilton*. New York Premiere, 2015.

Moore, Olin Harris. "Mark Twain and *Don Quixote*." *PMLA* vol. 37 (Jun 1, 1922): 326.

Mora, G. Cristina. *Making Hispanics: How Activists, Bureaucrats, & Media Constructed a New American*. Chicago: University of Chicago Press, 2014.

Morales, Ed. *Latinx: The New Force in American Politics and Culture*. New York: Verso, 2018.

Neruda, Pablo. *Canción de Gesta*. Buenos Aires: Sudamericana, 2003.

Palés Matos, Luis. *Tuntún de Pasa y Grifería: Poesía Afroantillana*. Barcelona: Gráf. Manuel Pareja, 1974.

Parker, Alan. *The Commitments*. 20th Century Fox, 1991.

Pattee, Fred Lewis ed. *Philip Freneau: Collected Poems*. Seattle: Kindle Direct, 2020.

Paz, Octavio. *The Labyrinth of Solitude*. Translated by Lysander Kemp. New York: Grove Press, 1991.

Pedreira, Antonio S. *Insularismo. Ensayos de interpretación puertorriqueña*. Internet Archive. https://archive.org/details/Insularismo

Petrie, Daniel. *Fort Apache: The Bronx*. 20th Century Fox, 1981.

Pietri, Pedro. *Pedro Pietri: Selected Poetry*. San Francisco: City Lights, 2015.

Piñero, Miguel. *Short Eyes*. New York: Hill and Wang, 1975.

Outlaw: The Collected Works of Miguel Pinero. Houston: Arte Público Press, 1975.

Porter, Katherine Ann. *The Collected Stories of Katherine Anne Porter*. New York: Harcourt Brace, 1972.

Povod, Reinaldo. *Cuba and His Teddy Bear*. New York: Samuel French, 1986.

Prescott, William Hickling. *History of the Conquest of Mexico*. Mount Pleasant: Arcadia Press, 2016.

——. *The Conquest of Peru*. Mineola: Dover Editions, 2005.

Quiñones, Ernesto. *Bodega Dreams*. New York: Vintage, 2000.

Raymont, Henry. "An Impassioned and Popular Writer." *New York Times*. Oct 22, 1971.

Reed, Ishmael. *The Haunting of Lin-Manuel Miranda*. New York: Archway Editions, 2020.

Rodó, José Enrique. *Ariel*. London: Forgotten Books, 2012.

Rodriguez, Rodriguez. *Hunger of Memory: The Education of Richard Rodriguez*. Dial Press, 2004.

——. "The Invention of Hispanics and the Reinvention of America." Bradley Lecture, The American Enterprise Institute, April 14, 2003.

Ruiz de Burton, Maria Amparo. *The Squatter and the Don*. Houston: Arte Público Press, 1997.

——. *Who Would Have Thought It?* Houston: Arte Público Press, 1997.

Salazar, Miguel. "The Problem With Latinidad." *The Nation*. September 16, 2019.

Sánchez, Luis Rafael. *La Guaracha del Macho Camacho*. Madrid: Ediciones Cátedra, 2005.

Santayana, George. *Character and Opinion in the United States.* New York: Scribner's, 1924.

——. *People and Places: The Background of My Life.* Glasgow: Good Press, 2021.

——. *The Last Pilgrim: A Memoir in the Form of a Novel.* Cambridge: M.I.T. Press, 1924.

Sartre, Jean-Paul. *Saint Jean: Actor and Martyr.* New York: George Braziller, 1963.

Schroeder, Barbet. *Barfly.* American Zoetrope, 1967.

Silva Gruez, Kirsten. "The Errant Latino: Irisarri, Central Americanness, and Migration's Intentions." In *The Latino Nineteenth Century: Archival Encounters in American Literary History.* Ed. Rodrigo Lazo, and Jesse Alemán. New York: New York University Press, 2016.

——. *Ambassadors of Culture: The Transamerican Origins of Latino Writing.* Princeton: Princeton University Press, 2002.

Simek, Lauren. "The Sounds of Narrative in Longfellows's *Evangline.*" In *Reconsidering Longfellow.* Christopher Irmscher and Robert Arbour, eds., 90. Teaneck: Fairleigh University Press, 2014.

Simon, Paul. *Songs from The Capeman.* Music Sales America, 1998.

Soboroff, Jacob. *Separated: Inside an American Tragedy.* New York: Harper Collins, 2020.

Spicer, Jack. "Imaginary Elegies." In *The New American Poetry: 1945-1960,* ed. David Allen, 147. Berkeley and Los Angeles: University of California Press, 1999.

Spielberg, Stephen. *West Side Story.* 20th Century Fox, 2021.

Stavans, Ilán. *The FSG Book of Twentieth-Century Latin American Poetry: An Anthology.* New York: Farrar, Straus, and Giroux, 2012.

——. *The Norton Anthology of Latino Literature.* New York: Norton, 2010.

Steinbeck, John. *East of Eden.* New York: Penguin, 2003.

——. *The Short Novels of John Steinbeck.* New York: Penguin, 2009.

Stevens, Wallace. The Collected Poems of Wallace Stevens: The Corrected Edition. New York: Vintage, 2015.

——. *The Letters of Wallace Stevens.* New York: Knopf, 1966.

Swarns, Rachel. *The 272: Families Who Were Enslaved and Sold to Build the American Catholic Church.* New York: Random House, 2023.

——. "My Church Was Part of the Slave Trade. This Has Not Shaken My Faith." *The New York Times,* June 17, 2023.

Tennenbaum, Frank. *Slave and Citizen: The Negro in America.* New York: Vintage Books,1947.

Thomas, Piri. *Down These Mean Streets.* New York: Vintage, 1997.

Tyler, Royall. *The Island of Barataria: The Governor of a Day.* N. P.: Reprint Services Corp, 1999.

United States Census Bureau. "U.S. Census Bureau Guidance on the Presentation and Comparison of Race and Hispanic Origin Data." 2003.

Valdez, Luis. *Zoot Suit and Other Plays.* Houston: Arte Público Press, 1992.

Vargas Llosa, Mario. *La Fiesta del Chivo.* Madrid: Alfaguara, 2016.

Vasconcelos, José. *La Raza Cósmica.* Madrid: Editorial Verbum, 2021.

Vincentelli, Elisabeth. "'Cape' of Good Hope." *The New York Post.* August 8, 2010. https://nypost.com/2010/08/08/cape-of-good-hope/

Wagner, Dennis. "Ulysses S. Grant 1872 - American Slaveholders in Cuba." *State of the Union History,* July 2, 2020. http://www.stateoftheunionhistory.com/2020/07/ulysses-s-grant-1872-american.html

Warren, Mercy Otis. *The Ladies of Castile.* Scotts Valley: CreateSpace Independent Publishing Platform, 2015.

Whitman, Walt. *The Complete Poems.* New York: Penguin, 2004.

——. *Democratic Vistas, and Other Papers Hardcover.* N. P.: Andesite Press, 2015.

Williams, John. *The Redeemed Captive.* Carlisle, MA: Applewood Books, 1987.

Williams, Stanley T. *The Spanish Background to American Literature.* New Haven: Yale University Press, 1951.

Williams, Tennessee. *A Streetcar Named Desire.* New York: New Directions, 2004.

Williams, William Carlos. "An Informal Discussion of Poetic Form." *Revista de la Asociación de Mujeres Graduadas de la Universidad de Puerto Rico* (July, 1941), 43- 45.

——. *In the American Grain.* New York: New Directions, 1925.

——. *Many Loves and Other Plays.* New York: New Directions, 1961.

——. *The Autobiography.* New York: New Directions, 1967.

——. *The Collected Poems of William Carlos Williams, Vols. I & II.* New York: New Directions, 1986.

——. *The Farmer's Daughters.* New York: New Directions, 1961.

——. *Yes, Mrs. Williams.* New York: New Directions, 1982.

Wright, Richard. *Pagan Spain.* New York: Harper Perennial, 2008.

Zimmer, Jonathan. op-ed, "Judge Sotomayor, a Mythic 'Hispanic.'" *L.A. Times:* June 12, 2009.

INDEX

Guntower, The 176

H

Hamilton 43, 84, 185-186, 194-199,
  236
Harding, Scharon 138
Harvard University 58, 103-117,
  150, 152, 199
*Haunting of Lin-Manuel Miranda,
  The* 197, 236
Hayden, Robert 81
Heal, Edith 191
Hemingway, Ernest 151, 153, 215,
  217, 234
Henna, Julio José 188, 193
Hijuelos, Oscar 51, 75, 153, 234
Hinojosa, Rolando 98
"His Excellency General
  Washington" 142
Hispanic Heritage Month 53, 80
*Hispanic View: American Politics
  and the Politics of Immigration,
  A* 33, 233
History of New York, The 150
History of the Conquest of Mexico
  149, 234
History of the Conquest of Peru
  150, 236
Holman, Bob 134, 233
Hoover, J. Edgar 29
Howells, William Dean
Huckleberry Finn 21, 151
Hudson, William Henry 199, 235
Hughes, Langston 81, 153
Huffington Post, The 58, 121, 234
*Hunger of Memory: The Education
  of Richard Rodriguez* 115, 236
Hunter College (Center for Puerto
  Rican Studies) 17, 37, 197
Huntington, Samuel P. 52, 58-61,
  64, 87, 104-5, 111-116, 235

"Hymn to Love Ended" 218

I

Ichaso, Leon 172-3, 177-182
"Imaginary Elegies" 1, 237
"Imaginary Translation from the
  Spanish" 218
Imus, Don 83
indohispano 29
Innocents Abroad 151
Insularismo 191, 236
In the American Grain 39, 186,
  192, 238
*In the Belly of the Beast: Letters
  from Prison* 175, 233
In the Heights 194-198, 233
"Invention of Hispanics and the
  Reinvention of America, The"
  20, 229, 236
Irisarri, Antonio José de 93, 237,
  241, 242
Irving, Washington 104, 150, 135
Ishiguro, Kasuo 199
Island of Barataria, The 143, 237

J

Jackson, Helen Hunt 148, 235
Jamestown 144
Jefferson, Thomas 143, 212, 235
"Jewish Cemetery at Newport,
  The" 150
Jíbaro island state 62, 64
Jiménez, Juan Ramón 14, 189
Joli, Mayra 64
John Jay College of Criminal
  Justice 82
Journal for Hispanic Policy, The
  108
Joyce, James 48, 92
Juliá, Raúl 173, 181

O

O. Henry (William Sydney Porter)
148
One Hundred Years of Solitude 22,
234
Old Man and the Sea, The 151, 234
"On the Rising Glory of America"
138, 139, 233
O Pioneers! 148, 233
Our Town 194, 195
"Oye Como Va" 11

P

Pachuco 3-5
"Pachuco and Other Extremes,
The" 3
Pagan Spain 153, 238
Palés Matos, Luis 16, 17, 189-194,
198, 215, 236
Papp, Joseph 172-176, 179-
180,183-184
Parton, Dolly 201, 203, 204
"Passage to India" 149
"Paterson" 92, 191, 192
Pattee, Fred Lewis 140, 141, 236
Payne, John Howard 143
Paz, Octavio 3-5, 27, 42, 63, 64,
102, 112, 129, 236
Pearl, The 153
*People and Places: The
  Background of My Life* 153, 237
Pew Research Center 196
Picasso 93
"Pictures of Columbus" 140
Pedreira, Antonio S. 191, 236
Pietri, Pedro 108, 109, 179, 236
Piñero 171, 171, 173, 177, 182, 235
Piñero, Miguel 37, 79, 171-84, 233,
235
Piscopo, Joe xi

*Pizarro in Peru, or the Death of
  Rolla* 143, 234
Poems of Philip Freneau, The 139,
141, 234
Poetry Society of America, The 83
Ponce de León, Juan 12
Porter, Katherine Ann 151, 169,
236
Porter, William Sydney (O. Henry)
148
Postmodernism 80-81
Pound, Ezra 124, 187
Povod, Reinaldo 173
"Prayer to Columbus" 149
"Preludio en Boricua" 191
Prensa, La 163
Prescott, William Hickling 149, 236
"Presencia Latina" 108
Princeton University 58, 138, 141
"Problem With Latinidad, The" 32,
236
Proud Boys, The 63
Public Theater, The 72-73, 185
Puente, Tito 11
"Puerto Rican Obituary" 108

Q

Queen Isabela 103
Quevedo 104, 133, 187, 190, 192,
218
Quintanilla, Selena 11
Quiñones, Ernesto 48-49, 236

R

Ramona 148, 235
Raza Cósmica, La 15,42, 53, 238
Rebel without a Cause 162
Reed, Ishmael 197, 236
Reggaetón 43
Remezcla 204

Revista de la Asociación de Mujeres Graduadas de la Universidad de Puerto Rico 39, 238
"Richard Cory" 83
Robinson, Edward Arlington 83
Rodó, José Enrique 31, 236
Rodriguez, Estuardo 120,121
Rodriguez, Richard 20, 115, 229, 230, 231, 235
Rodriguez, Robert 12
Rodríguez, Tito 216
Rodríguez Feo, José 153
Roffé, Reina 44
Rosinante to the Road Again 153, 234
Ronstadt, Linda 11
Rubio, Marco 57-58, 234
Ruiz de Burton, Mara Amparo 148, 236

S

Salazar, Ken 119
Salazar, Miguel 53-54, 236
Salcedo, Diego 12
Sánchez, Luis Rafael 17, 201, 237
Sánchez Sugía, María Celeste 34
Santana, Carlos 11
Santa Rosa, Gilberto 11
Santos, Romeo 11
Santayana, George 116, 145, 151-153, 199, 237
Santos Febre, Mayra 17
Sartre, Jean Paul 174, 237
Saturday Night Live xi
Scott Feldman, Judy 119
Separated: Inside an American Tragedy 61, 237
Sewall, Samuel 137
Shakespeare, William 31, 132, 187
Schama, Chloe 79

Schomburg Center for Research in Black Culture, 36
Short Eyes 171-176, 178-183, 236
Simon, Paul 82-84,153,162, 197
Silva Gruez, Kirsten 93, 237
Simpson Street 195, 234
Slave and Citizen: The Negro in America 40, 188, 237
Smithsonian, The 79, 119, 123-126
Smithsonian Institution, The 119
Snoop Doggy Dog 43
Soboroff, Jacob 71, 237
Sóngoro Cosongo 234
Soto, Pedro Juan 196
Soul on Ice 175, 233
"Spain 1873-1874" 149
Spanish American Roots of William Carlos Williams, The 103, 104, 186, 191, 218, 235
Spanish Background to American Literature, The 131, 132, 141, 238
Spanish Civil War 14, 16, 153, 189, 193
"Spanish Element in Our Nationality, The" 149
Spanish Earth, The 153
Spanish Husband, The 143
Spanish Republic 149
Spanish Student, The 150
Spicer, Jack 14
Spy Kids 27
Squatter and the Don, The 148, 236
"Statistical Directive 15" 148, 236
Stavans, Ilán 79-80, 237
Steinbeck, John 153, 237
Stevens, Wallace xiv, 153, 237
Strand, Mark 217
Sun Only Shines for the Cool, The 175, 176
Surgeon of His Honour, The 143
Swarn, Rachel L. 41-42, 237

www.ingramcontent.com/pod-product-compliance
Lightning Source LLC
Chambersburg PA
CBHW071850270326
41929CB00013B/2173